About the Author

Nick White was born in the west of England, during the decade that English clubs reigned supreme in Europe and Holland became the best team never to win the World Cup.

A sports fanatic and lover of the outdoors, he also played cricket, badminton and athletics to a high level, but football was, and still is, his undying passion.

As a Chris Waddle/David Beckham floating winger, he plied his trade at school and university level before playing for a French Sunday league side, for LJT in Cannes, and in Catalonia for Gracia y Malfeito Advocats in a Barcelona Wednesday night five-a-side League.

Apart from football his interests include finance, walking, reading, writing, cycling, running, cricket, travelling, languages and thinking.

His other published work is 'How to write killer adverts. The secrets of the mail-order gurus'. He lives in Paris and London, amongst other places, and supports Southampton, Aldershot Town and Barcelona, as well as any other team that dares to play beautiful football.

SUN, SEA AND SEXY FOOTBALL

The Life and Times of British Footballers Abroad (British Football's 'PTs')

NICK WHITE

Foreword by
Kenneth Wolstenholme

Invextus

An Invextus Book
First published in Great Britain in 2001 by Invextus

ISBN 0 954 1610 0 9

Typeset by Avon DataSet Ltd, Bidford on Avon B50 4JH
Cover artwork prepared by Colourpath
Printed and bound in Great Britain by
Biddles Ltd, Guildford, Surrey

Invextus Property Associates Ltd
7–11 Minerva Road
Park Royal
London
NW10 6JH

Contents

Foreword

Nick White is a brave man to have decided to write this book with its intriguing title of 'Sun, Sea and Sexy Football'. Few footballers writing their autobiographies would dare go into that subject. In fact few, if any footballers write their autobiographies. They hire a ghost writer who is a reasonably experienced journalist.

The writer of this book is a keen football supporter and it shows. He has approached a number of players and managers, past and present, and asked sensible questions so that he could find the true facts about life at the very top, and life in the ordinary mill of our football and football abroad.

Some of the players written about will not be all that well known to a lot of the readers, and this is because Nick White has not concentrated on the big stars. Yes, he has interviewed a number of the high class players, but he has also gone out of his way to find out what life is like outside the world of stardom. He has even included the story of a lady playing football for Friends of Fulham before she had a spell in Finland, and has since ended up as a hard-working official in her home country, England.

It is a fascinating book, showing how widespread football's popularity is, and I wish the author well with his book because he has worked so hard carrying out so many interesting interviews. We can all learn a lot from his work.

Kenneth Wolstenholme DFC and Bar

Introduction

There comes a moment in all our lives, a moment that marks, transforms, creates and shapes our view of life and the world, and our way of thinking and being for the rest of our time on this planet. A searing light of discovery and exhilaration, of the revelation of our path ahead, a moment of the realisation of the beauty and frailty of our hopes and dreams, a moment that stays in our hearts and minds forever and makes us the complicated mass of skin and bone that we are.

For some it is their first kiss, others their first love, for many more the birth of their first child. For me all three of these came at once, a month before my tenth birthday. It was during the 1982 World Cup in Spain – Scotland versus Brazil. Sure, I'd watched plenty of football before, but little did I realise that what I was about to witness in that Scotland v Selecao game was to touch me for the rest of my life.

Being an expert, and a noisy one at that, I fancied Scotland to win. They had, after all, assembled arguably their finest ever squad under the inimitable, fatherly gaze of the legendary Jock Stein. Included in this squad were the holy trinity from Liverpool, Souness, Dalglish and Hansen, as well as an array of talent from Alex's Aberdeen Army, the likes of Willie Miller and Roy Aitken, not forgetting of course John Wark and David Narey. And it was Narey who opened the scoring with a 'made in Brazil' 25-yarder to put the Scots 1-0 up.

Then it happened.

For the next 70 minutes, the life and world of a boisterous, enthusiastic and impressionable sports-mad curly-haired (nearly) ten year-old boy was turned upside down by the most exquisite exhibition of sublime footballing perfection I had ever seen. No hacked clearances or stodgy back-passes to indigest from Socrates, Zico, Junior, Falcao, Eder and co. Only a reinvention of football physics, a feast of feline grace of the Brazilian players as they expressed their whole being, by way of a joyous, dancing, swaying carnival of beautiful samba football, silky subtle skills, dazzling control and breathtaking passing. Oh yes, and those flowing yellow shirts, seemingly woven from gold and fitted as tunics for the gods.

Four goals and a million magic moments later, the Brazilian blitzkrieg was temporarily over, and eleven shell-shocked Scots trudged off the field shaking their heads in dazed bewilderment (as I was), questioning their knowledge of the rules of football, so little occasion had they to have influenced the outcome of the game. But in the presence of genius, no rules apply.

Two moments stood out for me in that match. Zico's free kick was one, but the other was a goal so perfect in its conception and execution, that I can still close my eyes and conjure up its image today. Eder of Brazil, flowing down the left, saw the Scottish keeper Alan Rough slightly astray, and without breaking stride or thought, caressed the ball in a perfect arc over Rough's head and into the goal, as if caressing the face of the woman he adored. Exuberance, exhilaration, emotion, melancholy, tenderness, joy – all encapsulated in that goal.

For me that moment *was* my first kiss (although a Dutch girl called Monique supplied the real thing a few years later). But they were similar in that I can still touch and sense them. My first love (she came soon after Monique), and my first child was and still is football.

But as with all first loves, loves based on mutual infatuation, loves bereft ofmortgages, children, hire purchase, keeping up with the Joneses and the Child Support Agency, there comes the bitter intrusion of reality. In this case, Brazil broke my tender heart after beating Argentina in a scrappy game in which Diego Maradona was sent off (my first sighting of the next genius). Brazil then faced Italy in the best game of the tournament, the best game of the last thirty years (although France/Brazil in 1986 runs it a very close second), perhaps the best game ever. It finished 3-2 to Italy, the critical moment being the suicidal Brazilian sideways pass across their own 18-yard box, intercepted and slotted home by Paolo Rossi. What a tragic waste! It left me feeling like the boy who'd fixed a date with the beautiful blonde from school, she'd stood him up, but he kept waiting at the youth club entrance in the forlorn hope that reality could be kept at bay. For the first time, but not the last, I felt sorrow at the death of beauty.

Nevertheless the penny had dropped and I spent every spare moment kicking a ball, the Gola one I'd won at the village fete, copying the Brazilians and feeling their joy, pleasure and elation flow through me each time I played. Much of the time it was on the village green with my friends, in the back garden with my family, or even with our dog, practising my Cruyff turns whilst avoiding her biting tackles. On my own, I'd juggle a football or tennis ball, or if I'd knocked them over the next-door neighbour's fence, a plastic bowls jack with holes in. I'd volley it against the garage door, or curl unstoppable free-kicks into the top corner of the angle between the pear and the apple tree, all the while keeping up a frantic running commentary, through rain, shine, frost or snow. I'd play until my legs, feet and brain could give no more, until the sun, that big yellow football in the sky, put itself to sleep for another 90 minutes.

As one of Thatcher's children growing up in the 1980s, turbulent times abounded as the world lurched unsteadily towards a 21st Century that many thought the human race would not be around to see. Out of the television popped a multitude of insane imagery, a cacophony of chaos: Northern Ireland; ETA; the Falklands; the miners strike; SOGAT; Libya; the Iran/Iraq war; unemployment; the Rainbow Warrior; Lebanon; the PLO; hostages; African famine; Live Aid; Chernobyl; AIDS; mutually assured destruction; the day after; the Evil Empire; Kings Cross; Herald of Free Enterprise; Piper Alpha; Tiannaman Square; the Sandanistas and South American agony; General Noriega; Irangate; and various assassination attempts, some that failed to hit the target, and others that were catastrophically successful.

Into this uncertain, unstable, care-worn world to which I was exposed came my own galaxy of stars of the sporting solar system: the entire Saints side; Hoddle; Liverpool; Spurs; Gower; Willis; Botham; Richards; Garner; Coe; Ovett; Thompson; McEnroe; Connors; Faldo; Lyle; Mansell; Davis; Ginny Leng (!) and hundreds, if not thousands of others. Their winning, and winning in style, was a tremendous inspiration to me, and encouraged me to play sport and enjoy every moment. I was, and am, immensely fortunate to do so.

As for football, my passion for the beautiful game mellowed and matured over time like a fine wine. As I entered my teenage years, the attendance at my first match beckoned and permission to go to a game was granted, albeit reluctantly. For, dear reader, football hasn't always been the glitzy rock-and-roll popular culture vehicle that we know and love today – far from it. The 1980s marked the nadir of the glam-free and glum 1970s, and reality was to bite brutally in that decade, at Bradford, Heysel and Hillsborough. Football was the convenient whipping-boy for all that was bad in the country. Instead, in and around the terraces, it became the ultimate manifestation of society's deeper social ills.

But such thoughts were far from my mind in November 1987 when I went to my first game, Aldershot versus Grimsby at the Recreation Ground. It was another 3-2 thriller, like the Brazil/Italy game five years previously, but a world apart in all but scoreline. That said, the feeling of the momentous savouring of a first-time experience at both occasions was just as great, and whatever they tell you, nothing can beat watching it live – except, of course, playing.

Aldershot's poor performances, like the inexorable decline of the morals of a nation into a bearpit, had a ring of inevitability about them, something that Spencer Trethewey (remember him?), Aldershot's potential new 19 year-old millionaire chairman and wannabe Silvio Berlusconi, did nothing to halt. But I enjoyed many special moments watching Len Walker's red and blue army over the years that I went to see the Shots at the Rec. The pre-match ritual was always the same: watch Saint and Greavsie at lunchtime; catch the one bus to the station, with my transistor radio clamped to my ear listening to Grant Coleman, John Hughes and Norman Murphy on Radio Solent; laughing at John Duncan, from 'When Saturday Comes', and his humorous look at the football world; keeping up to date with the other news; get the train to Aldershot; go into the ground; buy the 'Shots review'; and take my place in the 'kop' in anticipation of the afternoon's events.

It was a procession of stars past and future: Terry McDermott at Exeter; Sammy McIlroy at Bury; Steve Sherwood at Grimsby; Steve Moran at Reading (a heart-breaking 1-1 derby draw at a packed Easter Monday Rec – they got a penalty in the 95th minute!); Matt Elliott of Torquay and Darren Peacock of Hereford. And for Aldershot, Steve 'Wurzel' Claridge (yes, he had long hair in those days!) and a certain left-back by the name of Chris Powell - whatever happened to him?! And throughout this time my friend Mike, a rabid Man City fan who worshipped Paul Moulden and Wayne Biggins, was writing to Mel Machin every week begging him to sell Steve Redmond and Kenny Clements. When I told him that Kenny Clements had played for Bury in the same game I saw Sammy McIlroy, it made his week!

But just as you think your childhood will last forever, reality intrudes again. Like Big Ben, the Houses of Parliament and Buckingham Palace, some things were taken as read, as part of the furniture. Liverpool's total domination of the English game was one of them and I could never imagine it being any different. This was the era when even Saints finished above Man United in the League – yes, a long time ago! And looking back now, Liverpool's last League Championship win in 1990 not only marked the end of an era for them, but a massive dividing line between my childhood and early adult life, although of course I didn't think or know that at the time.

Then came University, the move away from the small world I'd been inhabiting, and the realisation of there being a very big world to explore and learn in. Part of my degree course was French, the love of foreign cultures having developed from watching the different teams in the World Cup all those years before.

A year of life, laughs and loves as part of my year of study in France came and went all too quickly, but the happy memories remained, one of these from being a player in a local side. We were the Chelsea of our day, with amongst our number players from Cameroon, Scotland, Spain, Italy, Germany, and a Lebanese goalie who surprisingly hasn't yet been snapped up by a Premiership club! Then I moved on to a three-month summer work placement in Cannes, living in the same youth hostel as a YTS trainee at AS Cannes called Johan Micoud – he now plays for Parma in Serie A. Whilst there I played in a massive tournament for teams from the whole of the south of France at Le Cannet. Our team, LJT, got to the semi-finals. It ended 1-1 after extra time, under the burning sun and that unique azure-blue sky that anyone who has lived in Provence will know and love. We lost the penalty shootout that followed, and with it the opportunity to play in the final. I was to have taken the sixth penalty, but didn't even get the chance to miss, let alone score. It was all over by then.

But all that was temporarily forgotten after the final with the appearance of Luis Fernandez, at that time manager of Cannes, to present the trophies. Yes, *that* Luis Fernandez, he of the mythical French midfield of the 1980s, he of the ice-cool nerves in that never to be forgotten World Cup quarter-final against Brazil in 1986 where football really was the winner, and where his penalty, under the harsh gaze of the midday Mexican sun and a spellbound planet, took France a step closer to a World Cup triumph that should have been but never was. I joined with my fellow players in an unusual gesture of admiration, standing there in silent open-mouthed awe. For a very special moment all nations, and there were many, neglected enmity and bitterness and were united in the appreciation of a situation that transcended nationality and in some way touched the hearts and minds of all those present.

Following more study, many jobs and a spell in New York and Canada, I headed for Spain, or more precisely Barcelona, capital of Cataluna. The language was guttural yet lyrical, the people warm and friendly (so was the weather and the food), and the girls smiling and pretty, with their aquiline features, olive skin and laughing eyes. Their football was the ultimate expression of all this and more. Their history, their culture, their love, their life. All channelled into 'Barca'. It really was, and is, 'mes que un club'.

Apart from studying and a spell with the Red Cross, there was of course another football club to play for. My new side, Gracia y Malfeito Advocats, was a team of Spanish lawyers, one of whom was Marc, my 'intercambio' (language exchange). We'd meet every Thursday evening, me to practise Spanish and him English, and every Wednesday night I'd be the guest 'extranjero' (foreigner) in his five-a-side team. We played a fast, furious, technical game in the Pedralbes district of the city, once home to Maradona and his minions. We usually started at 9.30, although it was still roastingly hot, with a sprinkling of female fans in tow.

My funniest moment came when I was a sub one night. There was an incredibly pretty girl sitting next to me on the bench, she 'dropped her hanky', and we got chatting. As I was becoming ever more stuck in the honey pot of her bottomless eyes and chestnut hair, I heard my name 'Nee-coe-laaas', pronounced in that gritty Spanish way. Thinking that she was whispering sweet nothings in my ear I carried on chatting, but again was interrupted by cries of 'Nee-coe-lass! Venga!' I looked round and to my horror the game had stopped, all the players were staring at me, hands on hips, whilst waiting for me to come on as a substitute, and the fussy referee was reaching into his pocket for his yellow card! Having already done plenty of 'warming up', I rapidly took my place on the field and proceeded to score the most beautiful goal of my career: past two players on the half-way line, their keeper came running off his line towards me, and like Romario, I not only passed it round him but curled it as well, into the far corner of the goal. It was in the net before even leaving my foot. But we lost that game, and my 'fan' melted into the warm summer night before I could even say 'buenas noches'. So much for the Premiership being the sole preserve of fickle supporters!

After a few more goals, my team-mates started calling me 'Leenekeeer' but it was after the first game I played in that I had my best experience of playing abroad, and one that all those in this book can relate to. After I had scored the winning goal in our 7-6 victory (very Johan Cruyff!) my team-mates came and patted me on the back saying 'well done'. After the final whistle, Marc came up to me and remarked on how they were a big team, now that they had a 'foreign star' playing for them. He said it with such warmth and affection, that in spite of being from abroad I was one of them. To go to a foreign country, adapt to a strange language, and prosper in a different culture and mentality, but above all to be accepted and respected, in spite of your differences (and in my blond-haired blue-eyed case in Spain, a very obvious one!), as 'one of us', is a tremendous feeling and one that I will always cherish.

As you will read in the following chapters, the former and current players and managers experienced the whole range of emotions during their life and times abroad, particularly given the fact that until recently, advanced transport links that we now take for granted, and the 'global village', were mere abstract concepts. This makes their many achievements all the more remarkable. The world really was a bigger and harder to reach place back then, as I can vouch for on a small scale with my numerous pre-channel tunnel trips to France.

Although they come from different backgrounds, with different perspectives and ways of thinking, a common thread runs through their stories, even those for whom things didn't go according to plan. It is their hunger for life, their rejection of setting small, ultimately unsatisfactory targets with vast safety margins, their love of learning and of life, of trying something new, and their realisation that human intellectual, spiritual and emotional development only comes through a continuous pushing back of boundaries, setting and achieving of goals, always striving to improve and do better, and learning from each new situation in which they find themselves. This you will read in the pages that follow.

Football, for better or worse, has changed. Change is an essential and inevitable part of life, and those who do not embrace it are destined to go the way of the dinosaur. The Britain of today would do well to learn from the experiences of those in this book. Their tremendous successes were based on open-mindedness, adaptability, goal- setting, hard work, and respect for others.

It is a sad reality that those who are successful are built up and knocked down with alarming regularity. This is the true 'English Disease' and another form of hooliganism. The contributors to my book have certainly had their share of media coverage over the years, some good, some bad, but as you will read, their resilience and sense of humour has enabled them to emerge triumphant, even in the most bizarre situations!

I feel that current British players are missing out on a wealth of personal and professional experiences by not grasping such opportunities to play abroad with both hands: they very rarely, if ever, come round again. One look at a map of the world should be enough to convince them that although Britain is a wonderful place, it is but a small part of a huge planet full of possibilities and adventure. They may fall flat on their face, but that too is part of life, and if they showed the same qualities of character and determination that got them to the top of their profession in England, not only would they be a success, they would have a wealth of experiences and occasions to look back on with pride for the rest of their lives. Such things have no price and cannot be bought. David Beckham and others take note!

Every day when we get out of bed and leave home to face the world is a step into the unknown, but the qualities shown by those in the book are ones we should all aspire to in our lives - to make the world a better place, a world where the preservation of individuality and personal freedoms, as well as respect for others, is ensured for future generations. Vive la difference!

Why is football so popular? This fantastic game that unites the world to such an extent that wherever I've been, whoever I've spoken to, whatever country they came from, a common bond is instantly formed thanks to the world's Esperanto. This game that empties streets and shreds nerves in a 90-minute believe-it-or-not welter of emotions? There are many theories, but I have a compelling one. It is its capacity for the unexpected, and the need that this fills in so many of us. So many people in this world lead regimented lives. It starts at school and continues throughout life, with enormous peer pressure from family and friends preventing you from fulfilling yourself, following your dreams and being all that you want to be in life. And in the same way that many people identified with Princess Diana and her problems, many people see football as a ray of hope in their lives, something that isn't programmed down to the last detail as with so much else in life.

Why do you think FA Cup shocks are so popular? The best or biggest team doesn't always win, and ordinary people identify with this. The little guy still has a chance, in spite of the overwhelming odds and resources that are stacked against him. The nobility of the human spirit, of achievement and pride in one's efforts still shines through, in spite of being dismissed by the masses. But just remember one thing folks, football reflects life. There are winners and losers, and it's a tough world out there – for everyone. And what is to become of humanity if we do not strive to better ourselves? We become like East Germany was, that's what, for without the inventors, the thinkers, the doers and the entrepreneur risk-takers, this or any country is NOTHING. As for non-competitive games, the less said the better – I don't know whether to laugh or cry.

Football's powers-that-be must tread carefully and endeavour not to kill the goose that lays the golden egg. There is too much football being shown on television now, even for me. We should seek quality, not quantity, and aim to recapture some of the sheer naked joy a child feels when chasing and taming a football, that most capricious and elusive of lovers.

Through writing this book and speaking to so many former and current players and managers, I too have had some wonderful experiences, and like a small child eating chocolate ice-cream, have gorged myself on a feast of football stories. It is my hope with this book that you, dear reader, will laugh, cry, enjoy and learn from the experiences of a very special and almost extinct breed, the British footballer who has lived and coached or played abroad.

My next book will involve travelling around the world in search of new football-related experiences. Perhaps we'll meet in a youth hostel, where depending on my mood I'll be the one loudly discussing the relative merits of various teams and players from around the globe. Alternatively I'll be the quiet one sitting in the corner, reading a book, with a wry smile on my face.

Whichever incarnation of me you find, I look forward to meeting you, and in the meantime I wish you well and hope that one day all your dreams come true.

With the writing and compilation of this book, at one point a hazy possibility and now a reality, one of mine has.

Acknowledgements

I have been touched by the boundless generosity of so many people who have helped in the compilation of this book, but above all by two groups: firstly the twenty-three contributors who generously agreed to give their time and share their experiences with an unknown football fanatic, despite heavy schedules: and secondly all of you, dear readers, for investing your time and money in this idiosyncratic tome!

I am particularly grateful to Dave Thomas of the Torquay Herald Express, Matthew Fisher of Performing Artistes of the F4 Group and Rebecca of Chrysalis North TV for their invaluable assistance in helping me obtain interviews with several of the players in this book.

Also of great assistance, in some form or another, were the following people: Claire McGee at Glasgow Celtic, Carol at Nottingham Forest, Ann Romilly of the Football Association, Dick Wright at Leeds United, Peter Lorimer, Nick Bevan at Premier Management, Clare Wheatley at Arsenal Ladies, the press office of Millwall F.C., Lynn Harris at the League Managers Association, Audrey Gates at Oxford United, Nick Beer at the Exeter Gazette, Richard Walker at Watford F.C., John Lewkins, Rachel Addison, Raymond Sparks and Bryan Little of ProStar Management, Sue Banks at West Ham United, Jeff Weston of Jerome Anderson Management, Phil Mepham at Aston Villa, Keith Hunt at Camelot Marketing and Sheila Harris.

A special tribute to my family, friends, and all those sportsmen and women, and others, who in some way have touched my life with their kindness and wisdom.

To Stuart Goldsmith, Dan Pena, Chevalier Harry Schultz, Dr Vernon Coleman and Vince Stanzione, for guiding me to the right path.

To Eduardo Galeano, author of the best book ever written about football:

> *'Un saludo de un loco de futbol a un otro. Espero que nos encontremos un dia . . .'*

* * * *

The interviews were conducted over the course of four months, from May to September 2001, and whilst every effort has been made to ensure accuracy, some of the facts and figures may now be out of date or seem out of context. But rest assured, dear reader, that this will in no way detract from your enjoyment of this unique book.

* * * *

What does ‘PT’ stand for?

Readers curious as to the meaning of the ‘PT’ part of the title are best advised to visit the excellent free website of Chevalier Harry Schultz at:

www.hsletter.com

or contact him at:

cameleon1@compuserve.com

‘PT’ has several definitions which taken as a group define it. One of these facets is **P**erpetual **T**ravel. Visit the website to find out more!

Chevalier Harry D.Schultz, KHC, KM, KCPR, KCSA, KCSS is, according to the Guinness Book of Records from 1981 to the present day, the highest paid investment consultant in the world at $2,400 an hour ($3,400 an hour at weekends). Harry has lived for extended periods in 18 nations, and shorter periods in many others. Knighted five times, Harry is a man for all seasons and a true citizen of the world.

His newsletter, with subscribers in more than 90 countries, is now in its 38th year of publication. Its unique perspective on our tumultuous and wonderful world (at a tiny fraction of the cost of his hourly rates), will enrich you spiritually, intellectually and financially, and the true meaning of ‘PT’, a phrase coined by Harry himself, will become abundantly clear to those receptive enough, and ready, to understand it.

Paul Lambert

PLAYER

Borussia Dortmund, (Germany), June 1996 – November 1997

Paul Lambert was born in Glasgow, and spent nine seasons with Saint Mirren, his first professional club, before moving to Motherwell in 1994. He played for them until 1996, during which time he won the first of his 28 Caps for Scotland (correct at time of publication). We pick up Paul's story in May 1996:

"There was one player from Motherwell, a guy called Rob McKinnon, who had signed for Twente Enschede and was playing over in Holland at that time. I was out of contract and there was nothing coming up for me club-wise in Scotland, England or anywhere. So the agent that got Rob the move to Twente Enschede asked him if he could pass my number on, to see if he could help me. Then I got a phone call from him, and he said to give him ten days or so to see if he could find me a club to move to. He then came up with some trial games for me, including two with PSV Eindhoven and Borussia Dortmund.

Motherwell had offered me a new contract but I didn't sign it. They were down at Northampton at the time and I had made up my mind that I was going to play in these trials, but if they hadn't worked out then I would have come back to the UK.

I went to Eindhoven first and played in two trial matches. Everything went OK but I was played out of position as a right winger, and the coach there said that he didn't need a right-winger as such in my style. So I knew that I was going to Dortmund as a last throw of the dice. I went there and they played me in a central midfield position, things went well, and they offered me a contract.

Going to play abroad had always appealed to me. I actually

played for Motherwell against Borussia Dortmund in the UEFA Cup, so I knew what it was like in that stadium. I knew about the players they had in their squad even before I went there, and when I got the chance to sign there it was absolutely fantastic. But I never, ever in a hundred years thought that what happened to me there was really going to happen, and I was fortunate enough to play with some great people.

My family couldn't believe that we were going over to Dortmund, and even if things hadn't worked in football terms, I knew I was going over there to learn a different way of thinking, living and playing, so that was a major factor for me moving to Germany.

As for my German before I went there, I didn't speak a word! Never in a million years did I think I would end up in Dortmund. That just shows you – with football you just never know what's going to happen to you.

I didn't have a big welcome when I went to Dortmund. I just arrived from Scotland as another new signing for this team, somebody from Motherwell coming over probably just going there as a squad player. I knew that myself, but the most important thing for me was that I was going to learn another way of living and about a different culture. But once the games started things snowballed, and from then on my life over there got a lot better.

I went to school for a spell to learn the language, and at the time my wife and wee boy were still in Glasgow. Of course on the football field, you had to learn what everything meant, but to be fair everyone in the dressing room spoke English, which at the beginning made it a lot easier for me. Once my German improved I got more involved. I got on really well with every one of them, and they were a great bunch of people. You've got to try and learn the language when you're living abroad – it's so important.

Borussia Dortmund helped us a lot with the accommodation side of things, and they took me and my wife to look at some houses. Luckily enough I chose a really good place to live, which was great because it had a garden for my wee boy. The neighbours were absolutely fantastic, and we still keep in contact to this day.

I wasn't the only new signing that year. There was me, and a guy from Norway called Steinar Pedersen. We sort of came from the same footballing background, from unknown teams from small places. His career never really went the right way, whereas mine went that way (gestures upwards!) – it took off. There was another guy, Jovan Kirovski [AUTHORS NOTE: now playing for Crystal Palace], who was on Manchester United's books. He came to Dortmund but his career never really took off either. Wolfgang Feiersinger came too. He played in a lot of matches when Sammer wasn't fit, so there were a few of us who came at that particular time.

I got on fantastically with the president. I could never, ever say anything bad about that club because what had happened there was so great, and they were all very hospitable to me. I still go back there even to this day to watch games sometimes. I go to see the general manager, and if the president's there I'll speak to him. There are still some guys who I played with that are there now.

There was one thing that was really good with the media over in Germany. They let you have your own freedom, probably because I wasn't from that country and didn't speak the language really fluently, although I did quite a few interviews when I was there. For the interviews, they said that I could do them in English, and they would subtitle them. The press weren't intrusive either. They just asked me about the games and whether I was happy there.

When I first went to Dortmund, my debut game was as a sub in the German Cup, which started before the Bundesliga season. We got knocked out by a small team, losing 4-3, and when we went into the dressing room after the game, there wasn't a word said. I wasn't used to that, because in Scotland we tend to shout and talk straight after a match. But we never really said much at the time. It was discussed the next day which was strange, and hard to get to grips with, but once you were there you got used to it. It was just a different mentality.

Ottmar Hitzfeld was without doubt the best coach I ever had. Nevio Scala came later and he was fantastic too. As for the training, everything was new to me. The warm- ups were different but the professionalism was top-draw. The coach and other members of his staff taught me how to play in my particular new role, because I'd never played that way at Motherwell, where I was more offensive, and I went to a more defensive style of play, so he changed my whole game. Ottmar definitely gave me the success I think that I have today. The facilities were first-class and everything that you needed was there. That's the way professional footballers should be treated, the way it was over there.

On the social side, we also had team nights out planned, as well as visits to restaurants. Stefan Freund, who was injured, had his comeback game and we went to a restaurant afterwards. It was a great night.

As for the players, I played with and got to know Stefan Klos, who is over here at Rangers at the moment. We're good friends now and we got on really well over there too. There wasn't one player that I really didn't get on well with – everybody was in it together. There were also players like Andy Moeller, Jurgen Kohler, Mattias Sammer and Karl-Heinz Riedle there, a lot of the players who I'd seen on TV here in Scotland. Then you find yourself over in Dortmund, they accept you as one of them, and that felt great. They were really nice to me.

I think that defensively, Jurgen Kohler was the best I ever encountered. Jurgen was fantastic, and so was Mattias Sammer who was probably the best Libero in Europe at that time. Offensively Andy Moeller was fantastic, someone who obviously a lot of English people don't like very much! He was a fantastic guy and world-class player, a superb number ten. Those three were absolutely fantastic.

As for the best players, I was fortunate enough to play against Hagi, Zidane, Rivaldo and Thomas Haessler. But the one who gave me the hardest time was a guy called Milinko Pantic [ex-Atletico Madrid]. He was incredible. We played Atletico Madrid in the Champions League in Madrid and beat them 1-0, and I thought 'OK – I've got this guy', and everything was fine. Then we went to play them again in Dortmund and he kept on turning me, and gave me a really hard time on that particular night! I think he's been the one player in a game where I had to hold my hand up and say ' OK! I got roasted there!' I just couldn't get near him.

We always had lots of company as my wife's parents often came over, and so did her friends and our German neighbours. When your friends are a long way away and they come over, you appreciate them more, and when they go away it's a bit sad. When you're living in a foreign country, and it's just the three of you, you know it's down to you to make it work. Obviously it can pull you apart, but it brought us closer together and we definitely had a great time.

The way of life is very different over in Germany, and dead laid back! In Glasgow everything's 'rush rush rush', but over there it's very relaxed. Everyone goes out, sits outside at a cafe with a coffee, and doesn't get bothered, because if you did that in Glasgow you'd definitely get looked at. Even though there's only one team in the city, with 70,000 fans, there didn't seem to be as much pressure on you as there is in Glasgow. It's a massively supported club, but you could walk the streets and no-one would bother you, whereas here in Glasgow you just couldn't do that!

The memorable games were, of course, in the Champions League. There was the one when I scored against Widzew Lodz in Poland, and obviously the Champions League Final, against Juventus in 1997, which we won 3-1. That was a massive game for me. Playing against Schalke 04 was probably the Rangers/Celtic equivalent of the local needle matches, and we knew that they were our fiercest rivals. The games against Bayern Munich were big ones too, but every game over there was brilliant to play in, because of the atmosphere generated inside the grounds. We beat Schalke 3-1 away and 1-0 at home.

The only downside over there was that my baby son was prone to pneumonia and feverish convulsions. That was a major factor as to why I came back. He was in the hospital over there, and that's when the language comes into play because you don't know 100% what they're saying, and you're not always sure what's going on. They kept him in hospital for five days for a brain scan, and it was the only downside to the whole thing.

And that's why the move away from Dortmund happened, simply because my boy wasn't well. My wife was obviously very upset because of this and so was I. Then Celtic came in for me.

The transfer talks were on and off, and Nevio [Scala] tried really hard to keep me. He did everything to try and make me stay when I was leaving. He even brought my wife's parents over to stay to try and make me change my mind! Eventually the two clubs and I came to an agreement, and that's when I had to go on the telly after a game against Parma in November 1997 to tell the fans that I was leaving.

You don't know how people are going to react when you're going, but the fans gave me an unbelievable send-off in my last game. When we beat Parma, there were massive banners all around the stadium and people crying and saying goodbye. It was one of the best moments in my career. That last game against Parma was incredible. All the fans stayed in the stadium and didn't leave until I had done a lap of honour. On top of all this they had draped banners over my car saying 'good luck'. That was really one of the best things that ever happened to me, and up with winning anything, that's been the best thing I've ever encountered in my football career.

The local media couldn't believe what the fans had done for me. There have probably been players who have been with Dortmund all their career who probably haven't ever had that send-off, and Stefan Klos was saying that he'd never seen anything like it. But now I can always go back there, and if they know I'm in the stadium they sing my name.

After the Parma game, I had to sign the release forms from Borussia Dortmund before midnight. I was up in the general manager's office and I had second thoughts about doing it. I phoned home and spoke to my wife who had seen me on television. I was upset and said to her 'I don't know if we can leave here'.

The club gave me a pendant as a goodbye present, inscribed with my name, and the dates when I signed and when I left Borussia Dortmund. They were great to me.

When I was getting on the plane to leave Germany, I was thinking 'what I am doing?', because I was leaving something that had been so great for me, and that showed when I started playing for Celtic. At the beginning I was playing so badly it was unbelievable, and the emotion of it all took a grip of me for a few weeks. Even when I came back here to Glasgow, I was playing absolutely terribly for a few games. We lost our first three matches, and I was trying to get over what I had done. It was tearing me apart. But once you're here at Celtic and see how important and fantastic this club is, you start to feel good again. But seeing what was there in Germany opened my eyes to a lot of things.

My abiding memory of playing for Dortmund was the Champions League Final, and the way the fans treated me there. If it wasn't for Borussia Dortmund, I wouldn't be here at Celtic today. That's how much they helped me, and I'm always grateful for what happened.

Since I left, I've been over for some games, and I've been to Munich to meet up again with Ottmar Hitzfeld. I broke a bone in my ankle just before Christmas, and went over then. I made a lot of friends over there who are really important to me. I also went over to see Liverpool play against Alaves in the 2001 UEFA Cup Final.

The one thing that stays in my memory was actually signing for Borussia Dortmund and getting a contract there, knowing that I was going to learn from, in my opinion one of the greatest coaches in football, namely Ottmar Hitzfeld. I think that, obviously with winning things and the Parma game, the actual day that I signed the contract was the most memorable one for me.

It wasn't just my game but me as a person that developed as well, and I changed so much. You've got to grow up quicker over there, especially as I had a wee boy at the time, so I had to. It gives you more confidence, and when you have success on the field as well it definitely takes you up another level, both personally and professionally.

Everything about that move for me was just perfect. It was a great experience, not just personally but for the whole family. Especially at Borussia Dortmund, because everything for me about that club was fantastic.

As I said, nothing in Scotland, England or anywhere that I've done before or since compares to that. I think that's been the major turning point of my career, and if it hadn't happened I probably wouldn't be sitting here talking to you today!

That's the way I look at it, and I'm thankful for the really great fun I had there. And that's why Borussia Dortmund will always be a big part of me."

Paul Lambert is currently playing for Celtic, where he has been since the end of 1997, and lives in the Glasgow area with his wife and family.

Joe Jordan

PLAYER
AC Milan, (Italy), July 1981 – June 1983
Verona, (Italy), July 1983 – June 1984

Joe Jordan began his professional career in Scotland with Morton, before moving to Leeds in 1971, where he was a League Championship winner, made 182 appearances, and scored 48 goals during his eight-year spell at Elland Road, as well as winning the first of his 52 caps for Scotland, against England, in 1973. He then moved to Manchester United in 1978 and stayed for three seasons. We pick up Joe's story in the summer of 1981:

"My contract had expired at Manchester United, and although at that time you were free to negotiate a move elsewhere, there was still a fee involved for a transfer. In 1981, AC Milan contacted me with regard to the possibility of me playing there, I had talks with them, and signed for them in the summer of 1981.

It wasn't an easy decision to go, as Man United were and are a massive club, and I was doing very well at the time. I had just received the 'player of the year' award and was the leading goalscorer, so my personal game was good. But I was only looking to the future, and the future was that I was twenty-nine years of age, and it was the last opportunity for me to achieve an ambition of mine, which was to play abroad. There had been previous occasions when the opportunity had been denied me, as I had been under contract and even when your contract was up, in those days the club held your registration and you couldn't go, so this was a last chance for me. To get an opportunity to play abroad was great, but to play for AC Milan in Italy was one I couldn't really refuse. I was absolutely delighted just to get the chance.

I did get offered a new contract by Manchester United and Dave Sexton, the previous manager. Then there was a turnaround in the summer and the new manager, Ron Atkinson, came in and offered me an increased contract. Manchester United did want me to stay, I was playing well, it was a club that I'd always wanted to play for and I enjoyed my time there. So it wasn't an easy decision but it was my last chance to go abroad as a player. I took it and have no regrets.

I had played against AC Milan before, for Leeds in the 1973 European Cup Winners Cup Final, but it was the attraction and the experience of going and playing and living in another country that made me want to go. There was also the fact that players did get paid better in countries like Spain and Italy, but that wasn't just why I went. The financial side can't be ignored, either then or now, but I wanted to experience the lifestyle as well.

I didn't speak any Italian before I went there. It was a new experience and culture for me. It was also a big step because I had a very young family with three young children, the oldest of whom was three, and the others were two and a baby. It was a big commitment to go, but there was no hesitation. My wife was 100% behind me with the idea. Although we made sacrifices in order to go, there were no regrets. I think that I can speak for my wife as well in saying that it was one of the best decisions we ever made, to have taken that opportunity. I think we all benefited, even my young kids who were there, as they experienced the early part of their schooling in Italy. Even though it was a big decision, and sacrifices were made, we gained so much by going to live in Italy.

There was a rather large contingent of press and representatives of the club who met us at the airport when we arrived in Milan. It was and is the norm, then and now. In those days, it was a little different from now because the Italian transfer market for overseas footballers had only just re-opened the year before, and they were only allowing one foreign player per club, so that in itself made it into an 'attraction', bringing out the media and the fans. I think there is a reaction when the only foreign player arrives in the country. Having said that, it was a very good and favourable welcome.

I had a language tutor from day one who helped me to communicate, especially when I went to away games on the train with the squad. I never found learning the language easy. I eventually got to grips with it, although it took me all my time in Italy to do that, but it was something I wanted to do and I found it enjoyable. It was a challenge, both on and off the field. Initially, Milan set me up with someone to help me, but once I came back after pre-season training and I was into a normal day-to-day, week- to-week routine, I organised it myself, and had my own guy to help me with Italian lessons.

The club and officials helped me in every possible way. First of all, they arranged for us to see about half a dozen houses. We went out initially to sign for a couple of days, we came back to the UK, and went out again, me, my wife, and my eldest child. We spent some time with the chairman and his family, took a trip to the coast and spent some time viewing some property they had lined up for us, and from that we got a place in a little village outside Milan.

When I arrived at AC Milan there was a lot of confusion. It was difficult to tell what was going on because I couldn't speak the language, but there was a lack of stability in my period there. There was a change in ownership and of managers, but in spite of all this they were very good to me. They understood the problems that me and my family had because I was a foreign player, and the fact that they themselves had been in turmoil. So it was a very difficult time, especially the first year, but even though it was extremely hard, we got through it. I was delighted with the second year, whereas the first year was pretty bad. I learned a lot from that experience both on and off the field. It was something that you would never have experienced in Britain.

I quickly adapted and became comfortable with the lifestyle there. It's a fabulous way of life, especially for a footballer. You were made to feel very special and were welcomed, although they put an awful lot of pressure on players, particularly the foreigners. There was as much pressure as I ever felt as a football player during that spell, but it was something that I handled, and felt better and stronger for it.

Having said that, there were a lot of problems over there, because everything in the football world revolves around results. Learning the language was difficult, but the way of life wasn't a problem as I met a lot of nice people. The decision to go and live in a little village was a very good one. We were just one of the village people, even though I was a footballer and a 'celebrity'. I did have normality there, as normal as it possibly could be. But everything revolved around results, and at that time they weren't brilliant, and pressure comes from that, but we handled it and got through it.

The club president at the time was Signor Felice Colombo. He was the one who had been involved in the scandal [AUTHORS NOTE: the Italian football betting scandal of the late 1970s/early 1980s]. I think he was still a large shareholder when I arrived and was, to all intents and purposes, the owner of the club. He was a very nice man, all the promises he made to me he kept, and he was a great help. When I was away for two weeks or more, they looked after my wife and family. The president's wife came around every day to make sure everything was OK. It was really first-class the way that they took time out to make sure that me and my wife didn't have any domestic problems, and was very reassuring. It showed a lot of understanding, and I was glad that it was something that they did do because it made things that were difficult a lot easier to cope with.

I started the season very well, but then had an indifferent time. In spite of this they never ever, at any point, became discouraged. I didn't lose the support of the fans either, and they were fantastic. My nickname there was 'Il squalo' (the shark), so I had a great rapport with them, both then and now. When I go back, I'm always made very welcome. That was encouraging in the early days, and kept me going.

As for the media coverage, that was something that went on every day – it was just the norm. Before every training session there was a press conference, and it became part of your day-to-day remit, as it has done in England now, unlike before. You went to training, and had interviews afterwards to give the journalists the time that they needed. It is a big part of people's lives over there, and the Italian press do cover football well. It's not just on a Sunday either. They would write about the Sunday game and carry on discussing it all week.

The Italian players were vocal after defeats. During the early part of my time there, I wouldn't really understand what was going on but there were strong reactions to disappointments. They were also a very superstitious group. I think you could say that the Italians are superstitious, and that comes across in their football. That was a bit strange for me as I'm not a superstitious person myself, and I was never involved in a club with things like that, apart from with my manager at Leeds, Don Revie, who had his 'routines', but the Italians were paranoid about it!

I was lucky at the time I was there, even though there was only one foreign player per club, not like now where you might get six or seven foreign players in a starting eleven. The foreign players at the time were Liam Brady of Juventus, Rudi Krol at Napoli, and Herbert Prohaska at Inter. In my second year, there was Muller, Zico, Falcao, Platini and Boniek. Out of all those, I would say that Platini stood out, and he was a fantastic player. Once he had settled in, he went on to become European footballer of the year three times: that says it all. Zico was also a fantastic player. He was a Brazilian champion and really showed his class. Falcao too was a quality player.

The Milan players all helped me to settle in, and there wasn't anyone I didn't get on with. What we had there was a young element in the team, players who became the 'new Milan', people like Evani, who was on the fringes of the first team and Tassotti and Franco Baresi who were regulars. There were also other players who did terrifically well elsewhere: Romana, who went to Napoli and won the Championship with Maradona, was a terrific player; and Battistini, who went to Inter among other teams. As for the other Italian players, there was Altobelli and Tardelli. That year, we had two team members in the World Cup winning squad, Baresi, who was involved in the squad but never played and Fulvio Collovati, who did play. It was a strong Italian League at the time.

My first coach was Gigi Radice, but he was replaced around

Christmas time as things didn't go particularly well for him. Then we had a stand-in coach, Italo Galbiati, who is Fabio Capello's right-hand man at Roma at the moment, and has been ever since Capello took over from Sacchi in the early 1990s. We had those two coaches in my first year, and then we had Castagner take over.

It wasn't just the tactics that were different, it was the mentality as well. I think that's changed now. I don't think the football was far away from being a 'catenaccio' style at that time. The training was more programmed and took up more of your day. You were involved a lot more on the training field than at the club, due to having morning and afternoon sessions. I think my touch improved as a result of the training over there, and I became a better player both technically and knowledge-wise. I would have been stupid not to have improved because of the experience. I think that if you go and you open your eyes and pay attention you will learn a lot, and I think I did.

As for the needle matches, I played in three derby games against Inter Milan. My first one was good because that came very early on. It was in the Italian Cup and was a massive game, because they hadn't played each other the year before. We ended up drawing 2-2 and I scored. So that was a very big moment, because I think that got me off to a good start with the fans.

In the summer of 1983, Milan said that they wanted to make a change, and they brought in another foreign player, which made me surplus to requirements. I had a meeting with them, and they told me what they were doing. I had the opportunity to go to two or three different clubs, but the one that was recommended to me, and the one that I felt comfortable with, was Verona. I got a call from them, and it was reported in a newspaper that they were interested in me. I had meetings with them, and they eventually persuaded me to go to Verona. I was advised to go to them and it was a good move. When I left AC Milan for Verona, Milan were very supportive, and delighted for me that I was staying in Italy.

Verona is possibly the most beautiful city I've ever lived in. The club had a great team with a good family atmosphere and feel to it, and there was also a strong camaraderie. I was there for a year, and for a small side we did very well. It was a good team, with good players and a great manager in Osvaldo Bagnoli. I also made some good friends there, as I had done in Milan. We got to the Italian Cup Final, which was good and bad, in that it was my last game for Verona, but unfortunately we got beaten by Roma. It was a year of frustration for me, because I got a thigh injury which prevented me from being available for all the games, but for all that it was a brilliant year and a great place to live.

I was glad that I had the extra year in Verona. The one big disappointment for me was that I never had the chance to get over there earlier. I would have liked that, but then again to have done that, I would have had to sacrifice some of my time in England, and that would have been difficult, because I had some great years at Leeds and a fantastic time at Man United. I think I would have enjoyed spending more time in Italy, but I had three years so I can't complain!

My last game for Milan was in a competition organised by Silvio Berlusconi called the 'Mundialito', which involved AC Milan, Juventus, Inter Milan and Flamenco. All the games were sold out, despite them being friendlies. When I left both Milan and Verona, it was encouraging to see the players and fans show their appreciation of me. They hung out good-luck banners for me in my final games for them.

I do go back to Verona and Milan quite often. I went up to Verona last year after staying a while in Tuscany, and although I haven't been to Milan in the last six months due to my coaching commitments at Huddersfield, I'll be going back to the San Siro next Wednesday with my sons, who are in the Cardiff and Bristol City squads, for the Champions League Final, as well as for a long weekend sometime during the summer.

As for my memories of playing in Italy, there's an intensity about the game and a structure there to support the argument that it's the best League in the world. I know the stats will tell you that the Spanish League is the best, and it's very hard to argue against that. I feel that the Italian teams in Europe over the last couple of seasons have failed to deliver, but prior to that two-year gap, the Italian qualification ratios and performances in Europe have been exceptional. Italian football comes as a package. You can't have it without the intensity, the big crowds and the media attention. You can't have everything that goes with it without it being what it is, which is a game where there is an awful lot of pressure on people involved in the game, not just the players, but the management, the supporters and the media too, who are all expected to deliver. That's the recollection I have of it, these factors that make it and made it the best league in the world. The stadiums were marvellous, and the support I had at Milan was unbelievable. There was a great atmosphere about the game, and a professionalism about the players, things that have been spoken about here in England in the last couple of years that have always been the norm in Italy.

I think the players that have come to England from abroad, especially from Italy, have brought that professionalism with them. Whether it's with regard to the diet, the discipline they have there or the routines prior to training, they've certainly made a contribution. So all those things that I saw twenty years ago are coming across here, not by British players going abroad, like Paul Lambert who is one of the last and latest ones to go abroad. They're very few and far between now, because the players are now coming in the opposite direction. I never imagined that it would happen that way. I would say that the top foreign players in the Premier League have contributed greatly.

I still think it's unfortunate that players don't go abroad now because it is different, and it's difficult because there is as much money here in Britain now as abroad. But it's not just about money, and I think it's something that I certainly gained from. I also believe that if you don't play abroad, it's something that you would look back on and wish that you'd had that opportunity. Take Paul Lambert for example. He could have remained in Scotland and had a good life, but he went to Germany and changed so much, not just because he won the Champions League, but changing by playing and living in a different country at the top level. That's something that happens very rarely nowadays.

When I left Verona and Italy, I was thirty-two and had to find somewhere to live in England. We made the decision to come back because I felt I was still at an age where I could contribute to an English club, and if I had stayed in Italy any longer I wouldn't have had that. I came back, had no idea where I was going to go, and had one or two offers, the best of which was from Southampton. I got a three year contract and it was a great move for me which enabled me to play again at the highest level.

The one moment that stands out for me of my time in Italy was the goal I scored against Inter in the derby in the Italian Cup. That brought everything together at a time when I was trying to channel my energies into playing at the top level, in front of a full house in a derby game and to score a goal. It wasn't the winner but it should have been! It captured the essence of everything that Italian football is all about.

As for any advice I would give to players of today, if I was in my mid-twenties now and had achieved everything I wanted domestically, I wouldn't have any hesitation in going abroad. I can't say for other countries, as I haven't played or lived in them, but certainly as far as Italy is concerned I would say yes. Playing abroad was always something I wanted to do. Even if I was a wealthy guy in my mid-twenties at this moment in time, I would still do it because it's about achieving things, not just a bigger bank balance, but about experiences, not just medals, but all of those things. Above all, it's so that you can be in a position where you can go and do things, and you can look back on them with satisfaction. You'll also gain from the experiences you have away from football. I would certainly recommend it to anyone who was fortunate enough to have the chance to do it".

After returning to Britain from Verona in 1984, Joe Jordan had spells with Southampton and Bristol City, before moving into management in the 1990s at Heart of Midlothian, Bristol City and Stoke City. He currently divides his time between his duties as coach of Huddersfield Town and working as a match summariser for Channel Four's 'Gazzetta Football Italia'.

David Platt

PLAYER
Bari, (Italy), July 1991 – June 1992
Juventus, (Italy), July 1992 – June 1993
Sampdoria, (Italy), July 1993 – July 1995

MANAGER
Sampdoria, (Italy), December 1998 – February 1999

David Platt began his professional career with a brief stay at Manchester United, the club he supported as a boy, before moving to Crewe Alexandria in 1985. He stayed with the Railwaymen for three seasons until Aston Villa signed him in 1988. During his time with Villa, he won the first of his 62 England Caps, scored three goals in the 1990 World Cup Finals in Italy, and later went on to captain his country. We pick up David's story in February 1991:

"It was in February 1991 that Bari came over to watch a game which I played in – the Bari president actually came over too. They had made the initial contact through an ex-player of theirs, Gordon Cowans [see later Chapter], who I was playing with at Aston Villa. They said they were coming over, and asked me whether I would be interested in joining them. At that time I really wanted to go to Italy, so the initial contact was made through them looking for me. They had checked to see whether I was available and willing to move over to Bari, and obviously because of my positive reaction to this, they followed it through.

They chased and chased me, and just before the end of that

season I went over to Bari for talks. It was a magnificent contract offer, but one that I turned down as I believe that there were other clubs interested in me at that particular moment. In fact I knew that there was other interest in me in Italy at that time. After I turned them down, I came back to Aston Villa in the summer of 1991 with the intention of staying at Villa Park for another twelve months, having another good season, and hoping that a bigger Italian club would come in for me.

All these things clicked into place, but it was the persistence of the Bari president chasing after me, not so much the financial package, but what he was trying to do with the club, that persuaded me to accept it.

In terms of how my family reacted to the news, I'd been saying that I wanted to go out and play in Italy for a long, long time. I was more or less leading my family into what I wanted to do, so it wasn't necessarily the other way around. My girlfriend at that time, now my wife, came out to be with me in Italy a few months after I arrived.

I guess that given the stage I was at in my playing career I felt, after I came back from the World Cup, as though I was one of the top players in the world. I wasn't frightened of anything and I had a lot to prove. Going over to Italy I realised the extent of the quality needed to succeed over there. I did put myself into that category, because I did think that I was more than good enough to play in Italy, as I knew that I was good enough to play for my national side. At that time I was probably not at the top of my playing career but very high up in it.

I think Villa were sad to see me go, but it was a very amicable split. They realised that I wanted to further my career. I'd been saying for a long, long time that I wanted to go and play in Italy, but I don't think they wanted me to go, as they didn't need the money, but in all honesty it was the right time for me and perhaps for the club as well. A lot had changed and things had been broken up.

I hadn't been to Bari previously, apart from Italia 90, but I had been to Italy before on holiday. In terms of the Italian language, I didn't speak it properly. I had about ten lessons before I went out there. They got me past the first stage of saying 'hello' and 'how are you', but I think that in the first week of being out in Italy I learned a hundred times more.

I didn't know what to expect, but I went into it with a very open mind. I knew that I would have to go to the country, that I couldn't change their culture, and that I would have to change mine. I went into it with a vague understanding of what I had to do to achieve things. I hadn't heard a great deal of Bari, although obviously I'd been there before. People told me that it was a different world, in terms of the Northern/Southern split in Italy, but in all honesty I was very realistic and went into everything very open- mindedly so it wasn't a problem for me.

The reception I got when I arrived there was unbelievable. There was a massive amount of media attention, and a lot of supporters came up to see my first game which was in the mountains in a pre-season friendly, so there was a huge amount of support. After a couple of weeks up there, we went to Bari for the first training session. We had to have it in the main stadium and there were 20,000 supporters inside the ground. It was a massive public fanfare.

In terms of learning the language, the club helped me a great deal. The best way to learn a language is to be in the dressing-room by speaking it day in day out with your team-mates, but I was having lessons as well, and had them for about three months. It wasn't easy, but I practised it twenty-four hours a day, and the good thing about moving to Bari was that it wasn't like Rome or Milan, where you could get away with speaking English – you do have to speak Italian. Bari found accommodation for me, I settled in very quickly, and they made everything very easy for me.

It took me about three months to get used to the difference in the football, but once I'd done that I was moving on quite rapidly. I joined in the summer, so the season hadn't begun. We didn't start off very well at all, and although our season did pick up, unfortunately we were relegated at the end of it.

I got on magnificently with everybody: fans, players, officials, the board, and particularly the president. He took me under his wing, and we still speak on a regular basis. I could still go back to

Bari now, and if I walked onto the pitch they would sing my name, so that's one of the good memories I have of my time there.

I got on exceptionally well with the press, and my whole year there was a good one because I got on with everybody, and they appreciated the fact that I went out and tried to make myself 'Italian'. In fact, when Juventus bought me twelve months later there was a quote coming from them saying that they were actually buying an Italian! That was pleasing, because I think I had to do that. The English players didn't have a good reputation over there, but I think I helped to boost it up after that.

I think the most memorable game I played in was against Roma, at Bari, where we won 2-1. We were 1-0 down at half-time. I had actually been ill for two days before that match, and crawled off my sick bed and scored the two goals to win the game, the last one being in the 90th minute. The saddest moment for me was leaving the club. I'd enjoyed my year so much, and then having to leave wasn't a good thing, but I knew that my career was going on and I needed to move.

As for the star players, the best I played against was Franco Baresi. He was magnificent for AC Milan and never let anyone past him. He was both a good defender but nasty with it. If you got the ball past him, you didn't go past him as well.

The most striking difference for me between the game in Italy and the UK, is the patient way in which they start the game. It's much more tactical, with a lot less percentage play. If I played in midfield, they wanted me to be further forward, but I think I soon showed them that I could play in the centre of midfield and get forward and back, and once they realised through seeing me in training and in the games that they didn't have to change my or their way of playing to cater for me, it worked well.

I think there was a lot of difference in the fitness side of things. It wasn't so much the training methods or tactics, but the fitness coaching, and I noticed a big difference there. I think my game was altered a lot by playing abroad, as I became more tactically aware. In England, I had played a lot more percentage football, when I pushed on and left the central midfield areas a little bit open, but in Italy you get punished if you don't have a good shape, and I soon learned to be much more of a team player. So my game came on a great deal tactically as a result of my playing over there.

Towards the end of January/February 1992 it was clear that I was going to move. There was a clause in my contract which allowed me to go to clubs at a certain level. There were several clubs after me at the time: Juventus, Fiorentina, Napoli, Monaco and others, but I always knew that if Juventus wanted me then I was going to go there, and they bought me in the end. The fans were disappointed but they understood, especially after we got relegated. They understood too that you couldn't turn Juventus down. It's rather like playing for Coventry and joining Man United, there isn't a comparison really.

My memories of my final game? We played away against Roma, and it wasn't a very auspicious occasion. We got beaten 2-0, we were already relegated, but the supporters and the club wished me well, and I've still got a very good relationship with the club and the supporters. I've been back a couple of times since then, one of those being when I was coach of Sampdoria.

My one abiding memory of my time there was the first Roma game. It wouldn't have happened with an Italian player. No disrespect to them, but there weren't many of them that would have been ill for the forty-eight hours that I was before, and badly ill, and still played. The club doctor came to visit me and said that there was no chance whatsoever of me playing. I was actually sick on the pitch at half time. When I came out for the second half, I still managed to turn in a performance in the next forty-five minutes and score the two goals, including the winner in the 90th minute.

I then moved on to Juventus, and it was a difficult season for me. I was injured, plus the fact that there were four foreigners at the club [AUTHORS NOTE: prior to the Bosman ruling on overseas players, there were only three foreigners allowed to play in an Italian club team at any one time]. The manager wanted to play me in a different role, a role that wasn't really suited to me, and as a result I didn't play many games. I scored some goals, won the UEFA Cup and finished third in the League, so in spite of the problems I wouldn't have changed it for anything, but from a football point of view I wanted to leave at the end of that season.

I wanted to go to Sampdoria, and had the chance to join them when I left Bari. I had kept in constant contact with Roberto Mancini, who was their skipper, so when the opportunity came to join them I took it with both hands. In many ways it was my club, and probably the best two years of my career. From a football point of view, I got the captaincy when I was there. The manager, Sven Goran Ericsson, was absolutely superb, the players were superb, it was a strong dressing-room, we played good, enjoyable football, and the supporters were magnificent. It really was the two-year span of my career that I look back on now, and wouldn't swap for the world. It was marvellous: the club, the supporters, everything really. It was a great place to live, and the one mistake I made was coming back so early. Having said that, I wouldn't have won the things that I did with Arsenal, the FA Cup and the League Championship, but I wanted that period to last forever and a day.

When I went back as manager of Sampdoria, I hoped that it would be like it had been before but unfortunately a lot of things had changed, including the dressing room. In hindsight it would have been nicer to have had some time in England learning how to coach or being a manager in England, and not having the Italian dressing room problems, the language problems, earning respect etc.etc. On top of this there was the coaching badge problem, which they insisted was there even though it wasn't, and the media were fuelling that. It wasn't an easy position to be in, but a situation all the same that if I'd been stronger, in terms of myself and in terms of maybe having the required coaching badges and that kind of thing, it would have been something that I would have liked to have done. It was a no-win situation for me and the club and it was the right thing for me to do to resign".

After returning from Italy in 1999, David Platt was appointed manager of Nottingham Forest and stayed for two seasons. He is currently the manager of the England under-21 side.

Jimmy Melia

MANAGER
Al Shab, (Dubai), 1978 – 1981
Belenenses, (Portugal), December 1983 – November 1985
Kwayti, (Kuwait), December 1986 – December 1987
Dallas, (USA), 1990 – Present

Jimmy Melia was born on Merseyside, and played for Liverpool from 1954 to 1964, during which time he scored 78 goals in 287 appearances and won two England Caps. Spells with Wolverhampton Wanderers, Southampton, Aldershot and Crewe Alexandria followed, before he began his coaching career at Crewe in 1972. He had a three-year spell managing in Dubai (see below), but is perhaps best remembered as the manager of Brighton and Hove Albion, the team he took to the 1983 FA Cup Final against Manchester United, before losing the replay. We pick up Jimmy's story briefly in 1978, and then in October 1983:

"I went out to Dubai in 1978, and worked for three years as manager for the Al Shab club. The ruler of that state was Sheikh Faisal bin Khalid Al Qasimi, and I was on very friendly terms with him. I often used to go to his palace to stay! The team did really well and I took them from the Second to the First Division during my time there. As for foreign 'stars', they tried to bring in some from China, India, and Pakistan, but there weren't any outstanding players at the time.

I remember that it was a small, broken-down little club. They then built this new stadium after three years, just before I left, and my memories are of a lot of people I got to know, many of whom are still my friends. Sheikh Faisal, the ruler of Sharjah, is my best friend there, and anytime I go back I go and stay with him in the palace. I have a lot of good memories of going around Abu Dhabi and to Dubai. It was very interesting and another great experience that I've had in my life".

October 1983

"Well, it was a funny situation with what happened. I'd just been fired after taking Brighton to the FA Cup Final in 1983, and the job at Belenenses was open. I think Malcolm Allison was also interested in taking it. I looked at the paper and found that he didn't take the job for some reason, so I called up the Embassy in Portugal and got the relevant information on the job, and let them know I was interested. Within twenty-four hours they called me back, I was in Portugal, and by the end of that week I was the coach at Belenenses.

It was a good move for me because I wanted to get straight back into football. I'm always happy when I'm involved with the game, and it was a good opportunity to go and work abroad and learn a little bit more about football.

I didn't realise how big a club Belenenses was. It was one of the largest in Portugal at the time, and it had just done a 'Manchester City', going down into the Second Division. It was a great opportunity for me to get straight back into the game and to get working again, which I did. I got there at the end of October 1983 and by the end of May 1984, I'd taken them back into the Portuguese First Division. It was like walking on water for two years taking Brighton to the Cup Final, the best feat probably anyone could ever achieve with a club, and then going the following year and winning the Second Division Championship in Portugal. They were great achievements for me. The following year I finished sixth with Belenenses in the First Division. We only missed getting into Europe by three or four points.

I had a fantastic time, a great three years, and everything was going really well, but then I got another year there and things didn't work out as well as I expected. But I only needed to have stayed three more months to go into the Guinness Book of Records as Belenenses' longest-serving coach, because the most anyone had stayed was about six months! It was a tough situation, a difficult club to coach and difficult people to work for, but I had a fantastic time, a great board of directors, and the supporters were unbelievable to me.

It was quite funny getting used to the crowds over there. As soon as I walked out on the field during the first two or three games, the people just stood up and clapped me onto the field and I thought to myself that this was great! Then one game we played terribly and I thought 'I'm not going to get cheered out next time!' So I walked on the field the next game and they cheered me again, so I thought I'd better stay on as long as I could!

As for Portuguese, I used to speak 'um poco'. I could speak a little bit of the language and that helped me to get by, but I did have an interpreter with me. My assistant was Portuguese. I can't remember his name off-hand, but he was the player who injured Pele in the World Cup and he played for Benfica.

I didn't know that much about Portuguese football before I went there. All that I knew was that John Mortimer, who was a friend of mine was at Benfica quite a lot. He had been working in Portugal, and Malcolm Allison was at Sporting Lisbon. The Portuguese all knew about English culture and the English game.

I don't think a lot of people knew at that time about my arrival. I think the club kept it quiet because I think they missed out on somebody for some reason or another, so they wanted to make sure a certain player stayed, and as a result it was a quiet reception. Then there was quite a big report afterwards. In Portugal, you've got about ten different newspapers all full of football stories! There's something going every day on every page, so once I finally signed, 'A Bola', which is the main Sports paper over there, was full of the news that I was going to be the coach. I was never out of the newspapers over there. Every day there would be something in the press all about me, the team and everything else, and they were all nice to me. The reporters were all good, and people from the town and the club still call me even now. It was a great time.

When I first went to Portugal, I wasn't very happy. It was

raining every day, and I just felt that it was like being back home,. But by going to the local restaurants, just getting used to everything and getting yourself involved, you get to know the people and they get to know you, you know where and when to go. You also get to learn about driving on the other side of the road! It was a funny situation because they put me up in a five star hotel on the seafront, and I stayed there basically for the three years I was with Belenenses!

It was terrific, especially the third year even when we didn't do that well, because normally you last about two years in Portugal, and I was going for my third year. I've never known a president so upset when I got fired. It was the Board that fired me. I think you normally find that in football it's all about results, and if the results aren't good you get fired. That's the same anywhere in the world. I don't think the fans gave me a nickname, but I know they were always terrific to me. They used to called me 'Meester Meelliur'! I'll always have great memories of Portugal.

The memorable games were against Oporto. We played them in the Portuguese Cup and even though we lost the game, I think ours was one of the few teams that kept the score down to about one, which was good over there because no-one was allowed to win in Porto, as Bobby Robson will tell you! We went to Benfica and put up a good show against them, and against Sporting Lisbon, and always made it difficult. They were the big teams. Oporto had all the best players at that time. They had particularly good midfielders and defenders, six or seven of whom were in the national team. They were always difficult to play against and had excellent skills and ability.

The people were unbelievably nice in Portugal. In every restaurant and everywhere you'd go, everyone would know you. They would tell you exactly what the team you were playing were like and how they played. They were just football mad! They all knew everything about the game, because it's a religion over there, particularly in restaurants with all the waiters. I used to go to one hotel every Monday and one particular guy would tell me everything about the team we were playing next week, about all their players and what they had done!

The training methods were very different from England, and this was where I think I learned a lot about the game. In England, everyone played the same way at the time which was the basic 4-2-4, but in Portugal everyone played a different formation. In England we would defend on the half-way line, whereas in Portugal they would defend on the penalty box. It was still tight, and they were still using the one-point and the two-point scoring system, so a point away from home was a great result. They would play it very tight, and make it very difficult to break people down. Trying to get at them and behind them was tough because the opposition would always have nine people around the ball, and make it very hard for you to try and get a result at home. I learned a lot over there, and I wish I had gone over much earlier in life.

I've got to tell you one thing. When I was there, Liverpool were playing Benfica in the European Cup. Sven-Goran Ericsson was the coach, and we spent a lot of time together talking about Liverpool and football. And I've got to tell you, I think that bringing him in as manager of the England side was the greatest move in the history of English football because that guy knows the game. He understands people and I think it was a great move on the part of the Football Association. He understands different cultures because he has worked all over Europe, and I can't stress enough how good I think he is, and everyone will find that he'll be very successful. The country's lucky to have him

As for leaving the club, it's going to happen to us all. I related well with the fans, because I tried to play good attacking football which they liked. They always remember me, and I think they'll always respect what I did for the club.

The media coverage was very unfair at the time, because of the record that I'd had over the three years. They should have given me at least until the end of that season. I got a Championship medal for winning the Second Division and a prize for a North v South game that we won.

At the time, I think I was just glad to get back to England after I left Belenenses. There was a lot of day-to-day pressure, with everything you did and everywhere you went, there were people watching you. I was certainly glad to have a job back in England after being so successful.

It was a great experience. I gained a lot of knowledge and increased my understanding of football. I was so lucky to coach and manage a club like Belenenses. The experiences I had there certainly helped me in the future. It was a great time and a marvellous club, and I look forward to going back and I've been back many a time. They were good people and were great to me. I haven't really been in touch with the club for the last ten years since I've been in Dallas, but all of the time they've always been nice and invited me to the games. They always give me a warm welcome, make me feel at home, and introduce me to the supporters.

Just after that, I went straight to Kuwait in the summer and I worked out there for the Kwayti club. It was a great traditional club but they had just been relegated to the Second Division, just like Belenenses had been, and it was a case of trying to get them back up into the top flight. Things didn't work out at that club because there was so much politics involved, and people trying to tell you who, what and how to play, and I had to do what I needed to do. We eventually finished second in the League but only the Champions got promoted. It was a disappointing season, because we were good enough to be in the First Division, but because of the people around me it didn't work out. You're working with a different culture, they all want to do what they feel they want to do, and they want to pick players and put you in positions that you didn't need to be in. Once I found out that I couldn't do the job properly, I left after nearly a year.

After I had finished in Kuwait, I came back to Britain the following year and then went back out to Dubai to set up my own football camps. I was building them up nicely in Abu Dhabi, Sharjah and Dubai and Coca Cola were sponsoring me. I went to work for a friend of mine in some camps in Palo Alto in San Francisco in 1990, when the Gulf war broke out in Kuwait. I didn't want to go back, and these two kids turned up from Dallas to this camp I was running in the States and said 'we were told to come to this camp because Jimmy Melia was here'.

So I worked with them for a couple of weeks, and then their parents asked me to come back to Dallas to do some camps there. I went back, they sponsored me for about three months and they said that they wanted to start a new club, which we did. It was called Dallas Inter and is now called the Dallas Solars. We then built this club up with the development side, with boys from age eleven to nineteen, and that's where I've been ever since. I also coach two girls teams and two boys teams in the eleven to eighteen age group.

As for the game here, all Americans want to be successful, and the men's team is not that successful. But the women have got the best team in the world plus they've got the best girls at junior level in the world, because the women have been playing football for a long time, not like in England. I noticed that England are starting to build up now and get really interested in women's football. In America they have got some fabulous players. There is a girl I coach who plays for the national team and she's a great player. The girl's programme is unique.

My advice to any British manager with offers to coach abroad? I would say take it, and learn as early and as quickly as you can, because I think that anybody now in the football community will be able to get jobs if they've worked in one or two different countries, as the knowledge and experience of working abroad is completely different and brings a lot to your coaching skills.

I would love now, with what's going on in England, to be going to Italy or Spain to coach. I think it would be a great experience for everybody, especially when you think of all the foreign coaches in England, and they're all doing great! The French guys are doing well at Liverpool and at Arsenal. I think now that people are looking for this. Football clubs are looking for people with wide-ranging knowledge and different experience.

Will the US men's team win the World Cup? I don't think they're ready for that yet. I think they're fortunate that they can qualify because of the Federation they're in, but I do think there has been a big improvement, and what I'm seeing now is a change with the younger ones. In America, what they're concerned about is education first and sport second, but now I'm seeing seventeen and eighteen year olds playing with the national team, and people leaving school to do this, which they normally wouldn't do to play football.

People have got to realise that everything's changing in the world. You've got to get your minds right. They're going to have foreign cultures and coaches in England and all over the world, and this is going to help everybody.

I'll be watching the Greece/England games on Fox Sports tomorrow, but hey Nick, I've got to go out and do some coaching now! I hope England win tomorrow! Bye!"

Jimmy Melia currently lives in Dallas, USA where, as previously mentioned, he coaches local youth team football with the Dallas Solars at several levels.

John Charles CBE

PLAYER
Juventus, (Italy), May 1957 – February 1962
Roma, (Italy), November 1962 – March 1963

John Charles was the first British footballer to have played abroad, is still the finest British footballing export, and a worthy recipient of the title 'football legend', never once having been cautioned or sent off. He began his career with Swansea Town, in the city of his birth, before being signed by Leeds United in 1949. He was to spend eight happy years there, during which time he won a Second Division Championship medal in 1956 and the first of his 38 Caps for Wales, his debut coming against Northern Ireland in March 1950. The 42 goals he scored for Leeds in the 1953-54 season remains a club record to this day. We pick up John's story in May 1957:

"Kenneth Wolstenholme helped to organise the deal, but I think Juventus came to Leeds to have a look at me, and he recommended me to them. I definitely saw it as a challenge, and when they came for me I didn't know much about the club. Then I got to know a little bit about them, and found out that they were one of the best teams in Italy, so I thought I would give playing out there a try.

Well, coming from Swansea to Leeds, and then staying there for ten years, and then moving again was a bit heartbreaking, especially as I thought I was settled here in Leeds. I'd been playing for the juniors, then the second team, then the first team, and I thought I was going to be playing football here the rest of my life.

I believe that money played a big part in the transfer, as I think Leeds were short of funds at the time and it was important for them to obtain some transfer money because of the West Stand fire the year before [AUTHORS NOTE: a fire in the West Stand at Elland Road the previous year, which was under-insured, left the club in financial difficulties].

I had never been to Italy before I went to play for Juventus, and I remember asking someone at the time where Turin was! But once I found out, I thought I'd try it. I didn't know what to expect, but the only difficulty really was the language. To begin with, I didn't speak Italian and it took me a long time to learn it. I had also never heard of Juventus before, because in those days we never took any notice of foreign teams. We knew about Brazil and Argentina because we watched them on television. There were other teams, but Italy didn't get the publicity that they do nowadays. I went to Turin by plane, but you couldn't get a direct flight from Leeds or London to Turin in those days so I went to Paris, and then on to Turin.

There wasn't a big fanfare when I arrived, just a few reporters there who wanted to know who I was, but that was all. There was also the chairman and vice-chairman of Juventus there to meet me. The chairman was only twenty-two or twenty-three and his name was Gianni Agnelli. I think the family owned half of Italy!

I picked the language up as I went along just by mixing with people, going out to dinners, and by speaking Italian all the time. That way I got to know it. The club found a nice place for us to live. It was a little house on a hillside overlooking Turin, which was lovely. All the players lived around me in that district.

When I arrived, Juventus weren't doing very well in the League. I was lucky enough to play with an Argentinian forward called Omar Sivori, who came the same time as me, and we hit it off straight away. They already had a great player at Juventus, an Italian called Giampiero Boniperti. They were struggling before we went there, but then they put the three of us together, and all of a sudden we won the Championship the next year. Juventus were nearly relegated the year before, and then we won the Scudetto in my first season (1957/58). So in that year they brought a few players in, Italians as well, as we seemed to click, and like everything else, when you click, you do well, and we won the Championship.

The fans called me 'Il Buon Gigante', 'the Gentle Giant'. Apart from Sivori and Boniperti, we had a centre-half by the name of Cervato who played for Fiorentina, the Italian national team, and then came to Juventus. He was a great player as well. They were a very rich club and they bought the best players. I also got on very well with the club officials. Let's face it, they could all speak English so I was very comfortable!

The press were always around, and were at the ground each day. There was a reporter there every day, because the 'Guerin Sportivo', which is a Milan-based newspaper, wanted to know everything about you. I was hoping that the press and the fans would like me and I think they did. I think that once I started scoring goals and winning matches, I got them on my side.

The needle match was against Torino, and when I was there the locals were always telling me what a great side they were, not when I was actually there but before I was there. There was the plane crash of a few years before in which the whole Torino team was killed – they were supposedly the best club in Italy. But then Juventus came to the fore, and took over from them. We also played AC Milan and Inter Milan, and they were always hard games.

I think the Italians were a bit above us in terms of their football set-up and organisation, and the players were looked after so well at that time. When we got there, they asked how many there were in my family. I said I had four sons, so they gave me an enormous car to ride round in! All in all they looked after me very well.

The manager/coach at the time was a fellow named Brocic. He didn't change my approach to the game. He just used to tell me go out and play as I normally did. You did your training, and then on a Sunday he used to just tell me to play in my normal style.

We used to do morning AND afternoons for training, and that was the big difference between Juventus and Leeds. We didn't do it at the ground though. Instead we had to go away to a special training camp at the beginning of the season for a fortnight, where we had no contact with anybody. It was just football football football and it went on until 10 or 12 o'clock at night. There was nothing else to do but think about football. The trainer had a blackboard out all the time. He used to talk at you about tactics for about an hour, then we would have a short break and then we would go back and do it all again! The training was taken very seriously at Juventus I can assure you. You couldn't mess about, and they would be down on you like a shot if you didn't do something properly.

Did my skills improve when I was out there? Yes and no, because I think you're born to be a footballer, and I just think that everything came into place for me at the right time.

With being at Leeds, winning the Second Division and being promoted to the First Division, and then going to Juventus and winning the first Championship for years, they hadn't won it for about five or six years, and to win it again in 1961, was an incredible turn of events. The fiestas that were going on when we won the Scudetto were unbelievable! I think we had to beat Padova to win the Scudetto in 1958, and we beat them. At the time they were known as 'the Tanks', because all their defence were 6'5"! It was unbelievable – they even made me look small next to them! They also used to call them 'the Panzer Division'!

It was wonderful actually, being in Italy at Juventus. They looked after me terrifically well and I was lucky to go to such a good club. There are a lot of great clubs in Italy, but I think Juventus are one of the best. The lifestyle and the food was very different, but I suppose you've got to adapt to it, and in the end I got used to it and loved it.

When I went back to Leeds in 1962, Juventus weren't keen to let me go, but I wanted to come back to Leeds, where I wasn't born, but where I started off my football career. My stay at Leeds wasn't a successful one that time, but when you think of it Leeds had progressed as a team after I left and grew to be a great side. I moved back to Italy after that, to Roma, which wasn't very good really. Although it was a lovely place and the people were very nice to me I just couldn't settle there. I don't know why but I just couldn't.

When the fans heard I was going back to Leeds, they called me everything under the sun! They wouldn't believe me and said all sorts of things. To be fair to Juventus, they asked me if I wanted to go. I said 'yes, I'll go back to Leeds', and that was it. The press called me everything for leaving. As for my last game for Juventus, the fans were very good towards me. The thing is, I shouldn't have left! The club didn't give me a commemorative medal when I went because you only get a medal when you win something, and they used to love winning things. That is the big thing about Italy: they love to win and don't like to lose.

My memories of playing for Juventus? It was everything really. For a start the city of Turin was beautiful, the ground was marvellous, and the players I played with were absolutely great. The citizens of Turin were not like the people down South, more like our own people.

When I boarded the plane, I did think that I'd done the right thing and not the wrong thing. I thought that because I had kids I wanted them to be educated in England, which was stupid really because they would have been better off there learning Italian, and then they would have been speaking two languages.

I think the best time was when we won the first Championship at Juventus, and I won the first Scudetto so to speak. We played Padova in the last match of the season and I scored the winning goal to win the Championship, and that was a great thing. There were always meals for the families, for any little thing that happened. There was always a fiesta going on! After winning the Scudettos, it was all go all the time. Every night someone would invite you for Dinner, and you were always on the move.

I still go over to Turin, and as a matter of fact I'm going over this month. I go over every year to a friend of mine, a full-back who was named Boldi. He didn't play very much in the first team, and was more a reserve player. I was very friendly with him at the time, and I still go over there to see him now.

As for playing abroad these days, the thing at the moment is that English players now are earning as much as they did and do in Italy, so if they don't want to play abroad they don't need to go. They've got to think about it now and ask themselves whether it's better to go over there or stay where they are, especially as they are getting well paid. I went because of the money. It was a big adventure and the five years I was there were lovely ones for me and my family. I suppose it all depends on what the player thinks, how he feels, and if he thinks he can do well somewhere else. If he's not doing too well at his own club and he gets invited to be transferred, I don't see why he shouldn't go".

> *After returning from Roma to the UK, John Charles moved to Cardiff City, where he played until his retirement in 1966. He currently lives in the Bradford area, and does charity work in conjunction with the former players association of Leeds United.*

Marieanne Spacey

PLAYER

HJK Helsinki, (Finland), May – September 1989

Marieanne Spacey is a pioneer of the women's game in Britain and England's most capped player, with 91 international appearances and 28 goals. She began her playing career with Friends of Fulham, and we pick up Marieanne's story in May 1989:

"What happened was that a guy managing Millwall Lionesses at the time had been playing in Finland, and then he came back over to the UK to manage Millwall Lionesses. Louise Waller, who was playing for Millwall, had been out there the previous summer season, and HJK Helsinki, the Finnish club, said that if anyone else was interested it would be great to have them playing the next season. Whilst we were playing Millwall, Alan (their coach) asked me whether I was interested in a summer season in Finland, and I said yes, as long as it didn't interfere with anything that was going on with the English national side. So the initial contact was actually made here with a guy who had contacts over there. I was with Friends of Fulham at the time.

My family thought it was a great move, and were very supportive. My father had already been out to Italy with me when I'd been offered a contract out there, and he said that whatever I chose to do was my decision. If I said yes, he would come out with me and make sure I was OK, and if I said no that I'd come home with him. But playing Finland seemed a very good idea at the time, for the simple reason that there was due to be an England game and a training camp, and HJK Helsinki said that it wouldn't be a problem for me to go to this camp. They would fly me back to the UK for the game and training, and then fly me back to Helsinki. In fact they were so accommodating that it would have been churlish to say no.

At that stage, I had been in the England squad for five years and was a regular member of the starting eleven. We were also doing quite well at Friends of Fulham, having just got through to the final of the FA Cup but we lost. So it just seemed like a good move, just to get some experience of playing in another country. I hadn't even gone to Finland to play for England, let alone on holiday, so it was a completely new experience.

Before I went, I'd been in touch with Alan and Louise and they explained everything thoroughly to me. I had actually played in an international club tournament before that in Menton in the South of France, and when they asked if I would guest for Helsinki I said yes. A free trip to the South of France, and to play football, it sounded ideal! I played in this competition for HJK Helsinki and won the 'player of the tournament' award. That's when they said they would like me to play for them in the summer season as well. I got to know some of the players very briefly at this tournament, and they said it would be really nice to have me and Louise playing over in Helsinki.

We went over to Finland in May 1989. We had just finished the season here and from there it was straight across to Helsinki. There was no big fanfare when we arrived. We just sailed through the airport and we met up with Alan. He was over there at the time, and it was just like we were tourists, as nobody else noticed us at all.

The domestic arrangements were all sorted out for us. The club paid for an apartment for the duration of our stay, and found it before we went because they knew we were coming. They had a sponsorship deal with a cafe bar for our lunches, and another deal with a proper restaurant for our dinners. So our food was all taken care of, and we had a nice apartment where we could cook if we wanted. We were only a short tram ride outside of Helsinki, and it was an ideal situation, because it was ten minutes away from the city, ten minutes away from training and from the ground, and five minutes away from where we could eat. As well as this, our friends and some of our team-mates were around the same area, so it was ideal.

HJK Helsinki were doing well at the time although the season had only just kicked off. They'd had a good season the previous year, but the League title was a bit elusive for them. It was always between them and another team, PPP I think it was, and one other team as well, so the Championship was always very close. Helsinki had some very good players. One in particular was the Finnish national team goalkeeper, who I knew about because I had played against Finland for England in a home international. I knew the keeper because she had a fantastic game, and when we went over she made us feel very welcome.

The president was a fantastic guy for the women's side, and he couldn't do enough for us. He took us for trips to the Adidas factory and kit us out. He had contacts with this video store, so we could go out and get videos any night we wanted. It was fantastic. He did all this without making us feel like we were something really special, but it just made us feel very welcome and that was really nice because it was difficult to begin with. At the time I was twenty-two or twenty-three and away from home, and although you're loving it and enjoying the time, you're still away from your home environment. But we settled in easily and very well, which was good.

There wasn't a great deal of support for the game out there, but when we were over there it was very much on its way up as the English game was as well. So the games weren't that well supported, but there was a regular group of supporters who would always be there. They took to me and Lou very well, and called me Max as everyone does here. That's a horrible name isn't it?! It's just that Marianne on the pitch is too long and it just got shortened down to Max, and it went on off the pitch as well. Only now have I stamped my authority off the pitch and said 'Look! It's Max on the pitch and not off it!' It's not anything to do with 'Mad Max' either!

Our matches were covered by the press every week, which was good. In one of the games I scored a goal where I got the ball on the half-way line, and ran through and scored having beaten several players. That was hailed as a 'wonder goal'. I've still got the clipping now and I don't even know what it says! At the time I had it translated, and they described it as a Maradona-type goal. The following week, there were a few more fans at the ground, so I think my 'wonder goal' might have pulled in a few more people to watch.

One of the most memorable games was when we played in Lapland. We had to fly up there for a game, and even though it was June or July there was still snow around the edge of the pitch. It was cold, but it was just a great experience. I didn't see Father Christmas which I was disappointed about – he was obviously resting! It wasn't a fantastic game or anything like that, just another experience of being in Finland, of getting the chance to fly up to Lapland and come back and say that I'd been up there. There was snow on the ground in June, it was freezing cold and we were playing with three layers of clothing on! That was another good experience.

The Finns had a national League back then, which we didn't have in the women's game in Britain. We just had regional Leagues, whereas in Finland it was national. We were travelling by plane to a couple of the games and by coach to a few others, so the travelling was the big difference. That has evened out now due to the travelling we do to games over here. I think there were about eight or ten teams in the League. The football over there was of a good standard, and there wasn't a team that you would crush. They were very 'much of a muchness' in level, but everywhere we went there were a lot of local derbies. They weren't derbies like you would have here – it wasn't such a crunch game or grudge match mentality – but they were hard-fought, fiercely contested games. As for the crowds, you're probably talking the same as you get over here, with about one or two hundred people watching.

We played on the outside pitches to the old Olympic stadium in Helsinki, and if there was nothing else on people would come to watch. But at the time there was a lot of ice hockey, and that was the big sport, so we were really competing with that for the supporters. One time we played in an all-day tournament, which also attracted an all-day crowd element rather than just casual support. They didn't just wander in, have a look, and go home again. A lot of them stayed the whole day to watch our games, which was really good.

As for the stars of our side, the goalkeeper, Marianne Sulen, was an outstanding athlete and a great player. She was a gymnast, an acrobat as a keeper. A good shot-stopper, she was very confident and gave her team lots of confidence. She was also good on crosses and throwing out from the back.

The strangest thing for me in Finland was midsummer, which is a huge celebration over there. I've never known anything like it. On the midsummer weekend, the whole of Helsinki literally packed up, went to their summer cottages and just partied for the week! We didn't go to bed! We finished training on the Friday and they said 'Right. We'll see you Monday, you're free to do whatever you want'. It wasn't a case of 'You mustn't do this, you mustn't do that'. It was midsummer, and everybody could do exactly what they wanted to.

Louise had made friends the year before with one of the girls who played in the second team, because she had come over and played for Millwall. So they invited us to their house for the weekend, and it was just completely mad! We were in the sauna at 4 o'clock in the morning! We wouldn't dream of doing that over here. Then we were running around outside playing football at 6 o'clock in the morning, being bitten to death because the grass was long and it was damp at that time. Then you went back to training on the Monday morning with a stinking hangover and bites all over your legs, and they said 'Hi! Did you have a good time? OK! Now we work!' We usually played our matches in midweek with the odd Sunday game too, but that week we had no games, because everything was shut as it was 'midsummer'.

Our coach at HJK Helsinki was very good, and at the time we had a very talented forward called Anne-Marie. I was playing in midfield and he gave me a bit of a free role, where I wasn't playing in midfield and I wasn't up front. It was just in-between, in behind the forwards 'in the hole'. So that was really nice because it gave me a bit of a licence to roam that I didn't have over here. It was creative, but still keeping up with my defensive duties, because they had some very good, tough-tackling defenders and very defensive-minded midfielders. They would hold the midfield whilst I went off and did whatever I wanted to do between midfield and up-front. We played a 4-3-1-2 formation.

We trained four times a week at Helsinki. It was quite tough because Louise and I had already played for a whole season. When we got there they were still doing their pre-season fitness work, whereas we had just played a whole season and were being thrown into pre-season as well. They had this fantastic training facility which was behind the Olympic stadium in these woods. It was a sawdust track going all the way through the woods, up the hills and all around. As long as you stayed on the track, you knew where you were going and couldn't get lost, and we used to have to run around it twice as part of the training. It was about two or three miles, all up and down hill, which was very good. The only thing was we trained on cinders. That was quite tough, because it wasn't really a realistic game situation. You wouldn't tackle as you would on grass, whereas at Fulham we had grass training facilities. That was one thing, although two out of the four sessions we would train on grass. They were the ones we looked forward to!

HJK played a very continental style of football, in respect of the slow build-up, soaking up a lot of pressure and then hitting fast on the break. So as a forward-playing midfielder you had to be switched on all the time. You had to be adaptable, as they may have soaked up loads of pressure and be waiting for you to score that one goal that won the game. There was quite a bit of pressure, but in saying that it was enjoyable. You knew that everyone was pulling their weight, everyone was working hard for the team, and it was a very enjoyable experience on and off the pitch. We had a good time off the pitch, but did do well on it too.

As for socialising, the other players came round to our apartment a couple of times, and we had impromptu parties. They just turned up with drink or pizzas. I wouldn't say it was really outrageous, more just a nice gelling time where everyone got together and got to know each other. The thing in Finland at that time was that it seemed as if nobody went out Monday to Thursday nights, because when they go out to drink, they go out to drink until they can't drink any more! The Finnish girls were saying they couldn't go out and drink Monday to Thursday because no-one would ever go to work the next day! So on Fridays and Saturdays it was like someone had undone the leash. Everyone went out, and there was this one sports-type bar just outside the Olympic stadium where everyone seemed to go on a Friday and Saturday night. If we had a game, we would go there that night and the night after, and have a drink with our team-mates and all the fans as well.

There wasn't a major storyline in the local press when I left. It was more a case of 'Thank you very much, we've enjoyed having you here, we hope you've enjoyed your time and you're always welcome back'. It was left very much in our hands as to what we wanted to do the following year.

My final game was during an all-day tournament, and we won it, but we couldn't get the medals until a couple of weeks later. They were given out at a special presentation, but by then I was already back in England. A couple of months afterwards, England played Finland in an international game at Brentford, and the president of 'hoyyucoe' (that's how you say HJK in Finnish!) came over to give me my medal, which was really nice. When we left Helsinki we had a party at our apartment and everyone came along. It was just nice to have had such a good time with them all and to leave on such good terms with everybody as well. With all the players, it kind of got 'competitive' where they said 'When we see you at Brentford, we're going to beat you!' But it was all very good-natured. It was nice that we got to the stage of friendship that we could say that and nobody was offended or maybe took it the wrong way.

My memories of playing in Finland? The fact that it was midsummer, and we were playing at HJK in eighty or ninety degrees in the home games, and then we flew up to Lapland and it was freezing – that is a fantastic memory for me. It probably sounds really strange, but the climate of Finland is amazing, and it was so dark! The week after we were celebrating midsummer, everyone was telling us to get the game played quickly because it was going to be dark any minute! It was crazy!

When I boarded the plane to leave, I thought to myself that I'd had a thoroughly good time. We were well looked after, and had some great times with our team-mates. For the first couple of weeks, it was very much a getting to know each other basis. You had a feeling with a couple of the players that we'd come over to take their place, and there was maybe that bit of envy. But after we said that we weren't there expecting a shirt or a route straight in the first team, and that we were going to work for our places, that feeling went away. We accepted that we had to do pre-season training like everyone else, and we couldn't back out of that because we'd had a hard season. I think we played our part for settling ourselves in as well as the team-mates settling us in.

I think my favourite moment was the goal that I scored, because it was not just probably the fact that it was a good goal. It was the fact that all my team-mates, and it was my third or fourth game, were still getting used to our play and we were getting used to them. It was literally as I got the ball and started the run, that everyone stopped and watched, and I thought 'Well I'd better keep going because no-one's supporting me, they're all standing watching'. And when I scored everyone jumped on me, and that was when we thought 'This is it you know'. We hadn't just been accepted, but they realised that we had come to help them and to try and progress and win things, and that we weren't just there for any financial gain or anything like that. We were just there because we wanted to play for their team. I suppose that was a real moment of settling in. I think they came runners-up again at the end of that season. It was very close, but they just lost out on goal difference.

My future is in football in England, whether it be in a playing or a coaching role. The game in this country has progressed so much in the past five years, let alone ten years, and that's where my future lies. I've got too much experience and knowledge of the women's game at the moment to let it go to waste, and there's still a lot more I can learn. So at the moment I'd be an absolute fool to walk away from it because other people might hopefully benefit from it. I'm also part of the elite coaches programme, which is all centred around the national coaching foundation and the Football Association to mentor elite players into coaching. I'm part of the development of that with the under sixteens and the under eighteens.

I'd like to concentrate on this country, and say that in six to eight years we will possibly be front-runners towards winning the World Cup. We (Arsenal Ladies) are into Europe next season. That's fantastic for the game, and for us as a club it's tremendous. If we're going to be going out there representing the English club sides and doing everything we can to put English club football on the map as well as with the England national side, then that's great.

If I was giving advice to a young English female footballer on where to play, I think I'd have to tell them to take the English route, because there's so much happening now. Back in 1989 there weren't the opportunities that there are now in English football. Yes, if they're determined to go abroad then you can only say 'Good luck and go', but if they're not sure I would tell them to think again. Hopefully there will be a professional League here in the UK within two years, and there are academies, centres of excellence, and an elite group now starting up in September at Loughborough University. There are so many more opportunities now in this country, that if you were to go abroad you may not get a chance. I'm not saying that if you're abroad, you're out of sight and out of mind if you're playing well, but there are no scouts in say Italy or Finland to say that they're playing well. There's only your word for it, or the club's word, and with the choices available here I would definitely stay in England, unless you could play a summer season like some of the girls who go out to play in Iceland.

With the professional League in the United States, they hand-pick players, so there's no guarantee you're going to be chosen to play for your side. It might be that you end up playing, like a lot of the girls who are still on scholarships from Universities and a lot of them are doing really well. But there's no guarantee that when they finish their scholarships they will go into the professional

League. It might be a case of them doing very well, but the club saying that they aren't what they're looking for. Then they have to come home, and you don't know how much that might shatter someone's confidence. They could be doing so well at college, having worked hard educationally and on their football and fitness, and then you're told you're not what they're looking for. I just think over there, when you've got the professional League set up, you've got a much bigger chance of becoming a professional player than you have over there".

Following her spell in Finland, Marieanne joined Arsenal Ladies, winning a host of League and Cup titles. She is currently the Women's Football Development Officer with the Hertfordshire County FA, and works with the England Women's under-16 and under-18 squads. She is also a member of the national coaching foundation's elite coaches programme.

Frank O'Farrell

MANAGER
Iranian national team, June 1974 – June 1976

Before moving into management, Frank O'Farrell enjoyed a distinguished career as a player with Preston North End and West Ham, and also won nine caps for Ireland. His first coaching role came as manager of non-League Weymouth, the team he took to the FA Cup 4th Round in 1962. The first of his three spells as manager of Torquay United began in 1965, before he went to Leicester City in 1968, helping them reach the FA Cup Final in 1969, and win promotion as Champions to the old First Division in 1971. He then managed Manchester United from June 1971 to December 1972, and Cardiff City from 1973 to 1974. We pick up Frank's story in January 1973:

"I wanted to do something different after my time at Manchester United. I wanted to reassess what I wanted to do with my life, because of the experience I'd had there. It wasn't the fact that I was sacked, although I was disappointed with it, it was the way I was treated by them afterwards, with their taking me to the door of the Court before settling my claim for wrongful dismissal, a period which lasted nine months. I'd had a bad experience. My lawyer told me that I was legally obliged to sign on the dole whilst I was unemployed, and I had never done that in my life since I'd left school. And they were supposed to be the 'good guys'. So I had to reassess myself then, having met the so-called 'good guys' at Manchester United. I thought to myself that if these are the best then there's something basically wrong with football. I think I wanted to get away from that, not so much 'get away', but become independent of people like that. That's what I set out to do, and I think I achieved that later on.

I was anxious to get back working again after Manchester United, and my appointment at Cardiff City was a short-term thing. I went down there in November 1973 and stayed until May 1974. We stayed in the Second Division by drawing our last match with Crystal Palace. Just before that, in April 1974, Iran came in and offered me the job of manager and coach of the national team. Brian Clough had been offered the job before that. He decided not to go, and then they came over and interviewed me. I thought it might be interesting, and I accepted a two-year contract with them.

Brian only went there to visit. He didn't see much of it, but he made a quick decision that he didn't want the job anyway. He had left Leeds at that time, but it wasn't for him. I rang him before, when I was approached, and he said 'Well, you know, it's a possibility but I don't want to do it'. He gave me a little bit of information about it, and then one of the executives of the Iranian Football Association, a man named Shariat, came over, met me, and invited me up to a hotel in London. We spoke, he put the proposition to me, and I said that I'd go. That was in 1974. I told him that I was going to finish out my season with Cardiff. That was the important thing. After the last match finished, we safeguarded our status in the Second Division, and I flew out to Iran the following day.

My eldest daughter was at college at that time, but my wife and younger daughter came out with me. We brought some stuff out with us from home because we were going out for two years, but we kept our house in Manchester at the same time for when we returned. And it was kind of a step in the dark really, another football management job, but in a different environment and another country. It was the first time I'd done that.

I flew in to Iran at night-time. Somebody met me at the airport, took me to the hotel, and the first experience I had of Teheran was that there was a power-cut in the hotel! It was pitch-dark, and I wondered whether this a good or a bad omen! But after that they found me a nice apartment. My wife and younger daughter came out too. She went to school there, we settled down, and we met a good number of expatriate people. It was before the Revolution of 1978 and it was a good time.

It was quite a difficult brief to start with, because Iran was staging the Asian Games. Now that embraces all sports, and is a kind of 'Asian Olympics'. There was wrestling, which Iran are good at, running, athletics, and football. Football was definitely the main sport, and the brief was for the football team to try and win the football tournament. That would give Iran the greatest prestige.

The only thing was that it was very tight for time, because if I remember rightly the Asian Games were held in September that year (1974), and I didn't know one player from another. So I had to go out and see some club matches being played, get players into camp, arrange a few friendlies, and build a team that I felt was capable of winning the Asian games. I have to say that was kind of a 'mission impossible' really. The ground they built had a 120,000 capacity, and was called the Aryameher stadium. That was where the final was going to be, and the hope was that Iran would be one of the finalists, and possibly the winners of it. From the Iranian point of view, the success of the games hinged on the football team. So that was my brief, which wasn't easy.

I had never been to Iran before being offered the coach's role. I just went there for the first time to do that job. I was very fortunate in having an interpreter, although many of the locals spoke English. I always said later on that some of them were speaking English with an Irish accent after I'd been there! In the meantime I had learned a little bit of Farsi, the language, and had been assigned an interpreter, a man named Kiomars. He went to Leicester University in the 1960s and had been a Leicester City supporter, so he felt he knew me. I also felt some rapport with him because we used to talk about Leicester City. He was very helpful in putting across my points when I was giving tactical talks. He was with me all the time, and proved to be very helpful during my stay.

They also gave me four Iranian coaches, and my other brief was to pass on my knowledge and bring them on. Heshmat Mohajorani was my immediate assistant, and he took over from me when my contract ended. We qualified for the Olympic Games in Montreal in 1976 and he took it on from there.

I think the press felt that my brief was to bring on the Iranian coaches as well, and I wasn't going to be there for many years. It certainly wasn't going to be a long-term thing. Also I think at the time, the salary for me was a bit high, and the money was being supplied by the government to the football federation. The oil crisis affected the whole economy, and that came into it.

I found the players quite skilful. They were strong and the defenders were tall. It's a very large country with a varied climate. You get the hot dry summers and the very cold winters, with two feet of snow on your roof in the morning, and sometimes you had to play in cold conditions. And then up in the North, in Tabriz around the Caspian sea, it's wet and you get very green country. It's where they grow the tea, and it's a bit like England or Ireland. Down South, you've got the desert around Abadan and Awaz. So it's a very varied country and climate. The people looked different in each of the areas. In Northern Iran, you get the Kurd footballers. They're a hardy race, strong and bright. They're willing to listen and can learn, and they had the skills needed to progress their game.

I wasn't the first foreign coach to go to Iran. When I went there was an Englishman named George Skinner working there, and another man, Alan Rogers, but I was probably the first national foreign coach they had. They were very helpful to me during my time there, because they knew some of the players and were able to pass on their knowledge to me.

I also had a brief to go and visit Crown Prince Reza. He was supposed to be the next Shah, or ruler, of Iran, as he was the Shah's elder son – a nice boy. I went there a couple of afternoons a week, to his school in the palace, to teach him football. I also met the Shah and the Empress Farah. They were very nice people and he was a very nice kid, so that was a bit of an 'extra' doing that.

It was basically a case of the Iranians wanting somebody to come in who had knowledge of football elsewhere, give them a boost, and start them on the road to some success. That was the purpose of the appointment, because they had failed in the previous Asian Games and they hadn't done well in the World Cup. That was my brief, and I had to do that within three months of my going to a foreign country, without knowledge of the language or of the players.

So I got them into camp and watched them train and play their club matches. It gave me a knowledge of players who I hadn't seen, and I brought them into the camp and eventually played a few friendly matches, sometimes with European teams who were coming to Iran at the end of their season. Eventually I chose my number of players needed for the tournament. To cut a long story short, we won the final by beating Israel 1-0, and that was before a packed house of 120,000 in the Iranian capital Teheran. So I achieved my first aim, which was to win that tournament. There was great rejoicing of course, which was very pleasing.

Kambiz Atabay was the president of the Iranian FA. He spoke very good English, was close to the Shah, and was a very high-ranking official in the government. The secretary was a man named Hoshan Didiban and he was very competent. I worked mainly with these two people, although there were other officials there as well. My assistants were Mohajorani and Hassan Habibi, and they were with me in the camp all the time, and in all the talks. So in that way I passed on what experience I had to them.

The next brief after the Asian Games was to make sure that Iran qualified for the 1976 Olympic Games in Montreal, which they did. Then my contract ended, I wanted to come home, and I felt Mohajorani, who had been national youth team coach, was ready to become coach. He took over from me then, the other assistants joined him, and following on from that they went on to the World Cup in 1978 in Argentina, where they drew with Scotland! So they did well. They also got to the last World Cup in France, and one or two of the players are now playing in Europe.

I met the Shah after one of the tournaments, and he asked me 'What do you think we have to do to improve?' I said I think you have to get experience of playing against European teams to bring them on. You might not win a lot of games, but the players would gain very valuable experience playing against them. Then there would be the possibility of getting into tournaments, like Turkey, who are the next door country and play in European competitions. That was the kind of suggestion I made to him and the officials: play against the best, learn from them, and the players will see what sort of standards they'll have to attain.

They had about sixteen teams in the League, who played in Teheran, Tabriz and Abadan, so it was a national League. There were also a few clubs in Teheran, one of them being Pas, which was the Police team. We used to play there every Friday afternoon. Their League was formed in about 1973 and they had a structure of promotion and relegation. So they did have a league structure, with a team up in the Caspian sea, a navy team, one in Persepolis, and also one in Abadan. So all the major cities of the country were represented. They played in a League basis and used to get big gates, although the stadiums in Teheran and Shiraz held about 30,000. That was the average capacity, apart from the big main stadium in Teheran, which held about 120,000 spectators and had a running track. All the sports stadiums had those.

They had an English language paper, which was good for me because I couldn't read the Persian papers. There was a chap who wrote for the English-language paper, Kar Hushang Namazay, and he was very fair and spoke quite good English. Most of the expatriates who were there read that paper.

The Iranians were very fervent and vociferous supporters at the stadiums, for the League and international matches, and they would let their feelings out. If you weren't doing well they would boo you, and this happened sometimes in games where things weren't going so well, but overall it went quite well and I enjoyed my two years, as did my wife and my younger daughter. People used to say 'Oh, it's alright for you out there in the Middle East in the winter', and I'd say 'Yes, we've got two feet of snow on our flat roof!' They couldn't believe me but it's very high up there, about 6,000 feet above sea level, and the Alborz Mountains are in the backdrop of Teheran. There's one peak there where the previous winter's snow wouldn't disappear until mid-June, despite the hot weather, which gives you some idea of the heavy snowfalls you got in that area. It was a healthy climate though, quite dry and very nice.

We used to play a lot of East European sides, who had been to Australia and were coming back to Europe. We played teams from Bucharest and Romania, East Germany, Belgium, and then the youth team played in a tournament down in Shiraz in 1975. The Arsenal youth squad came over, with people like David O'Leary playing in that team. The funny thing was, I'm a Catholic you see, that they had Churches there. You could go to Mass in Iran, and the tournament was down in Shiraz. There was a Mass centre there, but there wasn't a Church as such, and the priest used to take Mass in his apartment. There were about four or five Catholic lads in the Arsenal youth team, and they asked me where they could go to take Mass! So I said I was going anyway and I took David O'Leary and a few more of them to Mass. At the time he was only a seventeen year-old boy, and I'm delighted to see that he's gone on and done very well, and is doing very well, at Leeds.

We also played Brazil a couple of times there against their youth and national team. I took the youth team to Kuwait for the Asian youth tournament, and we shared the trophy with Iraq, where they decided that rather than have a playoff they would share the trophy, and each team would have it for two years. I was also bringing on the youth players as well, and some of them graduated to the senior team. That way they replaced some of the players who'd been in the squad when I first went, they went on to Montreal to the Olympics, and to the World Cup games in Argentina in 1978.

As for the best players I had in the Iranian side, there was one very skilful forward called Ali Parvin, and he was a very clever player. There was also a young player named Hassan Rowshan, a very good finisher and he graduated from the youth team. There was also Pariz Gelikchani, a midfield player. Now he could have been a pro. He was very strong, a good footballer with good fitness levels. After the revolution, I think he went and played in the United States for San Jose. He was a very good footballer and could have played in England because he had the physique and the ability. The goalkeeper was talented too, and they were playing a good standard of football.

I don't know what effect the revolution had on the game there, because that came after I left (in 1978). I think Mohajorani had to leave, because he was a policeman, and I think he finished up working in the Middle East, in Kuwait or Saudi Arabia. He wasn't the only one who had to get out of Iran. A lot of them had to leave because they would have been judged to have been part of the system under the Shah. Mr Atabay also left, and he went to America. There was General Hojat, the head of sport, and I remember when the revolution took place that there was a picture published in the Western press where there were thirteen Generals laid out on the floor, and he was one of them. So he got executed. You know what revolutions are – they go too far and then they have to swing back again. People get hurt and shot just for being associated with the regime when the revolution took place. So it was a bit of a sad episode.

Being Catholics we used to go to Mass on a Friday, which was the holy day, and Sunday was a training day. That was a major difference. I used to let the players off for Friday, let them go home on Thursday and come back in on Sunday. So we went to Mass on Friday, because that was the holiday as it was in the Muslim country, and there were a lot of Americans who went. That's why we called it the 'American Church'. The traffic in the city when you went down to Teheran was unbelievable. It was so dense.

Walking through the bazaar was a wonderful experience, with the smells and the spices. To see them weaving the carpets and rugs, well, all that was new and strange. My wife and I used to go down there quite often when I was free, just to experience that. And the food, like the shish kebabs, was all strange but nice. I don't think there was any downside of the two years I stayed there. I think that was mainly because the job went well. It was like everything else in life. If you're in a manager's job and you're losing matches, life is hell isn't it? So being abroad and losing matches is probably worse because you haven't so many people to comfort you and talk to you. You can always find another manager here to talk to who might be in the same predicament, but when you're abroad you're kind of on your own. So it was crucial that the job went well, because if it hadn't gone well you can guess what might have happened. Football management's a precarious business you know!

In terms of my coaching skills, going out to work in Iran added to what I had already, and the experience was good. Whilst I was managing Iran, our team played against some other foreign countries, which I hadn't done previously. I also met Bert Trautmann out there. He was coaching Burma at the time, and his team were in the Asian Games. I had a good chat with Bert because he was at Manchester City beforehand. It was lovely to be able to meet Bert out there. All in all it was a benefit to be in Iran, and gave me time to assess what I wanted to do.

When I left the job I felt I'd done my stint, and had done what I'd been asked to do. By that stage, Mohajorani was capable of taking over. He was the youth coach and my assistant all that time, and I felt after my talks with people that I was happy to go. I did feel that Mohajorani was ready for it. I didn't particularly want to stay a long time out there. Two years was good. It was fruitful, it was successful, and I was quite happy to shake hands and say 'Thank you very much. I've done what you asked me to do, I've enjoyed being with you, and now I'm going home'.

The Iranian FA presented me with a very nice Persian rug, which I've still got. They last for ever of course! You can walk on them, and you don't do any damage. A lovely piece – all hand-made and very exacting work making all those stitches. They also had a bit of a leaving reception for me, and there were a few nice speeches. They gave me a nice farewell, thanked me, gave me a nice rug, and we left on good terms.

When I came home to the UK, I was invited back by Torquay to be their general manager, and I said I'd do it. That kind of thing suited me at that time. I brought Bruce Rioch in as the coach, and started him off in his managerial career. Just after that, I had an invitation to manage Newcastle United. But I made a deliberate decision not to go on the merry-go-round again, and I said 'No, I'm staying here. I'll finish out my time at Torquay and settle here'. There was also the fact that my wife had been very good and had followed me round my various jobs, and I thought well, in fairness to her, I'm not going to go traipsing around looking at new homes. So we settled down in the Torquay area.

It wasn't really a long enough stay in Iran to change me as a person, to say that I was attached to the place. It wasn't like that, it was like a long visit of which I enjoyed the experience. I also saw most of the country through going around and visiting the clubs. It was a very nice experience, insofar as I had achieved what I had set out to do, and they were pleased that they had achieved what they hoped to achieve by bringing me there, so it was a nice finish to the whole thing.

I wrote a letter to the Iranian FA when they qualified for the 1998 World Cup Finals in France. I had a very nice letter back, acknowledging the part I had played in building up Iranian football in my time there, and I was pleased to be able to watch them playing in France.

The high points of my stay were the culmination of the first year, since the first few months were difficult because of what was expected of me, and I suppose the Asian Games Cup Final, going with the team around the stadium with the trophy was another. The Shah and the Empress Farah were at the match and what with the emotion of it all, well, they were so pleased. They had built this great stadium, had seen their team gaining a victory, and I shared that with them. There was genuine emotion there, and I was part of that. It's something that I'll always remember. The players were so happy, and thanked me for helping them to do that. That was the best time.

A lot of the other stuff was routine; going to visit the clubs and talking to people. It's like any national team. You're not playing international matches every week, you're going and giving talks in different parts of the country, and that was very good because we visited places like Shiraz, Isfahan and Tabriz – all lovely cities. We saw much of Iran when we were there, and I could take my wife with me as well, which was nice. We also went to a place just outside Shiraz called Persepolis, to the ruins of the great Persian Empire. The bas-reliefs on the stonework were beautiful. You could see the curls of the hair and all the images of the conquered people coming to the Emperor, all on the walls of the ruins, and images of King Darius and Xerxes. It was all part of the history as well, and I enjoyed those kind of things.

I would say to anyone in football who was thinking of coaching abroad to go with an open mind and go with your principles. That's why you've been selected, because you obviously made an impact somewhere, and those principles carry you through. You may have to alter them a little bit, depending on what you find when you go there. You might be dealing with different characters. For instance, you could maybe bawl out an English or an Irish player, but out there no. They're kind of sensitive and you'd treat them a bit differently. You found out in the early days that they're a bit shy and in awe of you. Even though they're the best players, you have to nurture them, bring them on and encourage them, and occasionally give them a rollocking as well! But it wasn't so much that, it was more telling them what to do. You were their teacher: they would call you 'the teacher'. You were teaching them better ways of doing things, and I'd do that by encouragement and praise. And you hope that your interpreter is getting across your ideas, which Kiomars Soroushiari was able to do, because he spoke excellent English".

After returning to the UK from Iran in 1976, Frank O'Farrell had two further spells as Torquay United's manager before retiring from football. He now lives in Devon and last May completed a 70-mile charity walk from Paris to Chartres.

Tony Cottee

PLAYER

Selangor, (Malaysia), October 1996 – July 1997

Tony Cottee began his playing career with West Ham, where he was also born and brought up, and is best remembered for his lethal and productive partnership with fellow Hammers legend Frank McAvennie. A move to Everton followed in 1988, where he spent six seasons with the Toffees. He then moved back to West Ham in 1994, and we pick up Tony's story in May 1996:

"What happened originally was that Harry Redknapp, the manager of West Ham at the time, called me into the office one morning. The season had only just got under way: I think it was the week leading up to the first game of the season. He sat me down, asked if I was all right and told me that he'd had a call from an agent who was interested in taking me to play in Malaysia. So I just started laughing because I thought it was a wind-up! But he said he was serious! So I asked him what I should do. He said that I should speak to the agent and go from there. So I spoke to the agent, it sounded great and it was quite a good financial package. After that I just said to him to get the manager of the team in Malaysia (which was Selangor) to come and have a talk with me, or better still get him to fax a contract over so I could have a look at it.

I waited for about two weeks and nothing happened. In the end I went and saw the West Ham director Peter Storrie and told him I'd been waiting a while, and I didn't think that anything was going to happen. About two weeks later, Harry called me in again and said that there was another agent trying to sort the deal out. So I said exactly the same thing, that I wanted to speak to the manager or see a contract. This time I actually spoke to the manager and had a contract faxed over, so things progressed from there.

I'm married to Lorraine, and at the time our daughter Chloe was four and a half. We only had our daughter and not our twin boys back then which made it a little bit easier, what with just the three of us. My wife and I then flew out to Malaysia to visit the club. We were only there for two days, and we had to let them know before we flew back to England whether I was going to sign or not. We had a look round, and to be honest we weren't sure, but I don't think that we were ever going to be sure. But I thought that I wasn't really the first or even second choice striker at West Ham at the time, and I saw it as a new challenge. So we told Selangor that I would sign for them before we left to come back to England, and I think we had the best part of a month just packing up, renting the house out and selling cars in preparation to leave. We left in November 1996.

Both West Ham and I were really sad. When I went back there, I was looking to finish my career with the Hammers. I thought that I'd been at Everton for six years and I wanted to stay at West Ham. I am a West Ham boy who grew up as aHammers fan and was born there, but it just wasn't to be. I also think Harry needed some money in at the time. He spent quite a bit of transfer money buying Raduciou, Futre, and Dumitrescu, and it ended up that Selangor paid £750,000 for me. It was a good deal for West Ham and it was quite a good financial deal for me. so I think in the end that both parties were reasonably happy.

Fortunately I had been to Malaysia before, on tour with Everton in 1990, and the only thing I could remember about it was how hot it was, because at the time we seemed to be touring all around the Far East every couple of months, and one country was like another. But I had been there, and the only other thing I knew about the country was that they were building the tallest towers in the world, the twin towers. But beyond that, I didn't know anything about Malaysian football at all, so it was a real shot in the dark. It was also very exciting, as we didn't know what to expect.

As for knowing anything about Selangor, I didn't have a clue! I'd never heard of the team, and I didn't know anything about

Malaysian football. I just literally had to find that out before I signed for them. One of the main things I wanted to check was that the betting scandals and the match-rigging problems had been cleared up. They assured me that that was three years ago, in the past, and there were no longer any problems on that score.

My wife and I spent a bit of time travelling around before I joined Selangor. We went to Australia and New Zealand and we had a bit of a holiday for five or six weeks, which was wonderful. I reported to the club in the middle of January 1997 to begin pre-season training, as their League campaign kicked off in April 1997.

When we arrived, we had to do an impromptu press conference. They took some pictures of my daughter wearing the club scarf, which was nice, and that was it. It was a big deal for Selangor, because putting it in perspective, the biggest amount they'd ever paid out in a transfer was I think about £70,000, and now they had paid out £750,000 for me! It was a huge outlay for them, and was a big deal in the local papers.

I didn't need to speak any Malay, because fortunately their second language is English, as Malaysia was under British rule for many years. They spoke very broken English, but you could at least communicate with them. Some obviously spoke better than others, but I think half the time they couldn't understand what I was saying, what with my cockney accent! In the end I was lucky because Steve Wicks was appointed manager. I think the club wanted an English coach, so it out worked well for both Steve and me. Apart from me there were two other foreign players there. One was a South African and the other was an Australian, so that was good.

As for our housing, there were no problems with that. The club helped us get an apartment, they gave me a car to drive round in, and they looked after me very well.

When I arrived it was the start of the new season. I think the season before they won the Malaysian Cup. What happens in Malaysia is that they have a League where the top ten teams in the League split into two groups of five at the end of the season, and they all play each other again. After that they have the semi-finals and a big Final, called the Malaysian Cup Final, which they had won the year before. So obviously there were big expectations that the team would do well again, because of their winning the previous year, and the fact that they had a new big money signing in myself.

The owner/chairman was a fellow named Dato Aini. He was the man in charge and I got on well with him, as I did with all the rest of the staff. In the main, they couldn't do enough for me.

To be honest, I found the fans a bit strange because they were very interested in the English Premier League, and the games were broadcast during the week or on a Saturday night. But when the Malaysian games were played, they were very fickle. There was no real atmosphere, like what you get in England, but then there isn't an atmosphere anywhere like England in the world. But it was very different, and there were times when sometimes the other team would score a goal and they were clapping them! So I couldn't quite work out the mentality of the fans to be honest. It was certainly different to what I'd been used to. They loved English football, but I don't think they loved Malaysian football.

I did bits and pieces for the media out there. I flew down to Singapore to do a personal appearance, and there was actually much more of a reception for me down there in Singapore than in Malaysia. I think they love English football even more in Singapore than in Malaysia, and they really looked after me. In the main it was just the usual press stuff. Every now and again the cameras would turn up at the training ground, or you did the occasional personal appearance, but that was about it really.

My debut springs to mind as a memorable match. It was a good game, because we won 2-0. It was like the equivalent of the Charity Shield, and the opening game of the season. It counted as a League game as well, and it was also called the Charity Shield. I missed a penalty on my debut, and in my first game! I think they showed it live on Malaysian TV, so that was an interesting debut. We also won the equivalent of our League Cup Final, although they called it the FA Cup Final, and although I didn't actually score we won that 1-0, which was good as well. So those were the two main games. I think I only played in twenty-three matches, so they're the games that stick in my mind.

There were some Brazilians, Argentinians and Africans in the League. In the main, the foreign players were the best ones, but there's no way that anyone in England would have heard of any of them, because they were real 'journeyman' players. So there was no 'big name' as such in the Malaysian League. There was certainly no one that I could say that I'd heard of when I went there.

I've always said that I found it tough out there. The hardest thing to come to terms with was the weather, but also the defenders because I was the record signing. So every time a defender was up against me, it was like Cup Final time for them. I had a similar experience when I went to Everton as the record transfer fee, and because you are that 'record transfer fee', everyone seems to try that little bit harder against you. But the problem was that I didn't get the protection from the referee that I did in England, and even more so now. I found that in some games, I was getting kicked all over the place without getting free kicks, and they were pulling my shirt. It was difficult because of the lack of protection, and was a bit like playing against Tony Adams and Steve Bould fifteen years ago!

My best friend in the Selangor team was the Australian lad who played centre-half. His name was Mehmet Durakovic, and I got on really well with him. He was also my room-mate during away games. I think he's actually coaching back in Australia now. It was nice to have someone you could have a good laugh with and speak the same language with.

We went out as much as we could, and used to go to Kuala Lumpur, which was about five or six miles from Singapore. The rest of the time, our daughter Chloe was in a British-speaking school, which was good. But I've always been very much a family man anyway, and I don't socialise too much with the boys on the beer and all that sort of thing.

My main memory of being in Malaysia? I think just the culture shock really. Seeing four people on one motorbike, including the Mum and Dad and two young kids. Watching them chop the fish up on the floor and things like that. There was stuff that happened over there that would never happen over here, and it was completely different. There were dead cows on the side of the road, and it really felt like you were in a third world country. It was a wonderful experience from a life point of view, because it really opened your eyes, but from my footballing point of view it was totally different.

They built the team around me as much as possible. Having said that, I did feel at times that some of the local players were a bit reluctant to pass to me, because they didn't want me getting too many headlines. I did get that feeling, but you can't prove it, and you can't say too much. But I think that Steve Wicks was trying to get them to play to my strengths as much as possible, and obviously as a goalscorer, if you score goals you'll win games.

I think I just had to pace myself a little bit more in the games over there, but it was hard to adjust to the heat, and it was very difficult to play in those conditions. In a way it was almost impossible, because you couldn't breathe. It was ninety-two degrees and 95% humidity. You couldn't get that second wind that you do when you play in England. The fitness that I built up in Malaysia was totally different to what I had before. When I went back to Leicester I was so unfit it was unbelievable!

I think the style of football they played is the same as when you play continental football, and with Malaysian football the standard wasn't as good, but it was no different to the Italian or Spanish League, in that they build up from the back much more, play in midfield, and when the ball comes to the forwards, you have to work hard to hold the ball, whereas in England it was much more direct and positive. So it helped me a lot because I felt it improved my game in terms of holding the ball up and bringing other people into play. I then used that to good effect when I went to Leicester, and I think it helped me to get two or three years at the end of my career at Leicester that I didn't really expect.

They played with three at the back, and I was often man-for-man marked, which made it very difficult for me. You had to have a good touch and good skills, otherwise you just lost the ball. In the main, I played with a strike partner. I think it's very difficult when you're playing against a man-for-man marker, because even if he's a poor player, just the fact that someone's grabbing hold of your shirt and hanging on to you makes it difficult. I just had to learn how to hold the ball up, whereas in England it was a different style of football.

I always say that from a life point of view, for me, my wife and my daughter, it was a great experience. From a football point of view it was hugely disappointing, and on that score I didn't really enjoy it as much as I expected.

I went back to Leicester in August 1997. It was a strange story, because the only way I got back there was because when I was at West Ham for the first time, one of my team-mates was Steve Walford, who was the first-team coach at Leicester and is now the first-team coach at Celtic, and I introduced Steve to my Dad when he was at West Ham. My Dad is an insurance broker, and Steve had maintained his insurance for about fifteen years with my Dad. So every now and then he rang my Dad up and asked how I was doing in Malaysia and he said that I wasn't particularly happy and wanted to come home. When my Dad said that to Wally, well Leicester had just won the Coca Cola Cup, and they wanted to build the squad up for the following season in terms of having a European campaign. And he said he would have a word with Martin to see if he was interested or not. So when my Dad told me I just laughed and said 'Don't be silly Dad! I'm not going back to the Premiership!' I thought I'd left the Premiership from West Ham, gone to Malaysia, but to finish my career off I didn't think there was any way I would come back to the Premiership. Then Martin rang me one day out there, I spoke to him, and Wally also rang me three or four times. Altogether, it took me about five or six weeks, but I eventually managed to get myself out of my contract with Selangor and sign for Leicester.

I think the Malaysian press were a bit disappointed when I left, because I'd gone out there as, you called it, the 'great white hope'. I went out there, and they had a lot of expectations, because I had cost so much money. The fact I was leaving upset them a bit. In effect, I played my first game in April and my last game was in July, so I'd only really been playing there three months. I think they were disappointed with the fact that I'd hadn't been there that long. They didn't really always understand my feelings and how a foreign player would feel abroad. From a personal point of view, my wife had become pregnant, and she returned home. So I was living in Malaysia for five or six weeks on my own, which was a nightmare, and we didn't find out she was expecting twins until after I signed for Leicester. So my reasons for wanting to leave were a mixture of the personal and professional: not enjoying the football, wanting to be with my wife, and wanting the baby to be born in England, or babies as it turned out!

My last game for the club was the League Cup Final, the game I mentioned before when we won 1-0. And to be honest by that stage I'd had enough. I hadn't seen my wife for five or six weeks, and we had won the Cup, so I thought this was a good opportunity, after I'd seen the owner, to say that I needed to go home. Then I went home, and while I was at home, I think it was a two-week midseason break, I got my transfer to Leicester finalised. With the Cup Final and the midseason break, that's why I thought it was the right time, and being quite honest I'd had enough anyway, being away from home, because I'm very much a London boy and I did miss home.

So I didn't really have any time to get a presentation from the club. In my spell there, I actually received a nice gold watch, which is now in my trophy cabinet, along with a couple of other things presented to me by the rulers of Malaysia. We went to have a banquet with them, and I also got some nice gifts, not actually for what I'd done specifically at the club but it was just during the course of the season.

When I boarded the plane, I was thinking, to be polite(!) 'Thank god I'm going home!' We really enjoyed ourselves personally, but on a footballing level I needed to get back to the professional way of playing, which was obviously in England.

I think dealing with the hot weather, which happened in every game, that is the real thing that sticks with me. I think back to half time in each game, and in all the years I've played in England I've never really sweated that much. I'd look down and underneath me there was this big pool of sweat, and I'd never lost that sort of body fluid before. I think that sticks in my mind and that proves how difficult and hard it was. There wasn't actually an individual game where this happened, but just every half time. Watching all the sweat pour off you was just unbelievable.

What advice would I give a British Premiership player with offers to play abroad? I would certainly tell him, providing he was happy with it of course, to give it a go. I think Steve McManaman's a great example, obviously with the way he's playing in Spain. My situation was a little bit different because I was coming towards the end of my career, but a player in his prime, and using him as an example, Sol Campbell, I think the chance to go and live abroad and to go to Barcelona or Real Madrid or wherever it might be, would be a great experience.

From a life point of view, it just opens your eyes up and it makes you more of an adult really, which is great. On the playing side of things, if you're lucky to get a country that's a bit more educated from a footballing point of view, it's a wonderful opportunity, and in the main you get well rewarded. As you know, footballers get well paid, but if you go abroad you seem to get even better money. I'd certainly recommend it to any player."

After returning to the UK from Malaysia, Tony had spells at Leicester City, Birmingham City (on loan), Norwich City, and Millwall, his last club. He now lives in Essex with his wife and family, and divides his time between his family and various football-related media commitments.

John Barnwell

MANAGER
AEK Athens, (Greece), June 1982 – June 1983

John Barnwell was born in Newcastle, and began his professional career with Arsenal, spending eight years with the North London giants. He then moved to Nottingham Forest in 1964 and played there for six seasons before going to Sheffield United, his last club. John began his managerial career with Peterborough. He later had spells in charge of Hereford and most notably Wolves from 1978 to 1982, where he won the Football League Cup in 1980 and suffered a near-fatal car accident that same year. We pick up John's story in May 1982:

"The way that it progressed and developed was pretty straightforward. I had a three year contract at Wolves, and a further three years on top of quite a long contract. I'd had a very happy time at Wolves. We won the League Cup, we got back into Europe and everything was very exciting for everybody. But the club had begun to get itself into financial difficulties, and the chairman at the time attempted to sell Andy Gray – without my knowledge – and that led to some confrontations between myself and the chairman. And that was the beginning, when I look back now, of the end for myself, because it was a battle I couldn't win. I stuck by it and Andy Gray stayed with us. Eventually he went. He followed me out of the door a year later, and I was advised by my legal people that my contract had a few weeks to go, and he hadn't signed it, and although it had been on my desk for three or four months, I hadn't signed it. I was a young manager, and had gone up the ladder, so I wasn't fussed about it.

Eventually I was advised to terminate my contract, which I didn't want to do. But in the end I took the legal advice to terminate my contract, and I was advised not to work in the short-term because of mitigating circumstances on the settlement. As it transpired I went over to the States, messed around there for six months, coaching in the colleges, and I had a pretty good time away from the pressures of the game. But I thought it was about time I got back to real life, and eventually the lawyers got Wolverhampton Wanderers into a management arbitration tribunal in Birmingham. Unfortunately, the week that they got them into the tribunal, Wolves were put into receivership. So I ended up with not getting paid on my contract, and having a very large lawyers bill.

There was quite a lot of press flying about at the time about it, and it was at that time that I was approached from an agent in Greece who asked me whether I would be interested in talking to Elefteris Panayidis, the president of AEK Athens. At that time I was pretty keen to get back into a management role. I wasn't that keen on going abroad, but it was a big club. They were also guaranteed European football, which was of great interest to me, and I thought that it would broaden my knowledge of the European game. So I met with Panayidis, funnily enough half a mile from here! He owned some property in and around Lancaster Gate. One of his companies was Budget Holidays, and their headquarters were in Tottenham Court Road. So I went over there to Athens, and eventually I signed a contract. And that was me working abroad, with no knowledge of what was going to come about!

My parents thought it was a great adventure for me. I looked on it as a development of my football knowledge, particularly as it was a different environment. The experiences I had in a very short space of time were very helpful later on in my life.

I'd never been to Athens before, but had seen AEK play in the semi or quarter-final of the UEFA Cup against Derby County, and give a very good account of themselves. And that stayed in my mind, because when you think of Greece, you automatically think of Olympiakos and Panathinaikos. But AEK are the sort of Arsenal of Greek football. They're in the north, and AEK stands for

Athens Union Constantinople. There's also a Turkish background to it, and of course trust me to pick a club that had a Turkish background, because traditionally the Greeks have had a few problems with the Turks! That was very interesting in itself.

Greek is a very difficult language, but eventually, and this is difficult to believe, I taught myself to read it. I didn't understand most of the stuff I was reading, but they thought I did! Which I thought was quite clever! The first thing I came across was during pre-season. They come back five, six weeks before the season starts, their season finishes very late and they have very little midweek football. Although they've got a smaller number of clubs, the season is elongated compared with ours – the climate has quite a bit to do with that as well. They were due to go to Germany the day after I agreed to go with them. They had something like three weeks in Germany, which is a long time to be away. So I found myself, an Englishman, in Germany with a Greek side!

The club had provided me with an interpreter, and it took me some time, not as long as I thought, to realise that what I was asking the interpreter, he wasn't telling them. He would tell them what HE wanted to tell them, so he thought he was manager of the team! But anyhow, we got rid of him, and I was very fortunate that when I returned to Athens I met a friend who had written to me, very excited, a Greek man who I met in Chicago in 1965/66 when I'd travelled there with Nottingham Forest and had three months in America. His name was Spiro Kouras, and I used to call him Sam. He was a good restaurateur and I think he had about five restaurants over in the States, which he had sold and then moved back to Athens about three months before I arrived there. So he wrote to me, saying where to meet him, and I asked him whether he would like to be my interpreter. Of course the Club weren't too keen on Sam but they didn't have to pay him so they were quite happy about that! At least I had some protection, and he was great, he was brilliant for me. That was an advantage in the early days. No, I didn't speak the language, but I attempted to very quickly.

Very few, if any, British people had been coaching in Greece for any length of time. I think Vic Buckingham had been out there a long time ago, but the man who was there the longest, strangely enough, was Les Shannon, who had been there as a coach when I was there as a player. So I knew Les pretty well, and got some information from him. Les had just been finishing his third spell in Greece, and had been managing a club called OFI Crete, who played in the Greek Premier League. He told me that it was vital that you learn a bit of the language, that you adapt a bit to the way they perform, and that there are many varied things that you have to be aware of.

Some of the stuff I won't be repeating, because after some time there, there were a lot of accusations of manipulation of the Greek League, and I was massively misquoted and got into a load of trouble.

It developed when Denmark were playing Greece in the European Championships. Greece had to beat Denmark for England to sneak in the back door. I was asked a particular question, live on ITV, by Jim Rosenthal. Martin Tyler was also commentating in his early days during the second half. And the interest was that if Greece won, England would get through to Euro 84. And Jim Rosenthal, who now presents ITV's Grand Prix racing coverage, came over to me. I know Jim quite well, and he had been over for a whole week building the story up for the game. He'd been looking at them, running on the Greek History, with lovely shots of the Acropolis, the Parthenon, and Lycabettus Hill, with a Church on top, and lovely scenes of the mountains. Then he went on to eulogise some of the qualities of the Greek players, and how it would be all one-way traffic against Denmark. One of their best players was a centre-forward called Nikos Anastopoulos. I think he'd been the only ever Greek player to win the Golden Boot, for the most goals in a season, and Jim was going through all this. I said to him beforehand 'Jim, no underarmers right. No naughty questions OK?'

And anyhow, he didn't stay true to his word, because he said, and this was a broadcast I knew he could edit, 'Well Nikos Anastopoulos scored twenty-eight goals', which isn't a massive amount for the guy who wins the Golden Boot, they generally score a lot more. But the Greeks don't play that many games compared to other European countries. Then Jim Rosenthal said

'Well, Nikos Anastopoulos has got the Golden Boot, but when you listen to John Barnwell, there are cries of 'corruption''. So I said 'Well yes, twenty-eight goals isn't a massive amount, a bit of a fallow year anywhere else. And of course, Mr Daifas, who has Aristotle Onassis' wealth, is the owner of Olympiakos, which Anastopoulos plays for, and there are cries that perhaps Mr Daifas gets at the referees. When you look at the statistics, he scored fourteen penalties, but you look a bit further, he actually missed eight!' And I started laughing because I thought it was quite funny. Anyhow, that weekend they played, Denmark rolled Greece over, England didn't go through, and I had the weekend away in Britain.

I was coming back to Greece and was at Heathrow airport the Monday morning. I bought the Daily Telegraph, and Colin Gibson, who is now editor at the Daily Mail, had written a piece on the back page. I was sitting in the departure lounge reading this, and the headline said 'Barnwell banned by the Greeks'. So I thought 'What's this?' I was reading it through and it said 'John Barnwell has been charged by the Greek Minister of Sport, Kimon Kolouris, for bringing the Greek game into disrepute', and then it went on to say what I had said. So I got straight on the 'phone, there was one in the departure lounge, and fortunately I managed to get in touch with Spiro Kouras, and he said 'Oh Mister! The problems you have here!' And I said 'I know!' How they found out what plane I was on I don't know, because there was local press waiting for me when I landed!

Well I went straight off to the Sports Minister, with Spiros Kouras, and Mr Kolouris wouldn't see me. When I landed there, I knew Dennis Howell, at that time the Minister of Sport, and I had his private office number at the Houses of Parliament. His secretary at the time was a chap named Patrick Cheney, and he came on the line. I told him about the problems, and they got the transcript of Rosenthal's interview with me. What had happened was that it had been interpreted quite aggressively by Greeks in this country back to Athens. And the last thing I said to him was 'Well I've been in Athens for over a year now and I'm not aware of signs of corruption and that was my bottom line. So I've answered Jim's questions, and I'm out of jail'. But that wasn't the way they saw it. So it caused me quite a bit of consternation.

That is part of living in a different society, being more aware of what you can say and what you shouldn't say, and probably being a bit naive and sucked into a conversation I shouldn't have been sucked into. They took it extremely seriously, but in the end, that was right at the back end of my time at AEK, and that sort of helped to make my decision to leave.

One of the main issues for me came at the beginning when we were in Germany. We played five games, against very inferior sides, and we slaughtered all of them. We had some very good players – there were about twelve full internationals and under-21s. There was a young lad at centre-half, Stelios Manolas, who was an exceptional player. There were a lot of tall players in the side who would have done well in the English League but not in the Greek League, because the ball was never in the air! Then we came back to Athens, and in pre-season we played a Newcastle side with the likes of Keegan, Hibbett and Waddle in it, with Arthur Cox as the manager. They were a very good side, and we beat them comfortably on a Monday night. On the Thursday night we played Queens Park Rangers, with Terry Venables as the manager, and Glenn Roeder and Terry Fenwick playing. We slaughtered them too, and after the game in the reception area, Glenn Roeder asked me how many men we had on the pitch! We did the same with Rapid Vienna four days later. But three great wins, and all of a sudden I'm a big hero and the best manager they ever had.

But all those matches kicked off at 9 o'clock at night. That's why I was surprised when the Greeks played England, that they didn't kick off in the afternoon. Now the season started on the next Sunday, and we were on a big roll. We were playing away in the North and we kicked off at 4 o'clock. I'd told them to play a fairly high- tempo game and engage them higher up the pitch, and that's how we caught everybody on the hop. We were playing technical football at high intensity, and we looked a very good side. Playing at 4 o'clock in the afternoon it was absolutely boiling hot, and the humidity was immense. For a quarter of an hour, we looked a really good side, and then if you'd taken a shotgun and blasted them, you'd have thought they were all dead, because they just couldn't make the distance. They were still trying to play a closing-down game, and couldn't do it. We lost that game 4-1 and got absolutely slaughtered. I remember travelling back, because we had our own plane, and they used to fill it up with wealthy supporters, who flew everywhere with us.

I remember coming back and thinking 'Well, every game during this very hot period, which is about three or four months, is going to kick off at 4 o'clock in the afternoon – I'm just going to have a rethink'. And I did just that. What happened was that instead of playing high up the pitch, we tried to make our first confrontation to win the ball back on the half-way line, and if we didn't get it then it was about ten yards outside the penalty box. It took me about another month to get them into that way of thinking. So that was an education in itself. Here you are, you've got a group of players, you don't speak their language, and you've gone from coaching them one way of playing which they weren't used to. You get them playing in that way, and then you've got to change to another way. So very quickly, you've had to learn to adapt your coaching, be quick on your feet, and be very innovative in the way that you did things. So it was a good experience for me.

When I first arrived in Athens, they put me in a very good hotel, and were happy that I was going to be looked after. I was single at the time you see. So eventually they did two things. They found me a very nice place which they rented up in the Mountains, just in the North of Athens, in an area called Kifisia, which is where all the politicians and the city people lived. In was located amongst the very expensive houses. They also got me a weekend villa on the coast, in a place called Vouliagmeni, which is about two miles from the old airport. It was like a palace, a sort of high-quality seaside hotel. So I had the best of both worlds there.

I found the days totally different when I was managing there, because I had no say whatsoever in the procurement of players. Having said that, I did have a say in who could go. There were also transfer windows, which we never had back in England. So suddenly you could end up with three players, and four players out the door that you weren't so sure of. With AEK being one of the bigger clubs, they were always going to get better players and get rid of the ones they weren't interested in. I had no say in the financial side of the Club at all, which was a great weight off my back. There was no reserve team, and we only had twenty-four squad players. And the big problem for that, I found, was keeping the ones who weren't regulars in your side happy.

But with not speaking the language early on, there was obvious conflict. You didn't know what was going on behind your back. So there was that to contend with as well. I remember thinking, when there were about seven or eight of them, who were reasonable players, who needed games. And if I'd put them in and they weren't match fit....So I went to the right people, they had what we call a football director, and said that I needed to arrange a practice game. So they put a midweek game on for me with another local side. It was supposed to be low-key, but we had about nine or ten thousand people turn up! What was supposed to be just a private type match turned out to be a real pressure game, and that's just a totally different way of running a football club. To this day, I don't know how they found young players, because I was not aware of any youth policy. They did have a youth team, but I was never subject to it. They kept it well away from me, and I had nothing to do with it. There were twenty-four players in my squad and that was it. That was an experience in itself.

AEK were in Europe, as they had won the Greek Cup the season before. There were a lot of arguments about it, because there were all sorts of confrontations during that game, with seats thrown on the pitch and all sorts of things. I think the game was abandoned and put back on again. They managed to win the Greek Cup, and that got them into the UEFA Cup. The season before they'd finished sixth or seventh in the League. So by the time I got there, I think we were lying about fourth or fifth most of the time. Matches at home weren't a problem, because the players were really up for it. We played some really good football, scored very heavily, had a lot of pace in our game, and were an exciting team to watch. Away from home we couldn't win a game. We drew a lot but couldn't win a game.

We had some confrontations with the local press, because you were always misquoted, and there was nothing you could do about it. The manager didn't have an office as such. You had a changing room to yourself, and that was it. There was no need for one. But you needed one to do your paperwork, teamsheets etc. and meeting rooms for people. I had my interpreter with me, so that was always held as an area for the press to see me afterwards, and that generally went through the interpreter. I was fortunate that I had an interpreter I could trust, so he wasn't feeding me the bad stuff. But with me being English, there were those who weren't terribly fond of the English, so that was a difficult situation for me. I ended up perhaps with the reputation as being a little bit of a character although I didn't set out to be that.

The one home player they loved was Tomas Mavros, who was built like a bit of a slimmer Maradona, and was the top goalscorer in the country, a wonderful player. Tomas didn't speak any English, and he'd caused previous managers some problems, because they didn't play the way HE wanted to play etc. I particularly remember the first evening, because we started training at about four thirty in the afternoon, because it was too hot to do anything before. I remember going out and being introduced to the players. I recognised Tomas and pulled him to me, and through my interpreter I started a conversation. And he for some reason took immediately to me, he put his arm round me and the 5,000 people watching all applauded! So that was that. Everything that you did at the club was on the television or on the news that day. We trained on the main pitch, and played all our games on it. Imagine the state of the pitch. It was dry and athletics was going on around the edge of it all the time. You just had no control over what was going on there, and it wasn't the best environment for concentration.

I also remember doing a TV programme with my interpreter there, and the chap was asking me, 'Mr Barnwell, after one year, Ee Athina eeneh oreah, polee polee oreah – Athens is very good, very very good'. And he's not asking me, he's telling me! So I said

'Well, Athens, it can be like any Mediterranean city. When the sun shines it looks fantastic, and when it's wet it doesn't look so good'. This was because consecutive Governments had given building advantages to certain building companies, and then the next one would come in and stop building work. So there are buildings half up, buildings half down and rubble all over the place, and it's a really strange mixture of really beautiful things and some quite ugly. And I said to them, and this was live on Greek Television, 'Well. I don't know quite what you're trying to do to Athens. I don't know whether you're trying to build it up or pull it down'. I thought it was quite funny – absolutely not! My interpreter looked at me and said 'No! Oh dear!' Then the interviewer asked me what I thought of Podosferistis, the Greek footballer, and he said 'He's good isn't he? polee oreah – he's very good'. I've just explained to you that we couldn't play away from home. They think that Greek wine, Retsina, is fantastic, and it's £2.50 a bottle. 'Well, your players are like your Greek Wine'. The interviewer looked at me, the audience went quiet, and I said 'They're bad travellers!' I thought that was funny, but again no!

So the interview finished and Sam came over to me, and he said 'Oh no Mister!' So I was driving down Sygrou Avenue, which is like Oxford Street, and they had what they called Peripteron, which is a news agency, a phonebox, and basically a place where you can buy pretty much everything. There are always loads of people around them. I was just pulling up to one in my car. The Greeks love their papers – they've got loads of them. They have one national paper which is a huge thing, with colour on the front and back. I could just see the headlines, and I thought 'Goodness me! I'm on the front page!' And what they'd done, they had cut my head off, and I was in my training kit of AEK, which was called Zita, the sponsor. They had cut my head off it and put the Wolves logo on my head! They used to call me 'Mr Barney', because they couldn't get 'Barnwell' on the page with the Greek lettering. So they called me 'Mr Barney – the wolf, the criminal'! So I went to Sam and asked him about it, and he said 'Oh! You're in real trouble now!' I asked him why that was, and he said 'It's not what you said about the Greek player, it's what you said about the Greek wine!' I had to go on television again and explain to them that I hadn't really meant it that way, that it was just a bit of fun, but they couldn't see the humour of it. So I got myself into a little bit of hot water over that!

The better players were in the big three teams, Panathinaikos, Olympiakos and AEK, because they had the most money. They were only allowed two foreigners per team back then. They had some pretty strict rules about foreign coaches. If you were dismissed as a foreign coach during the season, you couldn't go and work for another big club. They had some good rules in actual fact. There were some outstanding players that suited the Greek League.

I think they've developed considerably over the last fifteen years. There are also more Greek players now playing in European Leagues, which encourages the Greek player to widen his horizons, his thinking, and his football development. The problem we had in the big cities was one of space to play, particularly with training grounds, because they hadn't got enough pitches, and that was a difficulty for them. Whereas further out in the other cities, it wasn't as bad. They also have problems with the investment in football. There are technically some very good players, and we've seen one or two come over into the Premiership and do reasonably well. During my period there, I only really concentrated on players that I had in my squad of twenty-four. I trained some exceptionally gifted and athletic players, and technically they were very good. They had all the ingredients to make top players. What they lacked was tactical awareness and perhaps a bit of the physical aspect of the game. But I think they've improved considerably since those days.

The fans seemed to take to me pretty well. They're used to foreign coaches. I think at any club they'll prefer a national in their own team, that goes in any country. But I think if you're winning matches, they don't care who you are or what country you come from, and I enjoyed them. They were massively aggressive and at away grounds, downright frightening. I would have a guard around me as soon as I came out of the ground after a game, and they were armed. But the guard would take you to the coach, and escort you out of the ground. The supporter violence over there was considerable, and a lot of it wasn't publicised.

As for my departure from AEK, I think a few things had built up. I wasn't overly pleased with a couple of players that had been pushed onto me in the transfer window. They were good players, but they gave me a problem. I knew I had the majority of the players on my side, which was not a usual thing for a foreign coach. The thing was building quite nicely, but I knew that we had to strengthen in certain areas, particularly to help Mavros up front. The problem was that I inherited the foreign players, two of whom were English. One of them was the boy Ross from Everton, and the other was Tommy Langley of Chelsea. Now Tommy was a very good player, but he didn't kick a ball for us, because they couldn't unload the third foreigner who was signed before both of them. He was a Bulgarian, and there was some Eastern Bloc contract thing involved, where they owed money and he wasn't allowed to play, so I just had the one foreign player playing, and the Greeks didn't really take to him, because he wasn't technically gifted. He was an aggressive midfield player who could win the ball and get it on its way. I thought he was useful and I kept playing him, but they didn't like him. That caused me some problems with the supporters, a little bit of anxiety, but I stuck by my beliefs on that one.

I wasn't dismissed there. I think we lost one game at home against Salonika, which would never do of course because of the North/South thing. I think we lost 1-0 to a team called Larissa, a very good side. That was the first one we lost at home, and the crowd were baying, not for me but for the president! So I met him in Athens the next morning, and said 'Look. I think to save your own neck, I wouldn't be upset to resign'. There were a lot of tears shed. They call you the 'Mister' there, and he said that I was the best Mister AEK Athens had ever had. So I said to him that I thought it was time that we parted company for everybody's benefit, and if you have another look at the contract, we'll negotiate a settlement. So that's what happened and then I went. It was the experience of managing very good technical players who wanted to be organised, but in truth it was against their nature. They liked the individual flair, they liked the individuality of putting their personality on the game, and that's something you have to come to terms with.

I wasn't aware of the media reaction when I left because I didn't stay long enough. What I actually did was meet the president in his offices, which was what clubs do in the middle of the City: their main offices are never at the ground. So I went to meet Mr Panayidis, 'Terry' I used to call him, in the AEK office. I had already booked a flight for the afternoon, so I was going regardless. We had a conversation, and he didn't want the thing to happen. He informed the secretary to settle with me financially, of which there was a fair bit of bargaining that went on, and eventually he looked after me very well. So there were tears flying about, and all I wanted to do was go downstairs, get up to the apartment, get my bags and go to the airport. I shook hands with them, went downstairs – it was a really hot afternoon – and there were three policemen around the car. What you did in Athens, if you couldn't park at the parking station, was to park on the pavement – imagine doing that in Oxford Street! And when I went out, three police officers were around my car calling me all sorts of nasty names! So I had a few words back to them, got in my car and off I went. I then went straight up to Kifisia and packed my bags. I went to ring 'Terry' Panayidis when I got up there, but he'd gone. I wanted a few more words, because I wasn't that happy with the settlement and the way it transpired, but in the end I went straight off, got on a plane and went back to England.

When I look back on it, I enjoyed the experience but I wouldn't do it again. I can't really explain why. It was a learning process, one that I was pleased that I experienced. I also had a run, albeit a short one, in the European Cup. The experience of playing under very difficult conditions, for an Englishman, gave me some flexibility in my thinking, and I enjoyed all that. What you have to remember, and I think this is the major reason I enjoyed it, is that I had a very serious car crash in 1980 when I was at Wolves. I wasn't 'left for dead' but the doctors thought I wouldn't live through it. Anyhow, the surgeon patched me together again, and I wasn't allowed to do any physical training for two years. I was running Wolverhampton Wanderers in the First Division, and that obviously had some effect on me. So when I went to Greece and the warm climate, I was able to have a morning walk, then a run on the beach in warmish water, have a swim every day, and do all the things that went with Mediterranean living. Physically speaking that pulled me round, and I was extremely grateful for that.

What advice would I give to a British coach going abroad to work? First of all, if it's one of the bigger clubs, there's not a problem. The problem with that is first of all, make sure you have a solid contract, and one that is good for you if there is a parting of the ways, because I doubt you're going to be there for the rest of your life. Then you must be on solid ground, and take top-class advice from places where you can go to get that, and they should nearly always go to us, the League Managers Association, because we can guide them into the right areas to go. The other thing which is essential, absolutely essential, is that you must attempt to learn the language. That is absolutely major, because although it's alright to use an interpreter, you've got to get the feel of what things are about. Even if you're just attempting to learn it, they will appreciate that as well. So I think they are the two main issues. And to end on a humorous note, as I say to colleagues, whatever you do, don't have a fitted carpet!"

After returning to the UK from Greece, John Barnwell had further management spells at Notts County, Walsall and Northampton Town. He is now Chief Executive of the League Manager's Association, a position he has held since July 1997.

Dr Paul Balsom

Dr Paul Balsom is currently the exercise physiologist (fitness advisor) and match analyst for the Swedish national team, as well as a national instructor for the Swedish FA. He holds a UEFA A licence coaching certificate.

He played for Torquay United at youth level in the late 1970s, and obtained a BA Honours degree in Human Movement Studies at the South Glamorgan Institute of Higher Education in 1986. During his post-graduate studies at Springfield College, Massachusetts, he played football at both semi-professional and NCAA college level. He was awarded a Doctor of Medical Science degree from the Karolinska Institute in Stockholm for his dissertation 'High Intensity Intermittent Exercise', which was published in 1995.

Dr Balsom also runs his own company Exsurgo AB, which specialises in sports science and IT services in football, and his own website www.soccerfitness.com

He has presented his work around the world, including UEFA fitness training courses for Europes' head coach educators, and at meetings for Premier League football fitness trainers in both England and Italy. He has also presented his work in a workshop format to several Premier League clubs including both Liverpool and Manchester United.

We pick up Dr Balsom's story in 1979:

"I played at Torquay United in the late 1970s and early 1980s, but only as a youth player. I never took the step up to full-time pro. As for the fitness training exercises we did, it makes me wince to think about them, especially with what I know now! It was the classic set-up. We were running around the 400-metre track and doing sit-ups until we could hardly walk! It was slightly different then compared to now because at that stage the youth team wasn't as connected to the first team as it is today.

I was very interested in all sports and at the age of sixteen, in addition to playing badminton, rugby, cricket and table tennis on a regular basis, I played or trained for football either at school or club level six days out of seven. This often involved four 90 minute games per week. Looking back I'm very grateful for all the support and help I got from my parents which made this possible. I was keen to study sport after I left school but my careers master at Torquay Boys' Grammar school told me that the only real option would be to study to be a Physical Education teacher. Which evidently, he advised against. In 1982 I was awarded a place at Loughborough University to study civil engineering but, at the last minute chose instead to accept a place in Cardiff a year later at the South Glamorgan Institute of Higher Education (SGIHE), now UWIC, to study for a Bachelors degree in sport. The course I did at SGIHE, from 1983 to 1986, was a three year programme then called Human Movement Studies, which allowed for a specialisation in sports science in years two and three.

My interest in the science of football started off in Cardiff, where I became interested in time-motion analysis. This involved investigating the movement patterns of football players during a game. I designed a computer program which facilitated the registration of these movement patterns, which made it possible to analyse them in more depth and generate so called activity profiles. One of the details I focused on was to compare the movement patterns of individual players, not only playing in different positions but also at different levels of the game. The results from these studies, amongst other things, were in agreement with the findings of some previous studies which concluded that football was a form of high intensity intermittent exercise. At that time this type of exercise was not well documented in the physiological literature. There was, however, a couple of studies about intermittent exercise published by a group of Scandinavian researchers in the late 1960s.

From 1986 to 1988 I studied for my Master of Science degree in Health and Fitness in America at Springfield College, Massachusetts. During my time in the States I played football semi-professionally outside the college, with a team called Bridgeport Italians in Connecticut. I trained at the college in the week and then travelled to Connecticut for games at the weekends. The standard of the training at the college was relatively poor. What the Americans were doing at that time, was trying to take the American Football type of what I'd call 'steered' training, where just about everything, that could be, was planned, and put that into a 'soccer' situation. Even here the fitness training was performed in the form of running 'laps' without the ball with no special training for strength or speed.

I spent part of the final year of my Master's degree in California doing my field work at a health and fitness centre in Los Angeles. During this time I also helped the late Justin Fashanu, I became his personal fitness trainer. At that time Justin was recovering from a knee injury. Justin worked hard to try to get back to the top and his level of fitness was very impressive, but his knee always gave him problems. I can assure you that I was to say the least 'shocked' to hear of Justin's suicide.

I also spent some time with one of the big American Football teams, the Buffalo Bills. Their fitness trainer was an ex-Springfield graduate who I got to meet. The training for them was completely different from 'soccer' because there was a lot of muscle work in the gym and speed work on the field. It was very professional, and at that stage they had specialised fitness trainers. They also worked very hard on their diets.

I finished my Masters degree at Springfield by doing some research on football (soccer) players, trying to design a football specific fitness test.

After this work I decided that I wanted to do more research on science and football. I wrote letters to eminent professors around the world, and the most positive reply I received was from Stockholm. I basically jumped on the next plane to Sweden to meet Professor Björn Ekblom at the Karolinska Institute.

It wasn't until I came to Stockholm that I was really able to push my ideas forward. At the end of the first year at the Karolinska Institute, 1989, a PhD programme entitled, *'High Intensity Intermittent Exercise: Performance and metabolic responses with very high intensity short duration work periods'* was drawn up by Professor Björn Ekblom and myself (see www.soccerfitness.com/hiie). Although at this time there was similar work being done by Professor Clyde Williams and his research groups at Loughborough, and by Professor Jens Bangsbo at the August Krogh Institute in Denmark, it was somewhat of a relatively new area of research in the field of exercise physiology.

The main aim of my studies was to increase our understanding about the physiology of playing football. After the work I completed at SGIHE I learnt that when playing football, players work at high exercise intensities for only very short periods of time, anything from a couple of seconds up to 10 seconds in extreme circumstances, in between which they're resting (standing still, walking or jogging) for longer periods, sometimes for more than 30 seconds. This 'start/stop' intermittent type of exercise carries on throughout the game. I spent the whole six years of my PhD studying this type of exercise and completed eight laboratory controlled studies on high intensity intermittent exercise all of which were subsequently published in international scientific journals (www.soccerfitness.com/balsom).

The exercise protocols that were used involved either repeated over-ground sprints (up to 40 metres) on an indoor running track or repeated bouts of high intensity exercise (6 seconds) performed on a cycle ergometer. During these studies we took muscle biopsies, to investigate what was happening in the muscle, and blood tests to investigate what was happening in the blood, before, during and after intermittent exercise. Performance was also measured in an attempt to relate what we found in the muscle and blood with the onset of fatigue. I experimented with different work to rest ratios, with work periods between 2.5 and 6 seconds and rest periods between 30 seconds and 2 minutes. Interventions like experimenting with different types of food intake, administrating supplements such as creatine and regulating the availability of oxygen to the muscles, were made. It's not possible to go into detail about all the results here but the studies with creatine supplementation and Erythropoietin deserve a mention.

Creatine supplementation, to enhance the performance of football players, has been the subject of many articles in the media over the last few years. Creatine is a substance that is present in a normal diet. For example, relatively high levels are found in meat and a person who consumes a normal carnivorous diet will ingest about a gram of creatine per day. Creatine is partly stored in the muscles as creatine phosphate which is a very important source of energy during very high-intensity exercise. It is interesting to note that over a hundred years ago a whole book was written on creatine supplementation. The interest in creatine supplementation came to light again in the 1970s following the work of a group of researchers in Stockholm headed by Professor Eric Hultman. These researchers observed improvements in the performance of high intensity exercise in subjects who were administered 20 grams of creatine per day for a six day period. One of these researchers, Dr Karin Söderlund, started to work in my department, Physiology III, at the Karolinska Institute.

We decided that, because of my research interests it would be interesting to see if creatine supplementation could enhance the performance of high intensity intermittent exercise. We therefore carried out several studies to investigate this. We did in fact find significant improvements in the ability to perform repeated bouts of short-duration high-intensity exercise on a cycle ergometer in controlled laboratory conditions as a result of creatine supplementation. And I emphasise the fact that we used a cycle ergometer, because for most subjects who are administered creatine supplementation there is a marked increase in body weight by anything up to 3 kilograms in a week. We know today that the main reason for this increase is water retention.

A problem then with creatine supplementation for football players is that any potential performance enhancement on the football field may be contradicted by an increase in body weight. So in fact, I've never stated, and there is no documented evidence to show that creatine will in any way enhance the performance levels of football players. What I have done, however, is to administer creatine to individual players, where I've been able to have personal contact with them, and been able to monitor their progress.

There are many things and specific issues to think about when administering creatine. For example, we know that some humans do not store any of the ingested creatine in their bodies. They're what we call 'non-responders'. On the other hand, vegetarians tend to store more of any supplemented creatine than meat-eaters, because they normally have lower daily intakes of creatine in their diet.

The conclusion from our studies on creatine supplementation was that yes, we did find that in controlled scientific studies during very specific exercise conditions with repeated short-duration bouts of high-intensity exercise, performance was enhanced, suggesting that creatine phosphate plays a key role in the fatigue process during this type of exercise. The subjective feedback from the individual players that I have worked with is, however, varied. Some players have said that 'yes' they have felt an increase in performance during training and matches, but it's not been possible to measure this objectively. One thing that we mustn't forget is what is known as a 'placebo' effect. If I'd administered them a similar looking substance, in this case for example sugar, as creatine is a white powder, instead of creatine, maybe they'd have said the same thing! Some players have said that they didn't feel any differences after the creatine supplementation.

In another study, Erythropoietin, otherwise known as EPO, was used to increase the availability of oxygen to the muscles and the effects on performance during high intensity intermittent exercise was investigated. [AUTHORS NOTE: EPO is a protein that stimulates the production of red blood cells which after a six-week administration period causes an increase in haemoglobin concentration of around 10% and a subsequent increase in aerobic capacity of around 8%].

In our study with EPO, we concluded that performance of high intensity intermittent exercise could be enhanced if the availability of oxygen to the working muscles was increased. In practical terms this suggests that the aerobic capacity of football players is an important component of their fitness profile and needs therefore to be trained to and maintained at a relatively high level (see also later). It should be noted that in controlled scientific research experiments, similar to the ones described above, the aim is to gain a better understanding of how certain physiological mechanisms function during different types of exercise and in particular the role that they play in the fatigue process.

The administration of EPO in sport is in fact classed as doping, whereas creatine is not. In general, performance-enhancing drugs in football is a very controversial subject. UEFA has drawn up a list of so called 'banned' substances. These substances are divided into different groups. For example, central nervous system stimulants, substances with an anabolic effect and blood doping. If a banned substance is detected in a urine sample of a player following a randomised drug test then the player concerned is said to have been tested 'positive' and depending on the type of substance found banned from the game for a period of time. In the last year a couple of high-profile football players have been found guilty of taking banned substances and the whole issue of performance-enhancing drugs in football has been widely publicised. To the best of my knowledge no Swedish player has been found guilty of taking a banned substance although one of the players from the national team was recently involved in a positive drug test scandal but later cleared. At the time of writing this article I have no reason to believe and have seen no evidence to suggest that Scandinavian football players are taking illegal substances to improve their performance.

I think that one very important area of research in this field is to find methods to distinguish between naturally high levels of a substance stored in the body and high levels which have been artificially increased through the administration of a banned substance.

When I first came to Stockholm Professor Ekblom was already heavily involved in football. He was a leading international name in the field of football physiology, and at that time was working closely with the Swedish FA and one of the Premier League sides

Hammarby IF, based in Stockholm. So it was a natural progression for me to become involved both at Hammarby and the FA, which I did in 1990 and 1992 respectively. In Hammarby I coached their under 18 side while at the FA I started working as the exercise physiologist with the Swedish ladies national team.

There were two main aspects of working with the ladies in that respect. One was to find out what these players needed to do to take their game forward in terms of fitness. The other was to think about how a national team should prepare before an international game or tournament, taking into account such things as; making sure players were eating correctly, discussing with the coach how many times they could train per week, monitoring the intensities of training, deciding on the best time of the day to train, what to do with the substitutes after the game etc. I'm still working with many of these small but important details today.

I'm currently the head sports science instructor for the Swedish FA which amongst other things means that I'm in charge of the fitness content of the coaches' education programme. I'm also now the exercise physiologist and match analyst in the mens' national team with whom I've been working since 1998. In my role as match analyst we currently use an interactive computerised-video match analysis program. Part of my work as a match analyst involves filming all of the matches that the national team plays using a special camera with a wide angle lens. This film is then 'transferred' onto a computer and the game is 'digitalised', which means that with the help of the software 'any' event that occurs during the match can be registered and later retrieved from a database. For example, we register all goal scoring opportunities and at the end of the analysis, at the push of a button, all goal scoring opportunities can be retrieved and viewed on a TV screen or through a video projector on a big screen by the coach.

The number of national teams and top-class clubs who use a computerised video-match analysis system is increasing rapidly. Many clubs now employ a full-time match analyst. The tools that are available for analysing matches are also improving. Some of the top clubs in England have recently started to use a system whereby images from eight cameras which are installed at the ground are processed for each home game. The information that can be gained from such a system is mind blowing. For example, in addition to being able to replay intricate tactical details, every player is tracked throughout the whole game and information such as the total distance covered and time spent sprinting can be retrieved. In a recent match with the national team, one of our midfield players covered a distance of over 14.5 kilometres.

Working as an exercise physiologist in the national team is somewhat different from working as a fitness trainer in a football club. When the national team are together we don't perform any specific fitness training. The major part of our training focuses on tactical strategies, so I have to make sure that all our players are working at appropriate exercise intensities, by that I mean not too high or not too low, so they're as close to peak performance levels as possible for the game on a Saturday or a Wednesday.

An important issue in Swedish football is the education of the players and coaches about health and fitness related issues. I consider this to be another one of my most important roles with the national team. Sometimes I take the opportunity to discuss relevant issues on an individual basis. This may, for example, be at 11 o'clock at night after our last meal for the day or directly after a training session. On other occasions it may take the form of a very brief formal lecture to the whole group. I believe that it's important to talk to the players as often as possible, to give them small tips, and to take the time to hear a little bit about how they're training in their club sides, what they're eating, etc.

There are four coaches working with the national team: two head coaches, Tommy Söderberg and Lars Lagerbäck; the goal-keeping coach, Lennart Ljung; and myself. I should point out that in addition to the four of us there are several more non-playing members (staff) on the national team whose work and commitment is invaluable. These include a secretary, press officer, doctor, two physiotherapists and an equipment officer who travel to every match and a security officer and cook who travel to selected matches. As the fitness coach I am considered to be an integral part of the coaching staff. The two head coaches in the national team are the ones who brought me into the national team set-up and I am very grateful to them for that. From the very beginning I have not only been able to, but more appropriately expected to, influence important aspects of our preparations.

So starting with, for example, the planning of the training: the best time to eat breakfast, the best time to train and to have lunch, the time between lunch and dinner, all details around the planning of the training. Just small details, things we can influence, and not just physiologically but also psychologically. For example, if we train at eleven what's the effect of eating breakfast at eight or nine, compared to how the players feel mentally? So it's always the 'human factor' as well, and not just the science.

I am also responsible for the fitness part of the coaching education programme in my work as the sports science instructor for the Swedish FA. In the first two basic courses the participants receive two 1½ hour lectures and a practical session per course where the basic principles about the physiology of football are introduced. Between coaching levels two and three there is a whole weekend of football physiology. The coaches meet on a Friday and leave on the Sunday after what is to say the least, an intense programme. In the next coaching level the coaches meet for a whole day, and in the last one which I present personally we meet for half a day and discuss amongst other things 'latest findings'.

One aspect of football training which has interested me more than any other is endurance training. One of the books I have written in English, 'Precision Football' [www.soccerfitness.com/precisionfootball], which has been purposely written more for coaches and players than scientists, presents some of the more applied research that I have done with intermittent exercise. One of the aspects that is discussed in the book is that of maintaining or improving levels of endurance by training with intermittent exercise as opposed to training with continuous exercise. If the coach chooses to use continuous exercise, for example a five or ten-mile run, which didn't used to be unusual in English football (especially when I was playing!), time can then be used as a measurement of performance. So basically you would say that the player who takes the shortest time has the best performance during that run. If, however, the coach decides that because playing football is a form of intermittent exercise and it is therefore more specific to 'overload' them with a form of high intensity intermittent exercise in the training, the problem then becomes how to measure how hard the players are working. For example, a five-a-side game, which is a form of intermittent exercise, can be a very good form of endurance training. But until recently, there hasn't been an easy way of measuring the work rate of the players during that type of training.

The main focus in my book 'Precision Football' is to show the reader that by using heart-rate monitors during training sessions, the amount of work being done by each of the players can be quantified. This applies not only for example in small-sided games where the aim of the session might be for all players to be working with high work rates to maintain or improve endurance levels, but also during tactical sessions during the day or days before an important game where the emphasis is on keeping the overall physical loading relatively low but still being able to work sporadically at match tempos.

Apparently the majority of the training that Liverpool did under the reign of the great Bill Shankley was basically playing small-sided games. What they were doing then is what I believe today, based on my scientific and football knowledge, to be the most specific and appropriate type of endurance training for football players. The players are getting both tactical *and* technical training as well as incorporating important mental aspects. Furthermore, by changing variables such as the rules of the game, size of the field and number of players the emphasis can be shifted from for example, the physical aspects to the tactical aspects. But it doesn't matter which one you emphasise, because all the aspects of football are still there.

Another important issue with endurance training is the risk of drowning the explosive capacity of our players, and by this I mean their ability to accelerate and work at high speeds, by performing too much and/or the wrong kind of endurance training. In general, if you test 10 000 metre runners, they have very low levels of explosive power. If you then test 100 or 200 metre sprinters, they have very low levels of endurance power. In layman terms it can be said that adaptations in the muscle which take place with training for explosive power are in conflict with adaptations which take place with training for long distance endurance using continuous exercise. If the major part of the endurance training takes the form of intermittent exercise, then the players stimulate their so-called fast-twitch muscle fibres and this helps to maintain as opposed to impair levels of explosive power and at the same time overload the cardiovascular system.

We may be losing a lot of talented players from the game because they're classed as too slow and rejected, instead of looking at what can be done to make them quicker. For some players, due to hereditary factors, it won't be possible to make them 'quick enough' but I feel the knowledge of training for explosive power in football is very poor. In Sweden I have seen elite seventeen and eighteen year old players whose speed over 30 metres is, to say the least, relatively poor. The question is, what's happening? It maybe that current endurance training methods in football are impairing the development of explosive power. Therefore we need to find a balance between the combination of explosive power and endurance, and also accept that in our team, some players need to be more endurance trained than others. Getting this balance right is also extremely important for 'older' players, by this I mean those who have already celebrated their thirtieth birthday. It's a common belief in football that players start getting slower once they have turned 30. As I often tell these players Linford Christie was 33 when he was the fastest man in the world!

In addition to my work at the Swedish Football Association I am also a part-owner of a company called Exsurgo AB [www.soccerfitness.com/exsurgo]. It's a company that my wife Susanne started in 1991 in her role as a sports physiotherapist. Most of the work I do through this company is educational. I have travelled to various countries around the world with my book 'Precision Football', together with the Finnish company Polar OY [www.polar.fi], the world's leading manufacturer of heart-rate monitors, presenting two day workshops about using heart-rate monitors in football.

I've been to Argentina, Columbia, Thailand, Japan, Switzerland, Finland and Russia as well as to some of the top Premier League clubs in England. The response has been very positive, because the coaches like the idea of using small-sided games to maintain or improve levels of fitness which is one of the main things that we teach them. A lot of the coaches we meet have been using small-sided games for many years, but now they learn that with the help of modern technology in the form of wireless heart-rate monitors, they will be able to quantify training intensities of all players who are wearing a heart-rate monitor.

An important issue with monitoring heart rates is that the intensity of all types of training both with and without the ball should be quantified. There's very little documentation, if any, about the amount of work that football players do in a week or a month, or even throughout a whole season. For example, during a training session there maybe a full-back participating in a tactical drill working at a very high intensity and a centre-back working in the same drill who may be 'serving' balls, doing very little work. With the help of heart-rate monitors it is possible at the end of a training session or the end of a week to quantify the physical loading of individual players.

In another book I've written in Swedish, *Fotbollens Träningslära* the first chapter gives a brief background into the way that the application of scientific knowledge in football has become more and more important. Already in the 1970s and 1980s the Brazilians were using scientists to help them with their preparation for the big tournaments. When I compare England to Sweden, I feel that there has been a big reluctance in English football to embrace this area of change. The Swedes are very eager to influence any aspect of a sport that can lead to improvements in performance. One of the reasons for this is that there are many restricting factors which have to be overcome: for example a small population (9 million in Sweden compared to over 55 million in England), long winters where, except for in the southern part of the country, it is not possible to play on grass between

November and March, and relatively poor training facilities, especially in Stockholm. Fitness is one of the things that the Scandinavians know they can influence, so from an early age the players are encouraged to look after their own bodies. The Scandinavians have a good reputation in the field of exercise physiology, and research on the fitness side of football was carried out very early on in Sweden. There are some very impressive experiments documented as early as the 1960s at the University College of Physical Education and Sports in Stockholm. In general, the Swedish team do not have any problems with fitness levels, although we can always do better in terms of speed and explosive power and, as previously mentioned, this is the area of fitness which is now commanding a lot of attention.

What I've noticed over the last couple of years in England when I've presented my work at football fitness conferences, is that the majority of the participants have been under 35 years old, and many of them have completed, or are in the process of completing, a sports science degree. They've been highly motivated and shown a high level of understanding. However, the same question always comes up, 'how can we introduce scientific changes into our club?' I've tried to give them a few tips but more importantly to encourage them to share their ideas and experiences amongst themselves.

I've heard very frightening scenarios. Some of these fitness trainers explain how they are only allocated very short periods of time at each training session at their club, barely enough so that they can jog around the field a couple of times for a warm-up. They have very few opportunities to implement their knowledge. I believe that the new breed of fitness trainers who seem to be infiltrating into more and more of the top clubs in England are very important for the future of the game.

Attitudes towards fitness coaches ARE definitely changing in England. Shortly after I returned to Europe from my studies in America, I visited one of the professional clubs in Devon because I knew the physiotherapist there. I met him, the assistant coach and the manager. We started discussing a few things about science and the reply I got was 'Well why do we need science? If you put the experience the three of us have in football together, it's over a hundred years, we don't need science!' That was a common attitude then, but it is changing. I believe that the combination of many years of experience in the game together with some modern scientific knowledge is a perfect match.

The younger fitness coaches that are being employed by at least the top clubs seem to be getting access to the younger academy squads, which I think is great, because what will happen is that the level of knowledge about fitness of these players will be much higher when they move up into the first team. In fact I don't think that it will be too long before players start realising the importance of a good medical team at the club and start making their own demands.

At least half of the Premier League teams England now have, or are in the process in building, state of the art training facilities with a sports science department. I've been fortunate to visit the ones at Manchester United and Middlesborough as well as see the plans for the ones at Liverpool and Sunderland. I must say I've been very impressed not only by the facilities themselves, but also by the attitude and knowledge of the staff working in them.

I was surprised when I spoke to Sir Alex Ferguson and the coaching staff at Manchester United during a presentation that I made at their new training ground last year. At the very beginning of the presentation I asked them what they thought that science had to offer them. Sir Alex was the one who spoke first and said that I wouldn't have been invited there two years ago. In the last two years, he'd been working with a sports nutritionist, and seen improvements in performance on the field of play. This had opened his eyes to the world of science and football. I think that this is the key. It is important that the coaches and players see results that are meaningful to them; it may of course simply be increasing fitness levels but it may also be reducing the risk of injury, or having more young players move up from the youth team to the senior team, or even extending the playing career of some of the older players by a year or two. Football and science is about looking at the whole package, which for me is to see players in harmony with their body. It's a little bit of a cliché, but if players feel good about their bodies, for example they feel strong, full of energy and 'sharp', then self-confidence and ultimately high performance levels will come naturally with that.

I believe that the fitness coach should become an integral part of the coaching staff. I don't think this is happening yet in England. That's the way I have it in Sweden, and that's the only way I'd work as a fitness coach.

As for the future I think we may see, players employing their own personal fitness trainers either on a full-time or consultancy basis. The fitness coach in a club should be, at least in my opinion, an invaluable member of the coaching staff. The question then is whether one fitness coach is enough for all the different types of players? Many players have written into their contract that if they get injured they can be treated by 'their own specialist doctors'. Maybe they should also start looking to seek expert advice about their fitness training to help prevent them from getting injured! I think my message to any sports scientist working in football is that you have to be careful about how much science you present to the players. A lot of the work that I do doesn't get presented directly to the players. If you bombard them with too much science, for example, you tell them that they've got to change this, they've got to eat that, they've got to stretch this way or run that way. At the end, you get little if any response. Instead it's a case of doing a lot of hard work or even research until you are as sure as you can be that, by affecting this or that variable, then performance will be enhanced.

A lot of the scientists working in football that I see are over ambitious and they want to go in and change everything. TOO MUCH TOO SOON! It's not just about science, it's about learning to respect and get to know the players, and trying to treat them as individuals, to get as much out of each player as possible.

A lot has happened to Scandinavian football since I first arrived more than ten years ago. At one stage in 1992, Denmark, Norway and Sweden were all ranked in the FIFA top ten at the same time, and Denmark actually won the European Championship. Not bad when you consider that the combined population of these three countries is less than 20 million.

Looking back on the last four years, working with the Swedish national team brings back many great memories. As our head coach repeatedly says 'It really is a privilege to work with these players'. I'm often verbally abused by the players (but this comes with the job!), especially during the warm-up or the second lap of the cool down. Whereas in English I can usually but only just about 'hold my own', in Swedish it's not so easy. On one occasion I was explaining to the players in Swedish that we were going to run in the 'channels', the problem was I used the Swedish word for 'canal' instead of 'channel' and it was nearly five minutes before we were able to do something constructive again as they found this most amusing.

For many reasons our 0-0 draw at Wembley with England during the qualifications for the 2000 European Championships remains probably the high point of those four years, although beating England in Stockholm 2-1 in 1998 comes a close second. (Incidentally at this match Glenn Hoddle referred to me as 'the video boy' as I was holding a video cassette when I was introduced to him, a nickname that one of our coaches still uses today). On a par with these matches is our recent 2-1 win against Turkey in Istanbul, where we scored both goals in the last five minutes, which was enough for us to win our World Cup qualifying group. I've never seen a crowd stunned to the extent that the one that night was. The atmosphere switched from that of a burning inferno to all but total silence!

In 2002 I will be travelling with the Swedish national team to the World Cup finals in South Korea/Japan. Our performance in the qualifications has been VERY satisfactory, we have played ten games, won eight, drawn two, scored twenty goals and conceded three. We have learnt a lot from the 2000 European Championships in Holland/Belgium and we will be rigorously reviewing our methods of preparation for the World Cup based on this experience. A final between Sweden and England would be nice! Of course I would want 'MY' team to win". [For the record, England haven't beaten Sweden since 1968].

Dr Paul Balsom is still living and working in Sweden

with his wife and three children, Sebastian, Benjamin and Alexander, as discussed above. He can be contacted by e-mail at info@soccerfitness.com

Phil Gray

PLAYER
Nancy, (France), August – December 1996
Fortuna Sittard, (Holland), January – July 1997

Phil Gray was born in Belfast, and first played professionally for Tottenham Hotspur in 1986. He then moved to Fulham in 1990, Luton in 1991 and Sunderland in 1993, as well as winning 26 caps and 6 goals for Northern Ireland. We pick up Phil's story in May 1996:

"Well, the Bosman ruling was just coming round that summer, so you could go abroad for nothing. I remember speaking to my agent, who's a good friend of Chrissie Waddle, and he said it would be good for me to go abroad. So I thought I wouldn't mind having a go at playing in another country. An agent from France contacted me, and asked me where I wanted to go. I then had a trial game over in France, just to see how I got on, but because my agent knew a few people in Europe, he found out that a few clubs were there watching me, including 1860 Munich and Osasuna. I think both of them wanted to sign me, and the German club wanted me to wait until the morning. But Nancy were trying to get me to sign as well. I more or less agreed everything with them and said I would sign in the morning. Then the German club said 'Don't do anything until we get back to you! Hold on!'

So we waited until 11 o'clock at night, and they kept on calling, telling me to hold on a while. They offered me a three-year contract to sign, whereas Nancy only wanted me to sign for one year. So I thought to myself 'Well, it's only for one year, and if I don't like it then I can always go back home. But if I signed for three years, then I could be stuck, and if I don't like it, then....' So I ended up signing for Nancy, which I'm glad I did.

Me and my girlfriend were looking forward to going to a different country. It was totally different, and I'm up for things like that. I'd just had three good years at Sunderland and at twenty-seven was probably at my peak as a player. I think I finished up as top goalscorer for Sunderland the three years I was there, so I didn't have a problem with going out to France. My contract at Sunderland had expired, and I don't think they were too happy with me going, because they had offered me a new two-year contract. But I wasn't terribly happy with that, because I wanted three years, and not just two.

I didn't know anything about Nancy before I went although I had heard of them before, obviously because of Michel Platini. He was at some of the games. We went there and they showed us round a couple of days before my trial game, and they flew Lisa, my girlfriend, over to have a look round. I played in the trial game, and signed for them the next day. They just wanted to see if I was fit before they signed me. They took me to the Excelsior hotel/ restaurant in the middle of town, the chairman, the president and the manager and everyone went. We didn't leave there until around half past two in the morning! I didn't speak French at all before I went out there, but my girlfriend did, and when she had a couple of glasses of wine, it seemed to come out better!

When I first came over, they flew me over to Paris, and then someone picked me up and drove me to Nancy. Then I just went down to the hotel, where we stayed for about three months. But we couldn't handle that, because it wasn't like living properly and didn't feel right. So we went and found a town-house in the middle of a big park, La Foret de Haye in Nancy, which was lovely. It had a big swimming pool, and it was only about ten or fifteen minutes through the park to the training ground.

When I arrived, Nancy had just got promoted from the Second Division. When we started off the season, we weren't doing too well, and then we won a couple of games away from home. When I left, I think we were lying about fourth bottom, but at the end of the season I think they got relegated by two points.

I got on well with the president and all the Board. One was a barrister and one owned a chain of supermarkets called Leclerc. I think they had signed a few other players that year. They also signed Christophe Robert, the former Monaco and Marseille player. He was the one who was in the scandal with Bernard Tapie, and he told me all about it! He was probably my best pal there. We used to go out with him and his wife, or round his house most weeks. He took us under his wing.

Lisa, my girlfriend, used to sit just outside the director's box, and she heard people talk very highly about me which was great. In the end I only played in about fifteen matches, because I missed a couple of games because the World Cup qualifiers were on, and I had to fly back nearly every month. In six months I played five games for Northern Ireland, and as France were hosting the World Cup, their domestic football didn't stop as they were already qualified. I think the manager Lazlo Boloni, he played for Romania a hundred odd times and scored forty goals, was a bit annoyed that he had to let me go, but I got on really well with all the coaching staff and the management.

As for the press, L'Equipe interviewed me a couple of times, but a couple of the lads used to give me stick because they kept saying 'You've got to start speaking French', although some of them spoke a little bit of English. One of the younger lads was actually a solicitor who was playing football. I went round to his house a couple of times, and he more or less tried to teach me French. We had a French teacher, organised by the club, who used to come around and try and do bits and pieces maybe three nights a week. In the end, we became really good friends with the language teacher and her family, and they used to invite us round for meals. So we enjoyed that, and we still keep in contact with her. As for my French, I got by on the football pitch. But when Lisa was with me, she usually did all the talking.

My most memorable match was probably the one against Bordeaux, which was an away game. We beat them 1-0 and I scored the winner after something like twelve minutes. We held on for the 1-0 win, which was excellent. Probably Monaco away as well, because we went down there on a Thursday and were there for several days. We stayed in an incredible hotel and went round the town. I went with Christophe Robert and he showed me bits and pieces here, there and everywhere. I had a few good trips, but they're probably the two most memorable ones.

Probably the best players I played against out there at the time were Leonardo of Paris Saint-Germain, who was an unbelievable talent, and Robert Pires who was playing for Metz. Also Rai, the Brazilian, and about half of the Bordeaux team. A couple of them ended up at Inter Milan.

The tactics at Nancy were a bit different to what I was used to. They used to play one main striker up the middle. Lazlo used to tell me to just stay in the middle. He wanted me to always play in the box area. We used to play with one on the left and one on the right. I thought Boloni was an excellent coach.

The training was totally different. We went out to the training ground in the mornings for football, then back in for school and gym work. We had all our training facilities there, with saunas, jacuzzis, and beds and restaurants upstairs. We also have a lot of gym work. Sometimes we would go to the ground in the morning and eat breakfast together, and then we'd go out training, and come back in and have lunch.

Afterwards we would go and have a sleep upstairs, and some would just have a massage or a sauna, get their feet looked after or just read the paper. Some would play head tennis or keep-ball, and sometimes have an afternoon session on the weights, and for that they had a special trainer who came in and gave us proper weight training. We then went round the circuits three or four times, and would end up going and having a sauna or a jacuzzi after that. I can remember going in at eight in the morning and leaving at five. It was a long day, but it wasn't 'hard' training. You had plenty of rest, and did everything in-between. They told us to drink as much water as we could and used to force it on us! And tubs of isostar too. So you could go in and lift twenty bottles of water if you wanted and ten tubs of isostar, and constantly keep drinking it. They just beat it into you about drinking water. Before I went there, I never used to drink water a lot.

I then moved to Fortuna Sittard in Holland around Christmas 1996. Before I went to Nancy in the May of 1996, Fortuna Sittard rang me up. They said 'We'd like you to come, as you're on a free transfer'. They then asked me much money I was looking for. I told them and they said 'Oh, that's too much. We're only a small club'. I then totally forgot about it. I got a call from Osasuna in May as well, but I wouldn't commit myself that soon. I don't know how they made contact with me to be honest, or how they got my number in France!

Then all of a sudden, they called me up again and said 'We're interested in taking you up to Holland. Would you like to come?' I said that if everyone could work something out then I wouldn't mind. I went and met them in Luxembourg, and I sat down and spoke to them, but the chairman said there was nothing he could do. So then I just got up and walked away, and that was it. I think they came and watched me a couple more times, including the game against Bordeaux and against somebody else, and then they rang and said they definitely wanted to take me. The Dutch club more or less sold it to me that everyone in Holland speaks English, they're all English, all the training will be in English and everything else will be in English. On top of this, Mark Burke and Michael Jeffries were there. I knew Mark Burke before I went to Nancy, and they kept coming to me and saying that there were a couple of English players there, and that I would get on well with them.

I was also talking to Ossie Ardiles at that time, because he wanted me to go to Japan. I was talking to him and Stevie Perryman, and he was ringing up on the one hand, and I was thinking to myself 'Japan? How about it?' We'd found it a little bit different in France, and we sat down and said that Japan was going to be a hell of a lot different. It would definitely have been a big change. So we ended up going to Holland.

Nancy had just bought Tony Cascarino back, and he came just after the Paris Saint-Germain game. I don't think the manager was aware I was leaving, I think it was only the president who knew. The manager was a bit disappointed when he heard the news, rang me up before I left, and said he was sorry to see me go. The first team coach, Jacky Bonnevay, who'd come from Marseille after they won the European Cup Final, was a bit sad to see me go as well. He was really kind to me when my folks stayed here.

Just before I left Nancy, my last game was against Paris Saint-Germain at the Parc des Princes. I actually scored the winner with a couple of minutes to go, and Michel Platini came in to see me when I was in the bath after the game. I knew I was leaving then, and he was chatting to me! He was just saying what a good game it had been, and a great result to come and beat Paris Saint-Germain in their own stadium. The Paris Saint-Germain supporters actually clapped us off the pitch. After my first year back at Luton (in 1998), Lazlo, the manager, rang me up and asked me whether I would like to go back!

As for the one thing that sticks in my mind from that time, it was probably playing at home against Marseille, and seeing their supporters behind the goal. It was just unbelievable, and nothing like you see in England. In England it's just scarves and that's it. but when I walked out to play Marseille, there were flares, flags, smoke and rockets. They must have brought five to six thousand fans to the game. The pitches were in perfect condition in France. They were so perfect it was untrue except for one, and that was Monaco, which was awful. So my best memories were of the pitches, the fans. Oh, and probably getting a liking of red wine as well! That was Christophe who got me into that!

I would say that being at Fortuna Sittard was totally different, and more like a Luton sort of club. It was more family run, with two offices, and an average crowd of around four thousand. They were always struggling against relegation, and the year I went I think they had just survived in the First Division by about three points (only one team went down). I went there, and they were as good as gold. I told them that if we weren't happy in the house, and my girlfriend wasn't happy because I was training every day, then I wouldn't be happy coming to work. They got us a beautiful house and car, and also gave us money to furnish the house and buy other bits and pieces. They were absolutely fantastic, especially when we went out and looked for houses.

The training was totally different as well. We used to start at three o'clock in the afternoon, and normally stayed at training until ten. At the time they had a very young squad, but some of them have now gone on to bigger things. There was Marc Van

Bommel, who's now the captain of PSV Eindhoven and a Dutch international, Fernando Ricksen, who's at Glasgow Rangers, and Patrick Paauwe, who's now playing at Feyenoord as a left-winger. We had some indifferent results there as well. The mentality of Dutch football is totally different. They would always keep the ball, no matter what. If you went away from home, they would be happy with a 0-0, and would just keep the ball.

I remember thinking in the first two or three games I played, that I was making runs into the channels and coming short and spinning. But I didn't ever get the ball because they were just happy to keep passing it to each other backwards and forwards along the back. And if the other team doesn't get it, they're just happy doing that. I couldn't believe what was happening and wondered whether we would ever get the ball forward! It looked as if some of them were scared of feeding that pass through that would give it away, maybe because they'd get a flea in their ear from the manager. They just played square balls and little passes here and there. They would pass it fifty or sixty times, and I wondered whether I'd ever kick the ball!

We had some indifferent results. We went away to Feyenoord, and drew 4-4. Henrik Larsson was playing for them, Ed de Goey was the goalkeeper, and Ronald Koeman was marking me! We got talking and I actually had a bit of a chat with him! I asked him what he was still doing playing at his age, and he said it was because he needed the money!

Koeman wasn't the most famous player I was up against, and there's a little story behind that. When I was a teenager I was a schoolboy player at Arsenal, and I knew a guy called Michael. He now goes European scouting for Arsenal. We were in the bar in Ajax, and I was just having a cup of coffee before our (Sittard's) game against them, and Michael was standing there! I asked him what he was doing, and he said he was there to watch Marc Overmars as Arsenal had been looking at him for the previous three or four months. I thought to myself that he was going to buy him, but Michael said that this was his last chance.

Then he turned round and said 'I need you to do me a favour, Phil. Just give him a little nudge in the tunnel and tell him we're here watching him!' So as we were walking out, I walked up to Overmars, tapped him on the shoulder, and I said 'Marc, a scout from Arsenal's here, and he says it's your last chance!' And they beat us 5-0! Beforehand he actually turned round to me and said 'If you let me score, I'll be very grateful!' At the time Ajax had a great side, with him, the De Boer twins, and Dani amongst others.

At Fortuna Sittard, I went out a lot with Mark Burke and Michael Jeffries. It was a totally different lifestyle and culture. For example after a game, when we were in Nancy, we used to have to go over to where the people would be, and they would introduce us to the fans and have a drink. Then all the young single lads would go out, and the players with wives would go down to the restaurant. But the Dutch players never really went out as such. Once they finished training, that was it, they went home and never really went out for a drink. You would maybe see the odd one in the main square having a drink on a Saturday evening. They were all quite young lads, and I was probably the oldest player there.

A few clubs wanted to sign me in the summer of 1997. I think Bradford came in for me first, and my manager Pim Verbeek didn't want me to go. This was in July, and I had come back for pre-season. It was at the end of September that Luton signed me. I think he had heard the news, because he pulled me into the office and said that Bradford had telephoned. Their manager was Chris Kamara, and I'd actually played with him during my first spell at Luton. He was very positive about the move, but Fortuna Sittard still didn't want me to go.

But then about three weeks later, Pim went upstairs and became director of football. The club brought in a young coach, and to be honest we weren't seeing eye to eye. Then the next minute, he pulled me into his office and said that the club was selling me to Luton, and that was it. I thought there and then that I was definitely going back to England. He didn't even turn round and ask me whether I wanted to go back to England. It was just a case of 'Oh by the way, Luton have come in for you and decided to sign you'.

At that stage, I had only played three games in that season. That was before the Sparta Rotterdam game, and I knew that Luton's manager Lennie Lawrence, my agent and David Kohler, the Luton chairman, had been at the game. So I played, and the two Chairmen agreed a fee. I went back with the lads on the bus, and the next day I flew back to England. I agreed my personal terms and then had to fly back, tie things up, and fly straight back again. And then Lisa moved us from Holland back home again to Luton.

As I boarded the plane to leave Holland, I was thinking that it was their choice to sell me. I would have stayed, because I had another two years left on my contract. So I think it was the money they got for me. They got £400,000, about 1.2 million Dutch Guilders, which for a club like that was a lot of money. I used to speak to Fernando Ricksen, and he also told me he'd never leave, but once a club came in with a big offer for him, they sold him, which was true for other players as well. They were just like a little selling club, but I heard they've got a new stadium with a pitch that is partly below sea level.

I would recommend playing abroad to any young British footballer, particularly if he likes to find out about a different culture and lifestyle. Talking about the French football now, they're number one in the world what with them winning the European Championships and the World Cup. A lot of their best players are playing abroad, but France is still a beautiful country to go and play your football in. I learned an awful lot when I was out there, about training and at every level. You have your low and your high points, but all in all I had a great time".

Following his return to the UK from Holland, Phil resumed playing with Luton Town for three seasons. A brief spell at Burnley followed before he finished his career with Oxford United. He now lives in the Luton area with his partner and young son.

Steve Perryman MBE

MANAGER
Shimizu S-Pulse, (Japan), January 1996 – December 2000
Kashiwa Reysol, (Japan), June 2001 – Present

Steve Perryman MBE was born in Ealing, and signed as a schoolboy for Tottenham Hotspur in 1967. It was the club where he became a household name, and during a glittering playing career with Spurs he won two League Cups, two FA Cups and two UEFA Cups. He also won the football writers 'player of the year' award in 1982, an England cap, and was awarded an MBE for his services to football in 1984. His first managerial position was as player-coach at Brentford in 1986. He then moved to Watford for two years, before eventually going back to Tottenham as manager in 1994. We pick up Steve's story in 1994:

"I went to Tottenham with Ossie Ardiles, as his assistant, and we were the first managerial team that Alan Sugar took on board after everything that had gone on before. We lasted about eighteen months. For whatever reason it didn't work out and we eventually left. Ossie went to Mexico and I went to Norway on a short-term contract. I'd had contacts there for the previous fifteen years as I'd done workshops there in the past. Anyway, I came home in the December of 1995 and didn't have a base then in England, having sold up. Ossie had also left his Mexican club by then, was at home in Hoddesdon, and he invited me to stay in his house over Christmas and the New Year, which was fantastic. Whilst there he had a phone call from a FIFA agent, who happened to be a good friend of both of ours and was an old England Amateur International, and he put to Ossie the chance to go and be a manager in

Japan. Ossie then turned round to me and said 'Do you want to join me in this Japanese adventure?'

I wanted to go and coach in Japan for several reasons. Number one, we were looked upon as failures at Tottenham, which I thought was a bit harsh. Because of the fall-out of everything that had happened before at Tottenham, that meant we were on the back pages of the papers every day of the week. There were all sorts of problems going on, and of course a lot of the players backed, and had a loyalty to, the previous management team. Since Ossie and I were the people to follow them, I think we got caught up in the fall-out of it all. So I was determined to join Ossie and prove that we could be successful together, and try and prove Tottenham wrong. I think you have to do it if you take a knockback like that. As well as this, the fact that I'd been to Japan twice as a player in the early and late 1970s with Tottenham Hotspur as a player and team captain and enjoyed the experience, made me think 'Well, I've heard a bit about this Japanese thing with Lineker etc.', and I thought I'd try it.

We went to an interview up in a West End hotel with about seven or eight of Shimizu S-Pulse's officials. They provided us with some details about the club before we went to that meeting, which was very useful: where the club was situated, the population, what the area was famous for etc, but in the end it was a case of us not knowing what we were going to. You couldn't have made the decision from the information they gave us. It was simply a case of whether we wanted to go and work in Japan or not. It just worked out to be incredibly lucky that we went to a very good club, albeit down on their heels a little bit in terms of results, which is usually the way you get a management job anyway. We were lucky enough to live in one of the nicest places in Japan. They grow oranges there, are famous for their green tea and you'd open the curtains and look at Mount Fuji every day. It was out on the coast, virtually in the countryside. People usually think about the traffic and massive cities in Japan, but it wasn't quite like that where we were.

I spoke absolutely no Japanese before I went out there. My wife and I had gone to Norway together and she and her children, who were twelve and nine at the time, came out to Japan with me. So it was a bit of an experience for them I have to say! A new country, a different city, a different culture, and because of where we lived there were no international schools, so they were thrown in at the deep end of the Japanese school system. On the flip side of that was that we didn't have to leave them at home. But that had its downside as well because they had to stick it out at school for a couple of months not knowing what was going on, so they were trying to adapt too. Of course the upside of it was that they learned the language. They did very well, and I think they learned a lot through the experience. Imagine yourself in that position, it's hard enough at that age anyway, but just try to imagine it. The Japanese use symbols instead of western-type words. It's not like it was in Norway, where if you didn't understand a word you could look it up in the dictionary and find the English equivalent. With all the Japanese-charactered signs everywhere, it's almost impossible to do that.

It was a big test for them, and by that time we'd had our first child. So on top of everything else we took a six-month old baby to this new country. Of course you have to ask yourself lots of questions, for example, do they have nappies? Obviously they have babies, but do they have the new type of nappies, do they have old cloths, I mean, what do they do? It all became clear once we lived there, but like with all situations, there is a settling-in period. Having said that the settling-in period in Japan, especially because of the circumstances of my family then, was particularly difficult, not least because we were put into a holding apartment which was tiny. There were five of us living in there. If you were sending the two kids to school straight away, then that would be a bit more room for most of the day. But that was just a place where we were going to live for just a month or so before we sorted ourselves out before moving somewhere else, and it was because of this that didn't want to send the kids to school locally. to that particular place. So you're on top of each other, you're in a new country, it's incredibly hot and different, and things can get a bit fraught.

To be fair, there was a big reception for us when we arrived, because of Ossie's name. The Japanese, I have to say, love a name, be it the name of a bag, a fashion designer, a pair of shoes, whatever. They're not obsessed, but they're very impressed with a name. Ossie Ardiles has obviously got a name in world football, with him winning the 1978 World Cup. So yes, we did create a few ripples in the press when we arrived, and rightly so because this was a very big move for an Argentinian and his English assistant to be going to this club in Japan. Of course, the Japanese did their homework. They looked into my credibility, found out about my nearly one thousand games and they felt that Ossie and I were a good combination.

I think that the Shimizu club was extremely well organised in lots of different ways. They were used to bringing in foreigners, because up to that point they had been a Brazilian-biased club. One of their first managers was Rivelino, another was the chap who was the national team's goalkeeper in Pele's era, who I think has just been sacked as Brazil's national team manager, so I think all the clubs in Japan have this affiliation to a particular type of country. Some clubs had links with European teams, taking people from Holland and France, whilst the other clubs, basically most of them, are influenced by Brazil. I didn't know that before I went to Japan, but I certainly know now that there's a very strong link between Brazil and Japan. I think there are over one million Japanese people who live in Brazil. There are actually a lot of low paid workers from Brazil living in Japan, particularly in the place where we were in Shimizu, which is a port area.

If Japan starts up something new, which is what they were doing with the J-League, they tend to look at what's happening around the world, make a decision on what they think is the best, and then try to emulate that. Most of the clubs made the decision that they should be like Brazil, and brought in Brazilian managers and players. Take Nagoya Grampus Eight for instance. Their first manager was really Toyota, as are most of the J-League clubs, who are owned by big corporations. Their first coach was Gordon Milne, and he decided to take Gary Lineker there. Vast amounts of money were being bandied about, and that European link has been carried on ever since through Arsene Wenger and the French players he bought here, although the last appointment they made was a Brazilian, so it can change. They tend to veer in one direction or another.

In Japan, the president does not have a financial involvement with the club. Having said that, our club was actually a bit different. The J-League was formed professionally in 1992. Those clubs had had thirty or forty years previously playing as Toyota, Hitachi, Yamaha and Nissan, but they had some football background and played in a semi-pro league. They had been employing Brazilian goalkeeping and athletics coaches, and these people weren't working for Nissan, so they were virtually professionals in a semi-professional league. Our area was then granted a licence to have a professional club. This was almost certainly because football had started in Japan in our area ten years before anywhere else, at the instigation of one particular man called Mr Hotta. He had a love of football, as well as some influence, and decided that football was a very good vehicle for Japanese children, to learn about teamwork and togetherness.

So by the time the J-League was formed professionally, it was worked out that over a third of the Japanese players that were being produced were from the Shimizu area, because of the school system and the fact that it had been played there earlier. There was no big employer in our area, and as a result the club was virtually taken up by the community: by lots of small shareholders, by supporters and smaller-type companies who didn't cause any waves on the Japanese Stock Market, and then local businesses. So this was actually the 'community club' of the League. In some ways, the J-League wanted this to be a flagship, or a model, because they wanted the J-League to survive on its own two feet, through the gate and through sponsorship, and not necessarily with clubs being propped up by the big companies that just wrote off two or three million dollars a year in debts. If that was the way things had progressed, then eventually the companies would have got sick of it and pulled out. So our club was a model in many ways.

That was definitely a different approach to appointing members of the board of directors, as opposed to a club owned by a big corporation. For instance the club I'm at now, Kashiwa Reysol, would have appointed a senior member of Hitachi to be president of the Reysol club board, or maybe even someone who worked for Hitachi, now coming to the end of his working days there. They would move their man into this position, because of some sporting link or particular ability. Shimizu wasn't like that, because there was no big company backer. It was a number of companies plus supporters. So the man put in charge was not that powerful. He was powerful because he was the president. You know what it's like in Japan, they are very respectful when you are the president of anything – you are somebody. He wasn't there by wealth or position, he was there because someone thought he was right for the job. We would probably see him, three, four, five times a year, no more than that, and he was always very respectful to us. But we'd have a more day-to-day involvement with the management team at the club, and they would report back to him.

It was incredibly difficult at the beginning. Results-wise, life-wise, everything, and nothing was smooth. If you have a cold and have to go to a chemist, you've got to find the right stuff. Likewise if you think about walking into a supermarket over there it's difficult to know what's what. What is flour? What is sugar? What is this? It's easy to pick up the wrong thing, you know, it's just these little frustrations. As well as this, the children and the people in Japan have always got colds because there's such a variance in the temperature. If your child has had a cold for over a couple of weeks, you take that child to the doctor, whereas in Japan you take your child to the doctor, and he says 'We're in Japan, that's what happens. Kids have colds.' You just have to grin and bear it with certain things.

The job was also difficult, because we were struggling result-wise and hadn't pulled up any trees. Halfway through our first season they called us into a meeting after a particular match. We lost that game 3-0 at home, which isn't very good in any country, and I thought the worst. Anyway, the president said 'We know this is a difficult situation. What do you need?' It was fantastic, because they sat back and listened to what we needed. Ossie was particularly good at putting his case across.

Eventually, as all clubs do, we went on this mid-season break up in Hokkaido up in the North, where they set up a training week. We had a camp together and from that moment on it all went right. We came back from the camp, got to the final of the League Cup and won it, and everything just flowed from then on. Everything got easier and smoother, not because they treated us any better because of the results – they couldn't have treated us any better anyway. Over time you get to know more people, your social life improves, you meet people who can baby-sit for you, you find Italian restaurants or places where you can escape from Japan for a couple of hours, and then it all took shape. It was fantastic after that.

At the media interviews, they had a local Japanese man who'd lived in London to act as our interpreter, and I think he was something to do with a travel agency. He was not the most accomplished translator, and put the English questions across in a very straightforward manner. He just kept saying to us 'We need Cup in hand! We need trophies! We need to win something!'

Since the J-League had started in 1993, and up until we arrived in 1996, the Japanese had spent a lot of money, and Japanese football was at the point then that the first three years had been a real honeymoon period. It was a case of you couldn't buy tickets or get enough of the supporter items that were on sale in every store. People wanted it because it was the fashion of Japan, but after three years that had died a little, and suddenly there came the reality. So by the time, we'd arrived in 1996, things were getting a bit more difficult.

But we started to turn things round with the League Cup win, which was in very good style, albeit we were 2-0 up with about five minutes to go and drew 2-2. Eventually, we were leading 3-2 in extra-time, and most of what you see in Japan is decided by the golden goal, but for some reason it wasn't like that in this competition. Anyway, we got pulled back to 3-3 against the Liverpool equivalent of the country at that time, who were all-conquering, but we won on penalties, in the national stadium, and live on television. It was a magnificent game, and of course there were a lot of celebrations afterwards.

We then learned that when you get success in Japan, you put it in front of everyone. You go to the local government offices, you're presented to the Mayor, to all the hierarchy, and you go and visit various sponsors as well. You go to their various offices in Tokyo, and you're treated like gods. We were also appearing on a lot of TV shows. This is all bearing in mind that they called Shimizu 'The football city of Japan'. Therefore you can imagine how desperate this city was to win something. They eventually won it, so you can imagine what happened TV-wise. Ossie was lauded as a good manager, I was praised for my job in coaching, and everything went from there.

Eventually when Ossie left I won a League Championship with them, which was their first ever. Ossie and myself had previously finished top of the League but lost on goal difference, so we were making steps forward all the time. That eventually led to my Championship win, which also lead to a Japanese FA Cup Final appearance, which they had never done before, but unfortunately they lost in the final. But the team we played against, a team called Flugels ANA and part of Nippon Airways, were actually one of the teams where the parent company got fed up with paying off the club's debts.

And because Flugels then folded after that Cup Final, we then went through to the Asian Cup Winners Cup, which we eventually won. From there, like in the old days in Europe, we went on to the Asian Super Cup Final, where we eventually played the Asian Champions Cup winners from Riyadh over two legs, and lost by the odd goal. Had we won that game, which we were incredibly close to doing, we would have qualified for this August's World Club Championship, which unfortunately is now defunct, but we didn't know that at the time. So this little team in Shimizu, which is like Coventry in terms of stature, was just one goal away from appearing in this World Club Championship, which would have been an amazing turnaround.

In the first year, I like to draw a line under the struggles of the first six months. From then of course, at various times you lose a couple of games, but in general we had a very good record. The great thing about it was that Ossie was very clever with the finances. To begin with, we didn't have the big backing from a major company. The club went through some money troubles, and was eventually saved at the last minute by the biggest local company in that area. That did not reflect the lack of success on the field, because we were being successful, but in terms of the money flow behind us it was not correct, considering what they had spent in the past, and probably wasted I'd have to say.

So Ossie was obviously enjoying his time there. He was enjoying the success and so was I, and I remember Ossie making a statement saying 'OK. If we are not going to have the money of the others, we must be more clever'. So now I'm listening, because I usually know most of what Ossie's going to come out with, and I thought 'Oh! This is new!' He then said 'So we have got to have a style. People have got to know what we stand for. We are going to play quick, passing football (a la Ossie's style!) We have a smaller squad than anyone else. We do not want red and yellow cards. We are not going to speak to the referee. We are going to take quick throw-ins, quick free kicks. We are going to play a very fast-moving high tempo game. We are going to do this, this, this, this and this'.

So he put it all across, and the players followed him to the letter. It was magnificent because this was a manager who, in his own way, had cleared the player's minds of everything else that they had heard before. Remember, these players had already been coached by a Brazilian, then a Japanese, then another Brazilian, and then an Argentinian with an English coach, and they had been influenced by all these different languages and messages. He also said 'We do not play offside, we do not cheat, we do not waste time, we do not run the ball to the corner flag. We don't do this or this, but we do this. This is how we play, and if you three centre backs (we varied between 4-4-2 and 3-5-2) pass it between yourselves, you do not pass it in a way where the ball bounces three or four times along the ground, you pass it SHARP – bang! Then it moves on to the next player, then the next, then the next, and when you keep doing that, you open up the spaces and we go. Then we go forward and we play'.

He just gave such a positive image to the players, and they responded very well. Then he was clever, because he never turned down the chance of an interview. He told everyone, including the opposition, how we were going to play. And after games, when we won in very good style, they loved our style in Japan, he would say we are the best and the quickest passing team in the League. We make more chances than anyone else. We receive less red and yellow cards than anyone else. In actual fact, because football is a new game in Japan, the reporters who cover the game aren't actually specialists, and as typically happens in Japan within a company or an organisation, you may be there one year, and then they move you. So we might have had a press room of thirty people following the game, and it might be their first year for twenty of them. Rather than them being able to criticise you, they just listen. They just report what you've said, which is a great responsibility, and you can use this to your own ends. It would spread our message, and by the end people had the opinion that Shimizu S-Pulse was the best team in Japan. I actually think we were, but the message and of course the image that we were giving to our home supporters was the same as when we were live on TV. So there was a lot of propaganda, but for the right reasons.

Our local rivals were about an hour away from us, but in the same county, and they were called Jubilo, a magnificent and very well organised club. Dunga was their captain. He was their leader, and the club followed him through thick and thin. He was exceptionally good for them, but I think he also had some negative points, because he was so ultra- professional that in my eyes he would cheat, and con the referee. The Japanese players would follow him and his actions to the letter. He was good for that particular club, and in some ways he was good for Japan, but I felt this was the wrong type of leadership. But of course Dunga was a very good player, and an immense influence in any game that he played.

The one negative thing that I found with Japanese players, was that through their culture of being very respectful towards each other, but also loving a name, they would go to close Dunga down and then realise it was Dunga. They then got two metres away and would think 'Well, this is Dunga. I can't possibly take the ball off him!' So I would describe to our players what respect is, which means that you must put him under as much pressure as possible, and test his ability as much as you can. If you then beat him or he beats you, you shake hands and say 'Well, we tried our best'. Show your respect that way, instead of laying down and dying in front of him.

In England, a young boy has a dream of being a professional. They start training with the team at about six years of age. They start playing in a League at about eight, and they chase the ball. Eventually it takes the form of some sort of semblance of a decent park game, and you have to fight your corner in every game you play. You have to run, tackle and chase. So you learn the bare facts of football very young in England, where you have the parents screaming on the line.

In Japan it all happens a lot slower. It's all at school, it's more controlled, with less pressure and less tempo, and players have the space in which to try and improve. By the time they get to the top level in Japan, and are thinking about playing international football, all these players from Brazil and England have had to scrap for that yard of space on the pitch. The Japanese haven't had to do that, and it almost becomes a new tempo for them.

So that's the difference. In England, players know football from the shop-floor level. They have to get down and roll their sleeves up and get dirty. The way the Japanese do it is to go through the school system, to the universities, and then they get spotted and join a club. They've got good intellects and they're a race that want to improve. They want to learn new things, and give absolute respect to the teacher that's teaching them, be it the schoolteacher, the swimming instructor or the football coach, and so it all happens a lot slower. If it's all Japanese footballers playing against each other, then it's no problem if they lack this shopfloor type of mentality. The fact is that now you've got foreigners coming in to teach the players. Of course we tried to drag up that tempo and speed it up, but after what you know from your own career, the process of speeding up their football education and experiences can sometimes be frustrating.

By 1999, I'd had three years as Ossie's assistant. Ossie then decided to leave, because he felt that as much as he loved it in Japan, he was losing touch with the real football world. He was also very disappointed that the Japanese national job came up after the French World Cup, and he believed that he had a chance for the job, and rightly so. But they decided not to give it to a foreigner who had done a really good job in Japan, and therefore to someone who knew the country and the players. Instead they gave it to a Frenchman, possibly because of the French World Cup win and because of Arsene Wenger, who had a good record in Japan. With that disappointment, Ossie decided to leave.

I then took over for another two years, which meant I stayed in Japan for a five year period. We only ever signed year by year, as do most coaches and players in Japan. As we had won the Asian Cup Winners Cup in the middle of the year in Thailand, which again was their first ever Championship in that sort of competition, the club offered me the contract incredibly early. In previous years it had always been left until October or November, whereas this time they offered it to me in June. It just made me think a bit more about my future.

The year before I'd been voted 'manager of the year', which was very nice, and all this success was coming, but I just thought about it again, especially as my wife was talking to me about the children. One child was born in Japan and our first child, six months old when we first went out there, was now 5 1/2, the other child was now three. They had just started Japanese school, and spoke Japanese, as did the older two children. The older two children both had two years with us there. All these positive things were fantastic, but of course they weren't getting an English education, and they're only going to be judged in England when they're going for a job by whether they had any GCSEs or A-Levels.

So they then went back to the UK to live with their father, but they still retain their Japanese. However we were worried about the two younger children needing an English education. We were good parents, and had been at home doing things with them, but we're not teachers. It was magnificent to hear two little girls speaking Japanese to each other, but at that stage they couldn't yet read English. We thought that if they'd been in an English school they'd have been reading by that stage.

As a result we decided at the end of the fifth year to make a change, and we came back to the UK at the end of December. I just returned to Japan about a week ago. I had about six months off and would have liked to have got a job in England. I did have some interviews, but for whatever reasons, nothing was quite right for both parties, and I eventually took the chance to come back to Japan. I'm here now, and my family are going to come out for the summer months, and then reassess it again at Christmas when I go home again for the holiday time.

The fans and the press were a bit shocked when I said that I was going to leave Shimizu. They knew that these two people, Ossie and myself, had given the club this style. Therefore, they wanted to continue that style, because it had been proved to be successful, and they were thinking 'What follows this?' When one manager leaves, his assistant takes over and it continues to work, as was the case with Ossie and me, it means that in five years the club and the supporters haven't had the consistent managerial struggles that some of the other clubs have endured. Some of them employed two or three different people a year, striving for the success, not getting it, and making a change.

Of course, that leads to upheavals. It's not just one man who comes in, it's all his staff, and then they're all out and someone else comes in, and all that that means in terms of new cars and new apartments. It takes a lot to make the changeover, and our club had not had that as it had been a fairly easy ride. Needless to say, they had to make the decision on someone to appoint as my successor. They employed a Yugoslav youth coach that was at the club, much to my surprise, because there was a man at the club called Mr Oki, 'Okisan', who was Ossie's number three and my number two. We felt that with him having five years of such good experience that he should have taken over. He could have continued the work. They decided against it, and went for another foreigner. To be fair, he's doing quite a good job so they made the right decision.

Having said that, I just felt that they should have had faith in their Japanese up-and- coming manager. When you think that the big stars of Japanese football eight years ago were Dunga, Lineker,

Stoijkovic and Leonardo, you find that nowadays people in Japan don't really speak about the foreign names. They do with regard to Italian football or with Manchester United, but when it comes to talking about the J-League, they have their own grown-up good-quality Japanese players, so they are the stars. That gives them the chance to appoint a Japanese national coach. They have ability, and this man has ability. If he didn't have ability, he wouldn't have survived with us for five years, and therefore I felt to give credit to him to be the next manager, but unfortunately they ignored it, but of course it's their money, their company and their decision.

I had a discussion the other night with the former football director of Shimizu, who has now moved on to another club. I asked him about the period at the beginning of my contract, when things weren't going so well, but they had confidence in our ability to succeed. Was it really like that, or was it a case of 'We can't afford to sack them? To sack them, we've got to pay them off, we've got to get someone new?' But he said 'No. No. We trusted what was happening. The results weren't right, but we could see the signs were good'. And as events proved they were more than repaid for that.

My last game in charge of Shimizu was an amazing event. It was the final of the Asian Super Cup. We were playing against Al-Hilal of Riyadh in a magnificent stadium. We lost 2-1 at home, but in Saudi there were 48,000 people there, all dressed in white robes. We totally dominated the game but unfortunately drew 1-1. Had it been 1-0 or 2-1 to us, it would have gone to penalties and then anyone could have won, but it just went the wrong way for us. This was the biggest game our club had ever played. Not only did they do fantastically well to get there, but when they were there they performed to an extremely high level. If you look at the two games, forget goals but in terms of performance, we were much the better team. The financial clout of this Saudi Arabian team was enormous. They had five Saudi internationals, one Colombian and one Nigerian international, and we played better than them. Remember, they were in this Super Cup Final because they were the best team in Asia, and we took them right to the wire. To get there we never lost one game in Asia, but unfortunately the only game we did lose was at home against Al-Hilal. Before that we had to go and win in places like Shanghai against a team coached by Lazaroni, the Brazilian's World Cup manager in 1990. We had to win in Seoul against a team called LG Cheetahs, and get results in some lesser places like Vietnam. We got some very big victories, so I think we can be proud of that.

The thing that sticks in my mind about coaching in Japan is the way that when you are teaching Japanese players, they give you 100% respect and attention and follow your every word. We went there with the right ethics, and if they listened, which they did, they came out of it with good ethics, because it was a big responsibility to have with how you shape someone's career. Some of the people we taught are going to be representing Japan in the 2002 World Cup Finals, which is a major event for them in their own country and they want to do as well as possible. So the respect that Japanese people give to their teacher was the most striking thing for me.

I sometimes worry about England because of the lack of respect for teachers compared to my younger days, the lack of respect for instance for policemen. I'm even reading that nurses are getting attacked late at night in emergency hospitals. Can you imagine that happening years ago? In Japan, you would not get those things because people over there have respect for each other. That goes in lots of different ways. Take litter for instance. I've spent some months back in England, and I've seen a car driving along. They finish a packet of cigarettes and throw it out of the window. That just wouldn't happen in Japan, so this place has a lot of good things about it. Of course there are some negatives. Sometimes I think that Japan is either twenty years ahead or twenty years behind the times. My wife had a baby here, and some of the things she went through were similar to what was happening fifty years ago in Britain. Her grandmother would tell her stories of when she had babies in England, and some of that still applies in Japan today. In some ways they're behind us, but they've retained a level of respect for each other which is wonderful.

The team I'm with now is called Kashiwa Reysol. Kashiwa is a suburban area of Tokyo. not far from Narita airport. The club is owned by Hitachi, so they're very powerful, and have a wonderful ground and training facilities. Despite all their power, they haven't yet won a League Championship, despite coming close in the past. I've come halfway through this season to help the current manager. [AUTHORS NOTE: Steve is now the manager of Kashiwa Reysol]. I won the 'manager of the year' award in Japan in 1999, this manager won it in the year 2000, and Hitachi have partnered us up to try and make that final step for this club to try and win the Championship.

I think that when you work abroad from England, people describe it to me as if they felt a surge of energy. I absolutely felt that, and part of the reason was because the life of an English football manager is different to that of a Japanese one. There are less games in Japan and fewer people play soccer in Japan. There was a list that came out in England the other day that had the names of seven hundred free transfer players from the PFA. They haven't even got seven hundred players in Japan! So that's the difference. You don't spend all your time running up and down motorways scouting and chasing players that you're never going to get. You must concentrate on coaching the group that you have.

If you are a coach, and that's your field of expertise, you should want to work in a country where you have the opportunity to express yourself. In England, you are a coach because of your football experience. Then you get pushed into negotiating contracts, sponsorships, and things away from what you do best, which is on the coaching field. On the other hand you can go to a foreign country and develop yourself as a coach. You can teach them, and whilst teaching them you have thinking time to improve yourself. I'd never met a Brazilian person before I came to Japan as a forty-five year-old, and my children have now met Brazilians. I've also worked with Brazilians and coached against Frenchmen.

I've had a wonderful experience coaching in Japan, which I may have got if I'd stayed in England, because now there's Arsene Wenger and the other foreign coaches and players in the Premiership. I can't say a word against it, other than you are away from your family and friends. My father died when I was in Korea playing this particular game, and I flew home. So for the previous four years, I did not see him as many times as I would have done if I'd been in England. So there was a price to pay, but if you're just judging my experience of coaching abroad on job satisfaction then what I've been through is magnificent".

After a brief spell in the UK, Steve returned to Japan, and as already mentioned, is currently working as manager at Kashiwa Reysol, a J-League side based in Tokyo.

Luther Blissett

PLAYER
AC Milan, (Italy), June 1983 – June 1984

Luther Blissett began his playing career with Watford in 1975, and the first of his three spells at the club at which he made his name lasted until 1983, during which time he won the first of his 14 England caps. We pick up Luther's story in May 1983:

"The initial contact was made directly with the football club. I didn't know anything about it, and the first I knew about it was when Graham Taylor called me here at Watford. I was just walking out of the tunnel, and he said to me 'I just want a quick word with you. We've had an offer from a club in Italy, but we're going to say to them that we want double what they're asking, and we'll see if they come back'. And that was it. My thoughts at the time were that I wasn't bothered, and wasn't looking to leave this place because we'd just finished second in the First Division. I was very interested but I hadn't even given it any thought about playing anywhere else.

In the end it all worked out well. I think Graham Taylor called me the following day and asked me to pop over to his house to see him. So I drove over to his house over the other side of Watford. I went up into his attic, which he had made into an office, and he sat me down and said 'It's about the team that came in and offered half a million pounds for you. We said they would have to double that, they've come back with a million pounds and said 'There's a million pounds, now can we talk to the player?' And so it's over to you. Do you want to talk to them?' When he told me the club was AC Milan, I told him that the least I could do is talk to them, and see if I fancied going. But at that time, I hadn't even thought I was going to go. It was just a case of talk to them and find out exactly what was involved.

By that stage, I had played in the England under-21s and the full international team. I had probably played about eight or nine games by then. It was a case of going to Italy, with the thought that it would help my international and club career. If you play in one of the better Leagues in the world against some of the best players in the world, something's bound to rub off on you. So I was looking forward to going, for the change of culture and the challenge of trying to succeed in a different environment.

I think everybody was quite sad to see me go, but I think the million-pound transfer fee made people feel a little bit better! Let's face it – a million pounds in those days was a lot of money, and I still can't believe that people will pay that sort of money for a footballer. I think it's unbelievable when you see the sort of sums now that are being bandied around, and it's quite worrying. For Watford to be paid a million pounds for one of their players, especially for a player that they had brought through themselves, was a great achievement for the club. It was wonderful for me to be given the opportunity to go and play in a country like Italy, and to play for a club such as AC Milan. After a lot of consideration, the deal was finally concluded. I think it was probably in the very late hours of the night that I decided, after long deliberations, that I would go.

It was a sad moment when I actually made the decision. It was not something I did lightly and I spoke to a lot of people about it. My parents said 'If you want to do it, and that's what you want to do, then fine, you've got our support. You go out and do it'. And it was pretty much the same at Watford. Graham Taylor and Eddie Plumley were saying 'Great. We'll have the million pounds, but if you don't want to go, we'll be more than happy to say 'Thanks very much but no thank you', and you stay here and get on with it next season'. It was really down to me, and I was under no pressure whatsoever. It was just a case of making a decision to further my education as a footballer.

I had never been to Milan before I signed for the 'Rossoneri'. Obviously you know what the Italians are like. You see loads of things on TV, you see them in the World Cup, and you expect them to be fanatical and really up for supporting their team. For me it was like going to one of the big derby games, Manchester United v Liverpool or Arsenal v Tottenham, and I feel that's what their supporters were like. They were very fanatical, very much behind their club, and nothing else mattered in their lives. So that's something that I wanted to go and experience.

The initial contact with AC Milan was made when we met in a local hotel. I remember it was a very hot day, and stuffy in this room. They had about four or five people with them, and there was me and the agent who was arranging the deal, as well as my accountant. We sat there with these people and we were trying to negotiate one thing and another to try and find some leeway. I just couldn't believe the things they were talking about. They talked about things, and I might as well not have been there. It was really a case of them getting on with what they had to do, and the player not really needing to be there. That was the initial contact, and when I actually met the president a week or so later, this was in London, he basically wanted to meet Elton John as well! It was one of those sort of meetings.

When I arrived in Milan, I was taken off the plane by a car which picked me up right at the side of the aircraft. I went straight through immigration ahead of everybody else on the plane, and as the doors opened to walk out, the masses of supporters that were lined across the side barriers was incredible, something I'd never experienced before. They were calling out my name, of sorts, because Luther is not exactly a name that Italians say very often! It was strange to hear it said in that dialect. It was quite an exciting time, with that first contact with all the supporters. That was the main thing, because it's the fans who are always the ones that make any football club. You could see that they were really fanatical supporters of their club.

My initial aim was to go out there, have a medical and a look around Milan, the pitch and the offices, and sign the contract. Then after having done all that I flew back to England. So that was as just the initial thing, and when I had to fly back out there full-time they organised an apartment for me. They put me in a hotel in the centre of Milan, and that was where I stayed for the first couple of months, well the first month at least, before I found somewhere outside Milan and moved there. They had contacts for the accommodation, and I told them what I was looking for. They came up with one or two places for me to go and have a look at, various different places to live. The club also came up with a car and they dealt with all those sorts of things. I just chose the car I wanted and that was it.

I didn't speak any Italian before I went there. It was just a case of taking one or two language tapes and learning the odd word or two. When I got there I started taking lessons, so it was a case of trying to settle into it as much and as soon as possible. I had lessons once or twice a week. It was difficult initially, because to pick up the finer points of any language is a massive thing, and because they were trying to teach you the grammar of it, I sometimes found it quite tedious. But I got on with it and again it was an interesting thing to be there and to be taught the language, and thinking that I was now going to be living there. So that was something totally different that I'd not experienced before.

AC Milan had just got promoted back to the First Division, after the recent bribery scandal and everything that had gone before. All their top stars had gone and they didn't really have any 'name' players there. They had Franco Baresi, who was a young lad coming through. You could see from day one that he was the best player they had, and that he was going to be something special. All the others were just very ordinary players, so in that respect AC Milan was no different to countless other teams. They were starting again from scratch, but I think the problem was that the supporters and directors were still remembering the great AC Milan sides that used to win in Europe and dominate their local League. So in that respect it was very difficult at the time because they expected me, being one person, to suddenly turn it around for them and it doesn't happen like that. You need a team around you to do it. So consequently my time playing for AC Milan wasn't that successful.

As for my meetings with the president, it seemed on the surface that I got on well with him. He's the one who says that the club wants this or that player and they went out and bought you. So they expect everything to go ticki-ti-boo. They expect it to go like clockwork, and everything to be fine. But when it doesn't work out like that, it's not so much that it's not going well for you, it's looked upon as his judgement doesn't seem to be right. They then tend to try and put pressure on you and say that you've got to do better. That was one thing, but you can only do so much depending on the circumstances that you're in.

With the press interviews, you got the odd one or two here and there that you had to do. Initially, when I went on one or two TV shows, I had an interpreter there because these were done in the first two or three weeks after I arrived. But after that, in the after-match ones, you did the best you could to deal with the questions that were thrown at you about the game. Often with things about the actual game you could understand what that was about. It's when they began talking about things, and you didn't know which way it was coming from, that it became a bit difficult. But when they talked about something like football, the terminology and the things that they say are pretty much the same, and you can pick it up fairly easily, so that wasn't too bad. It was just in general conversation, when they could be talking about anything and everything, that it was a little bit more difficult to follow initially.

My nickname at the time? They used to call me 'The black bomber'. I found that the supporters, as most supporters are when you go anywhere, are always 100% for you. But when things don't go well, they look at you as being the latest import and so-called 'big name', and you're the one to be the first they have a go at if things aren't going well. They knew that I had scored thirty three goals in England the season before I came, and I ended up scoring six goals over there in the thirty two games that I played in Italy. So they look at that and say that it hasn't worked out, but their thing wasn't to look and try to find the reason why. They just want to see you score goals, which I can totally understand. But there were reasons why I didn't get the goals, and a lot of it was to do with the way the game was played in Italy at the time. Thankfully it's changed an awful lot. Nowadays the game is far more attacking, and the forwards have more opportunity to show what they're able to do, which makes it far more attractive to watch. When I went there it was still pretty much the mentality of 'We've got the draw, let's keep the draw, and if we can nick it, let's nick it'.

When I started out there, we had a number of pre-season games, friendlies and Coppa Italia games, and it all went very well during the friendlies. I ended up scoring about eight or nine goals in the warm-up games leading towards the season, so I was thinking that it was going to be great, because we're going to have a go. But when the season started, there was a completely different attitude towards the game and it became very difficult. But the games that stick out are obviously the derby games, because when you arrive in the San Siro, with 100,000 people there, there are flares going off everywhere, the drums are beating, and the noise is quite unbelievable. You're on the pitch, there are players five or six yards away, and you cannot hear a word they're saying when they're shouting to you! So things like that are just fantastic. You walk out of the tunnel, and suddenly you see all the colour and all the faces, and the noise and smell of it all as well. It's the most unbelievable thing and captures all your senses.

There were a lot of great players over in Italy at that time. Michel Platini was one of them, and playing against him was unbelievable. The understanding that Platini had with Boniek, who was playing with him at Juventus, was quite incredible. Passarella was playing there as well, and you also had the likes of Falcao. They also had great players like the German Hansi Muller, and a lot of very talented players were playing there at the time. They were really the pioneers to what is now a very strong League in Italy.

The thing is, being in Italy, you might occasionally want something like fish and chips, and you just can't get it. But there are so many other things you can get, that you have to get into the lifestyle and understand that this is the way they do things. Those were some of the things you had to come to terms with. Some of the things that I couldn't get the hang of and I don't understand why they do it, was that you'd be driving in traffic and someone would stop and go and buy a newspaper, and they'd go and buy a coffee. The car would just be there, and you'd be sitting there waiting for it to move! Then they'd get their coffee, come back, get in the car and drive off! Things like that were very strange for me. It's just a totally different way of looking at things. Life over there doesn't seem to be as hectic. The pace of it seems to be just so much more relaxed, and they seem to enjoy their lives more.

Eric Gerets, the Belgian international, was the other foreign player who at Milan when I was there. We had the odd meal together, and you also went to a lot of these 'Milan Clubs', which were fan clubs all over Italy affiliated to the football club, and be their guest for the day. So you did mix socially with the players and go and do this sort of thing. Eric would probably have been the one player I had most contact with.

The manager obviously watched a lot of the games early on, and he could see the attributes that I had. I think in the pre-season games, the players actually played towards that. If you let players naturally do the things they do best, they will play pretty much to what they're capable of doing. But when the tactical restraints come in, and the fear factor suddenly sets in, and people think they can't afford to lose the game, then players don't play naturally or the way they should.

It was because a lot of the players were fearful of losing games, that I think they never went out with the attitude that they could win games, and consequently they didn't perform very well. We found this in many games when we were better than the opposition, and it was really just a case of flicking the coin in the air, and whichever side it dropped you might get the rub of the green that day. They were games that we really probably should have won. So tactically, I just think that for the fact that they had this fear thing about losing games was really stifling the players. It stopped them delivering what they were really capable of producing, certainly with some of the games, we probably could have a few more results if the players had been a little more relaxed about what they were doing.

You did your pre-season stuff and you trained in the morning. Then you had lunch, and went and had a lie-down for about three or four hours. You would then start again at about 4 or 5 o'clock, and work for another couple of hours. In the evening, you would have dinner, relax and take it easy, and then it goes and repeats itself the next day, and so on. So that was different. Some of their actual training routines, once the season got under way on the football side, meant that we did very little in the way of fitness work. They did little maintenance things to keep players general fitness going, but we did very little of really increasing or putting the edge on your fitness when the season got going. There was also a lot of technical work, stuff with the ball, and a lot of biometric stuff.

I think my game changed quite radically as a result of playing abroad. When I was playing out there, I was the only forward. I had my back to goal all the time, and you very rarely got to run the other way, because the ball was always played up to you, you laid it back, and went through for a return, but the ball would always end up back with the sweeper, and it would start again. And it would be very frustrating.

A lot of the training methods were quite good, but in the games it was just so difficult at times because you wouldn't get enough of the ball. As a forward I liked to run onto the ball, and attack people by taking them on, but with your back to goal all the time, the defenders are always favourite. You had a marker on you and there was always somebody covering, so it made it difficult for you all the time. There were one or two games where we got the balance a little bit more to the way I liked it, but we didn't really do it enough. When we did get the balance the way I wanted, we looked capable of winning games. Whether it was the coach or the players, or a combination of both I don't know, but they had this thing about risking losing the ball or giving it away at times to get the reward for it.

By the summer of 1984, Milan decided they wanted to change the two foreign players, me and Eric Gerets, and they were already looking to bring two new players in. You could only play two foreign players at the time, so my options were to stay there, and not play anywhere because there was no reserve team, or to leave. I had the opportunity to go to Roma and Torino, so it was a case of you move and go there or you stay and wait for something to happen, whether it be an injury or whatever, and get back in the team. But I'm a footballer, and what I want to do is play football, and if I'm not allowed to play then I don't want to be there. So my thing was that if they didn't want to keep me, I didn't want to be there. It was as simple as that. I wanted to get on, because the most important thing to me is my career and my enjoyment of doing the sport that I love, and that's simply that. But people asked me about the money, and I said to them that money has got nothing to do with it. The main thing has always been for me, and it still is to this day, if I enjoy what I'm doing, what you get paid is an added bonus to what it's all about.

My transfer was all over the papers, and I had journalists from England ringing me up talking about it. It was just always going on. It was very newsworthy, so they were the ways that you picked things up. And after that, once you've made your decision about what you want to do, you just get on with it.

Well obviously the supporters, as with a lot of things, were split when they heard I was leaving AC Milan. Some would say, yeah he should go, and the others said I should stay, but that's always going to be the case. They ultimately don't have the final say in anything. That's all done at board level. So they can voice what they think, but ultimately if the chairman or president, as in this case, decide that they want somebody else, then that's what they'll do. And for me, things had to move on. There was no point in staying there.

The last game of the season we played away at Udine. All I did at the end was change shirts with one of their players, and that was basically it. Once the game was over, I knew that that was pretty much it, because there had been a lot of things talked about as to which club I would be going back to, and there were several clubs mentioned. But my thing was, I knew Watford. I knew that I'd score goals at Watford, so I wanted to go back there.

When I left, it was a case of me wanting to go back to Watford, but reluctantly, because I would have loved to have given it a go in Italy for longer. But there's no point in giving it a go if you're not going to be able to play. If it had been a case, like now, of being able to have more than two foreign players, I would have stayed and fought for my place, but you can't fight for a place that's not there. The way I saw it was a case of getting out as soon as possible, and look after your career more than anything else.

My favourite memories of playing for AC Milan? Obviously the supporters. You get out there in that stadium. You walk out there in the San Siro, in the red and black stripes of AC Milan, and you're playing for them. It is the most unbelievable feeling in the world to be playing for that club, and walking out there onto the pitch. Other things, such as living in Italy, were just fantastic experiences. Their way of life is just so different. The food, the clothes, all these things are so different and very good. It was just a wonderful thing to have been a part of.

As I was boarding the plane, I was looking forward to getting my career going again when I got back to England. That was basically it. It was not a case of having regrets about anything. I made the decision and that was it. I will go all the way with that decision, until somebody proves to me that you've now got to go in another direction. My decision was to go to Milan, it didn't work out, and the opportunity was there now for me to come back to England for another club, and my choice was to go back to Watford and what I was looking forward to. So it was a case of 'Thanks for the experience'. I learned a lot about how to prepare for games, personally and as a team. I've kept that with me ever since I went to Milan, and for that I'll be grateful. But my main thing was looking forward to coming back and playing in England, and showing everybody what they had missed for a year.

Well the biggest things I remember were the day I arrived there initially, with all the supporters, and I walked out of the airport with all these hundreds of people there screaming, with banners, That was quite unbelievable and overwhelming, and obviously my debut game is a big memory too. That was against Verona, and Joe Jordan was playing for them. I actually said in the press conference before the game that I was going to score my first goal for AC Milan that day. I did score, and we won the game as well, so things like that were fantastic. They were just great things to happen.

If a British footballer asked me about to going to play for a club abroad, I would say go, but make sure the club that you're going to is geared up for success, that they've got good players there, and that they are looking ahead in what they're doing. I went to Italy in 1983, and it was basically to play for AC Milan. I'd not really given it a great deal of thought about the other players they had there, because again like everybody else, they think about all the great players that they've had, and you think those players were still there. But when I got there it was a completely different thing, and none of those great players were still at the club, and then it's very difficult.

As long as they've got good players there that you know *are* good players, then I would say go. As long as you get things sorted out and in place, you can go and have a great time playing abroad, because basically the English players can add a little bit of something different to the foreign game, wherever they go. They have this aggression, and this willingness never to give up. So they can add another dimension to what the foreign players have".

After returning from Italy in 1984, Luther rejoined Watford, and stayed with the Hornets until 1988. He then played for Bournemouth until returning to Watford in 1991 for one final season. Spells at West Bromwich Albion, Brentford, Bury and Mansfield Town followed until his retirement. He also had a further spell at Watford, as assistant coach to Graham Taylor until June 2001.

Luther now lives in the Watford area.

Colin Addison

MANAGER
Celta Vigo, (Spain), June 1986 – June 1987
Atletico Madrid, (Spain), October 1988 – June 1989
Cadiz, (Spain), January – June 1990; July – October 1993
Badajoz, (Spain), July 1996 – June 1997

> *Colin Addison began his playing career with York City in 1957, and stayed with the Minstermen until 1961, when he moved to Nottingham Forest. Six seasons and 62 goals later he went to Arsenal for a year, followed by a three-year spell at Sheffield United. Colin finished his playing career at Hereford United, during which time he also masterminded 'The Bulls' historic giant killing over Newcastle United in the FA Cup in 1972* [AUTHORS NOTE: yes, the one with the Ronnie Radford goal!] *Further management spells at Newport County, Derby County and West Bromwich Albion (assistant to Ron Atkinson) followed. We pick up Colin's story in June 1986:*

"I was initially approached by a Spanish agent based in London, who asked if I would consider a move to Spain to join Celta Vigo. Obviously, this was a great opportunity for me, so I flew out to Vigo with my agent, to meet the club's president and watch a couple of games. On returning home, I discussed things with my wife and family before accepting the job.

Football has always been an international game, but at that time, there weren't many British managers working overseas: John Toshack and Jock Wallace were definitely abroad, but there weren't too many others!

I'd never been to Vigo before I took the job there. At that time,

I didn't speak very much Spanish, but once I'd made my mind up, I soon got into it by reading phrase books, but by far the easiest way to learn a new language is by being in that country with the locals. Every day was a lesson when I was with the players; they were true professionals and a great help to me, although the club's Physical Trainer spoke very good English, which was a huge advantage! Coaching in Spain was a massive learning curve for me.

When I first arrived, the press met me at the airport! When Spanish clubs appoint a new manager, he is under immediate and fierce scrutiny! I spoke to the press every, particularly to Jose-Maria Garcia, who hosts Spain's most popular radio football show, and to 'Marca', the Spanish daily football player. There was a fairly sizeable reception to welcome me at the stadium, where I signed my contract before departing for pre-season training in the North of Spain.

Celta Vigo had been relegated just before I arrived. My task was to get them promoted back into the First Division at the first attempt – not an easy job by anyone's standards – and not without its pressures! The Spanish people are incredibly passionate about their football, so much so that they say the three most important people in any Spanish city are the manager of the football club, the president of the football club and the city's mayor!

We had a good start to the season, getting into the top six very early on. We stayed there, worked hard, won matches and were promoted at the end of the season. I always remember my first game in charge at Celta Vigo when we beat Logrones. It was, of course, wonderful to get off the mark with a victory. However, the most memorable game, without doubt, was our final game of the season in Bilbao, against Sestao FC, coached by Javier Irureta [AUTHORS NOTE: currently manager of Deportivo La Coruna]. We had to get at least a draw to be surer of gaining promotion, and we did just that with a 0-0 result. After the game, I remember Irureta saying, 'Celta fought like tigers and deserve their promotion'.

In Vigo, I inherited a great side with two very talented forwards; a Brazilian by the name of Balthazar and another called Lucas. Between them they scored around 50 goals that season and really set us up for promotion. The strike force was a massive advantage, but the side was full of talent.

In October 1988, I returned to Spain alongside Ron Atkinson at Atletico Madrid. We were together for several months until Ron left and I stayed until the end of the season. There were many memorable games during my time in Madrid. As one would expect, the most memorable were the 'Madrid derbies' against Real. They beat us 2-1 at the Bernabeu in a fantastic match. When we played them in the return fixture it was, unbelievably, an even better game, ending in a 3-3 draw. Beating Johan Cruyff's Barcelona 'dream team' in the Spanish Cup will also live with me forever. In a two-legged round, we drew the first match 3-3 in Barcelona, winning 4-0 in the second leg in Madrid. Obviously, everyone was delirious with excitement; after all, it's not everyday you beat Barcelona!

The following season I was back in Spain again, this time with Cadiz CF. When I arrived, they were struggling and lying second-bottom of the league. We worked hard, got out of trouble, and avoided relegation on the last day of the season. I left the club having achieved my objective of saving them from the drop, although I was back in Cadiz again 18 months later, this time to try and win them promotion. By that time they had been relegated (the season after I left!) and were struggling more than ever. I resigned in the October. Things had changed and I was unhappy that several things had been promised to me, but were never delivered.

In 1996, I returned to manage Badajoz, a Second Division side, and was there for a full season. We had a great season, only missing the play-offs by one goal! Extremadura pipped us at the post and were promoted to the First Division. To miss promotion by a point is bad enough, but to miss out on goal difference – and just one goal at that – was very hard to accept. The club wanted me to stay on, but before even accepting the job I'd decided to come home at the end of the season, whatever happened.

Overall, I look back with fond memories of my time in Spain, and am proud of my track record there. Successful with promotion at Celta Vigo; qualification for Europe and reaching the semi-final of the Spanish Cup with Atletico Madrid; saving Cadiz from relegation; then enjoying a tremendous season with Badajoz. My best memory? It has to be winning promotion with Celta Vigo. It was such a big game and a big day. I was a winner again – and loved every minute of it! Spain is a wonderful country with wonderful people. My family and I return regularly to see friends and enjoy our holidays there.

Should a British coach work abroad if given the chance? It depends. If your mind is set for a huge challenge and you're ready to undertake that and make the move into a completely new culture, with many different attitudes, then do it! After all, football is football wherever you go; the pitches are the same, the goalposts are the same – and it's always 11 v 11!"

After leaving Badajoz, Colin returned to the UK where he has enjoyed further success with Merthyr Tydfil, finishing runners-up to Forest Green Rovers in the Dr Martens Premier Division, Scarborough Town and then Yeovil Town, finishing as last season's Nationwide Conference runners-up. Colin is currently the manager of Nationwide Third Division side Swansea City. He continues to live in Herefordshire.

Stuart Baxter

PLAYER
Helsingborg, (Sweden), 1974 – 1976
South Melbourne, (Australia), 1978 – 1981
Landskrona, (Sweden), 1981 – 1983
Orebro, (Sweden), 1984 – 1985

MANAGER
Orebro, (Sweden), 1985 – 1986
Skapr Tromso, (Norway), 1986 – 1988
Halmstad, (Sweden), 1988 – 1992
Sanfrecce Hiroshima, (Japan), 1992 – 1994
Vissel Kobe, (Japan), 1994 – 1997
AIK Solna, (Sweden), 1997 – 2000
Lyn Oslo, (Norway), May 2001 – Present

Stuart Baxter, as can be seen above, has enjoyed a distinguished and wide-ranging career in many countries, both as a player and manager. He was born in Wolverhampton, the team for which his father played for fourteen years. As a player he began his career with four seasons at Preston North End from 1971 to 1975, and also had a short spell with Dundee United. We pick up Stuart's story in June 1975:

"Helsingborg was the first overseas club I played for. When I left Preston North End to go to Dundee United, and during my short spell with Dundee United, there was a coach there from Sweden watching one of our games. I then went down from Dundee United to Blackpool, and Eddie Quigley, who took me to Blackpool and was a very good friend of Brian Birch, was the coach who was watching me playing, and they happened to bump into each other at the training ground one day. He asked what I was doing there, and Eddie said that I was moving to his club from Dundee United. Brian came to my house very early one morning, and just knocked on the door and asked me whether, instead to coming to Blackpool, I wanted to play abroad. So I went and met the Helsingborg team who were at the Lilleshall training camp. I played a friendly for them against Sheffield Wednesday, and two weeks later I was in Sweden.

I was there for one year with Brian Birch, and for two years altogether. My immediate family, I think, were quite enthusiastic and thought it was a good decision. You've got to remember that at that time the English contractual system was almost penal. You would sign a two-year contract, but that meant that it was two years with a further two-year option on the club's side. Then if you wanted to go after those four years, it was also by 'pulling their nails out' so to speak. So for me to get out of that, and go onto the European freedom of contract, seemed to everybody around me like a very good idea. It definitely worked out well when I went there, and at the end of each contract I went to a new employer, without being smitten by the option rule.

As for the major differences of living and playing abroad for the first time, it was everything that was different. The way of life was very positive and I found the standard of living in Sweden to be very high. So we found lots of things as being very positive. The people were very friendly and made us feel welcome, so we didn't feel any great drawback there, but the football was very different. I remember being involved in all sorts of heated debates about the way that the game should have been played. I was a talker on the field, and always trying to help people, but all of a sudden I realised that they didn't want my help. My help to them seemed like nonsense. It was through this talking that I became a changed person, in as much as my views on how the game can be played, not how it should be played.

So I went full circle and went the opposite way, and then came back to a balance a few years later. That also helped me in my coaching, because during that time I evaluated everything, all the things that I thought were supporting walls in the building. It wasn't just 'Shall we put a window here or a door there?', I evaluated everything. I broke it all down and started thinking 'Well, should we do that? Is it right that people have said that to me? How did I feel when they said that to me?' It was a very enlightening process and I don't know if everybody who goes abroad does that or feels like that, but I think everybody to a degree experiences it. I knew how I felt when people told me not to lose the ball. I knew how I felt as a player, I knew what anxiety that created, and I knew how it felt when suddenly people were just telling me to stop kicking the ball.

That time at Helsingborg was on loan. Eddie Quigley was the manager of Stockport. Eddie was the manager who wanted to take me to Blackpool before I moved to Sweden. He then moved to Stockport and he actually brought me back. There were a few misguided managers who thought I could play centre-forward, and Eddie was one of them! It was very flattering, and I always had some small hope myself that it would work. I was quite good in the air, and people always used to want to harness that as a centre-forward. I wasn't useless on the ground, but they all thought the aerial capacity would be a good weapon. I never really got the chance to play there a long time. Eddie took me back, I was on loan for a month and then I went to Sweden. I think there were a few other people who tried me out as a centre-forward.

We had an English manager at Helsingborg, Brian Birch, and he left after one year. I stayed on until the end of my contract. I didn't really think I was going to stay any longer than that and I didn't have plans to. Sweden wasn't going to become my home, not at that stage. When I was coming to the end of my contract, there was an Australian manager, Dave Maclaren, who had seen me play in Scotland, at Blackpool and in Sweden. He'd been calling me all the time for about twelve months, asking me to consider going to Australia. I didn't want to at that stage and I said to Dave that I was happy where I was and didn't really want to go. But he kept calling and trying to persuade me. One morning he called me at 4 a.m., as they do the Australian managers. They tend to forget that there's a massive time difference, and he told me in no uncertain terms that it was the last time he was going to call me. Then he made me a very reasonable offer, and I went there, which was typical of me. It was feet first again, and a case of 'Well why not?!'

South Melbourne, the team I played for, did very well. We finished third in the Australian League, I was also selected for the Australian national team, and played ten times for them. Rudi Gutendorf was the coach. He was putting together a team irrespective of nationality, and we were going to salute the flag and take Australian passports for the Spanish World Cup in 1982. He wanted me to be the mainstay of the side. But the team fell apart due to some political thing that the Australian Government wanted the 'Socceroos' to give up their nationality, even though we were promised dual citizenship. That would have meant that we would have needed work permits to get back into our own countries if things went wrong, and five of the team weren't prepared to do that. We had a very good team. We beat Norwich City 4-0 in a friendly game, we beat Yugoslavia 1-0, we only lost 1-0 to England, and we beat Olympiakos 2-0 on tour, so overall we had some very good results. But that team fell to pieces, which was a shame, due I think to the political side of things. We weren't prepared to take that risk of being marooned in Australia if it all went wrong.

Christian Vieri's father, Roberto, also played in that side, and he was a very talented midfield player. We also had a Brazilian called Hilton Silva, and there were a couple of other English lads. One of them was Tony Henderson who had come from Sunderland, and there was a Greek lad called George Christopoulos. Alan Davidson, who also played, went on to Nottingham Forest – he was one of the Australian lads, and Eddie Krncevic, a Yugoslavian who later played for Anderlecht, was also a regular in the side. So it was quite an interesting team. Some of them stayed in Australia but didn't give up their passports, some of them went back to their home countries, and some of them gave up their passports.

Australia didn't qualify for the Spanish World Cup, and Rudi Gutendorf packed up his suitcases and walked away, which we were all afraid he would do. We got beaten by New Zealand, and they qualified instead of us. We had already thrashed them twice in friendly games. We thought we were going to get there, but these things can happen in football can't they?

I then went back to Sweden. Keith Spurgeon, an English manager, was at Landskrona. A fantastic guy. He's passed away now, but I had quite a relationship with Keith. I'd been back in Sweden two days, and he called me at my Mother and Father's house and said 'When are you going to come and see me?' I had never spoken to him in my life! I asked him who he was and he said 'I'm Keith Spurgeon, I'm at Landskrona, and when are you going to see me?' And that was how our relationship started! He signed me on the strength of a recommendation from Ron Newman, who was the manager of San Diego at the time, and had been trying to sign me for two years. Keith had managed Ron Newman as a player. So he said 'Look, Ron wants you and I'll offer you this', and then he offered me a contract. I was his player of the year.

Keith left at the end of that season, and went to work in Cyprus. He contracted Multiple Sclerosis, and I actually went down to Cyprus a few years later to work with him because he was becoming so poorly. I also went up to the north of Sweden to visit him two days before he passed away. His wife is actually living in the Stockholm area now, and she did come and see us play. Keith was also the coach of AIK Solna at one stage, so when I eventually went to AIK in 1997 it was a bit of deja-vu for the club. It was nice that people knew him. Lennart Johansson, president of UEFA and still the honorary president now, was the chairman when Keith was there. So it was quite an interesting circle to be in and Keith was fantastic.

I was there one year with Keith and two years apart from that. The following season I ruptured my Achilles tendon and was out of the game for a full year. I then got myself fit and played the rest of the following season before going to Orebro. Roy Hodgson was the manager, and he was there for two years. Alan Cork was playing for them at the time. Corky had broken his leg at Wimbledon, and he wanted to keep himself fit by playing on through the summer. He did very well, and was a good lad to have around the place.

As well as playing football, I'd been doing a bit of coaching throughout my career and started when I was at Preston. In fact I started when I was seventeen, and we played against the Army, the Royal Lancs regiment. They were stationed at the forward barracks in Preston, and we played them as preparation for the youth Cup quarter-final against Manchester City. Alan Ball was the manager back then, we went across and played them, and after the game they asked Alan if there was one of the first-team players that would fancy coming over and coaching the soldiers twice a week. And he said 'No, there's none of the first-team players but there's one of the best reserve-team players who would'. And he just said to me 'You'll do it won't you son?', so I said that I would. My father was a coach, and I expected to do that when I finished playing. In my mind I was never in doubt that this what I was going to do. I just started coaching there, and it was a something that happened at every club I was at, where I always asked if I could do a bit of coaching with the kids.

By the time I got to Orebro, I'd had my third achilles operation, Roy Hodgson had left, and the players wanted me to take over. The board at the club also said that. So I said I'd do it, as long as I didn't have to play. I didn't want them looking at me as 'Stuart Baxter, player/coach'. I wanted to make that transition there and then, and wanted to be looked at for my coaching abilities.

So I had one year there and we finished fourth, but I just felt that it was such a difficult job coaching players you'd played with, it being my first full-time coaching job. It was very demanding, in that it put a lot of pressure on my relationship with the players. It's a difficult enough job managing and coaching at any time, but it's even more difficult being a player/coach. Just ask Kenny Dalglish or Graeme Souness. If you take that position as your first job in football, then you realise that it becomes a very difficult scenario.

I just didn't want to continue that way. I wanted to establish my own coaching style, without the added pressure of trying to put your arm around one of your best mates because you're going to drop him, and running the risk of having other people you know very well wondering why you're distancing yourself from them. I didn't want that to hamper my own coaching development.

You do try your best, but it doesn't come out right. Either it comes out as 'You've changed since last year haven't you?' Or it becomes 'Well you haven't changed anything since last year', and they take you for granted. And getting that right in your very first year, well, I don't think I'm that talented to make that work out right. I wouldn't mind doing it again, knowing what I know now, but it's a very different scenario to what I knew then. In the circumstances I don't think I did badly at all.

As for my time at Vitoria Setubal, it was only a brief spell that I was in Portugal. Malcolm Allison was working there, and I knew him quite well. He was working with a physical coach I knew very well, Roger Spry, and Roger and Malcolm really just asked me to go there and help out. They were in the run-in, and I did a little bit of coaching with some of the players. They were split up in a group of small squads, and I was there just to keep it bubbling for the rest of the season. You couldn't really say I was employed by them but Malcolm just brought me out as a bit of a change to the face of the coaching. It was a very temporary thing.

I then became manager of Spakr Tromso of Norway, took them from the Third Division to the First Division in two years. At the time my Mum was quite sick and lived in the South of Sweden. So at the end of the year I went back to visit her in the middle of my contract negotiations with the club. Whilst I was there Roy Hodgson, who was at Malmo at the time, said 'Look. Halmstad have asked me to recommend them a coach, and I've just recommended you. What do you think?' So I said to Roy that I thought it would be perfect for me, because it would take me back to Sweden, closer to my Mum.

Halmstad had just been relegated from the Swedish Premier League when I arrived in 1988, and the chairman, who is very famous in Swedish football, was Stig Nilsson. He's one of the 'old school', and he pulled me in and said 'Last year we sold six of the best players. You have nothing to work with but the kids. We may buy a couple of Third Division players, but nothing else, because I am never getting in the situation again where my house is remortgaged to pay the debt to the club. Stuart, I don't care if it takes you one year or ten years. Get us back into the top Division, do it with a little bit of style, and you'll get my full support'. [AUTHORS NOTE: the town's nickname is 'Laxastaden' (Salmon town) and is the home town of pop group Roxette!]

He was marvellous, and we won the League the following year. So I was very pleased and that was fantastic. The young team we had became men very quickly, and we got promotion. During that year, obviously because we had a good young team, we provided six of the Swedish Olympic team that played in Barcelona in 1992. Most notable for the English people would be Nicholas Alexandersson (formerly of Sheffield Wednesday and now at Everton). I gave him his debut at the age of sixteen! We had another sixteen year-old who played for the Swedish national team, who went on to Blackburn, called Nicholas Gudenson – he now plays back in Sweden. Other players included Stefan Lindqvist, who went to Neuchatel Xamax, then came back to Gothenburg, and was the captain of IFK for many years. So we had a very good young team.

We also had a couple of very hardened pros in that team as well. The thing was though that the nucleus of the team was young. The first year was very successful, and with the team being young, that cemented a very strong respect for each other. For me to them for doing a man's job, and them to me as an enthusiastic and professional young coach. So it was a good working relationship, and worked for four years until I went to Japan.

The president of Sanfrecce Hiroshima asked a friend of mine to ask me to help arrange the training camp for Mazda. Imanishi-san, Kazuo Imanishi, was the president of the team for Mazda, and it was my last season for Halmstad, although I didn't know it at the time. It was at the beginning of that last season, in 1992, that this training camp took place. You've always got too much to do, and you don't want to be organising training camps for people, it's the last thing you want. I very reluctantly said yes, I would do it for him. So I booked a hotel with one of the directors, I put on a couple of training fields for him, helped him with his equipment, and then organised one game. I played my second team against their reserves. They were quite upset about that, because they had already played against two Finnish teams and beaten them, and they came over to us and rather indignantly pitched up against our reserves. I did tell them that two years before, six of the team had played in the Olympic side. This reserve team was top of their League, and wasn't much worse than our first team. Anyway, we thrashed them 3-0, and in typical Japanese fashion they then videofilmed every one of my training sessions for the next seven days! They watched our first team play and win in a League game on the Saturday.

Mr Imanishi did ask me at that time 'Look, we're starting a big professional League in Japan next year. Would you be interested in taking the job of coach of Sanfrecce Hiroshima?' And as you do in football, you say, look that's interesting and it's very flattering, please give me your card and we'll stay in touch, at that stage probably not thinking that I was going to take it. Then the season goes on, you carry on working, you start looking at the same group of players again, and now you've got another thing in your mind. You're thinking 'I wonder how it is in Japan?' Then you go, have a look around, you speak to people, and it starts becoming more interesting. So when he called me and asked me what I thought, I thought 'Yes'. It was right at the time when I was deciding what I was going to do, and I said I would take it. It was a good time to leave Halmstad, after four years, with me having done a lot for the club. And that was it. Again, typical me, feet first. And people said 'Blimey! You're going there, you've got one little kid and your wife. You've just got married again'. But exciting? I thought so!

When you're learning the Japanese language, nothing helps you. You don't learn it just by watching television and you don't pick it up on the streets either. It's a very difficult world to go to, Japan, and in the beginning you feel very helpless. Some people don't want to speak English and some people don't speak English. So you struggle along with your bits and pieces of English that they understand. The football games were OK, because I worked through an interpreter for the first time, but that became better as the quality of the interpreter I got improved. We won the

Championship the second year I was there. The interpreter was the local coach of Hiroshima University, so he was both linguistically efficient and football-wise he had an idea what I was trying to get at.

The Japanese are well known for their respect of those in authority, and that respectfulness just went throughout the social system. The older you get in Japan the more you're respected at work. It's not a case of it being the silly old buffer who sits in the corner and gets nothing. That 'silly old buffer' has all the experience and he's paid more than anybody in the company. They've got a totally different view on experience. You work in karate, you go through your gradings, and the higher you get the more you're respected. By the time you've taken your black belt and your sixth black belt or your sixth Dan, you may be quite decrepit and can hardly walk, but you're not any less respected than the Bruce Lee type of black belt. That attitude goes through their whole society.

The players and the fans were superb and the staff were efficient, clinically so! Steve Perryman has obviously said the same thing to you, and they can't do enough for you – they kill you with their kindness! The best thing I learned in Japan was how to play their game. The whole of life in Japan is a game, and it's about knowing how to conduct yourself. At the beginning, in the first year, I didn't know how to conduct myself. I conducted myself like a gentleman in Europe, but that wasn't a gentleman in Japan. Either you would be looked at as being a pathetic foreigner or as being a 'big mouth'. So it was a case of knowing how to play their game, reading between the lines, and saying things without saying them, use the shadow of the sword instead of the blade of the sword, that sort of thing. I became better at playing their game, I became better respected, and I also became better accepted.

I think Steve was quite right with what he said about how Ossie used the media to get his point across. I never criticised referees openly from the touchline. My standard was 'I don't want to criticise referees, but I want them to understand that the Japanese football baby is growing here, and if we don't teach the kid good habits, then he isn't going to grow in the correct way'. In that I'm constructively criticising the referees. That's the way I used to do it. I would give that message, and use about ten different examples of how they're not teaching the kid the right habits. They're not teaching our defenders how to defend if they don't penalise people for just stomping on people and running over and pulling shirts, and doing silly things like that. So yes you could use the media and criticise without criticising. You could criticise and be construed as being this very loyal servant of the Japanese system.

Once again, I could do that after a year but not in the beginning. I'd go into a press conference after a game at the beginning and say 'Listen – I thought that referee was flipping useless!' and they would say 'Oh yeah? You did, did you?' I couldn't read what they wrote, but they would be saying that this big-mouthed foreigner was criticising their more than adept referees. But a year on I would say 'Look. I don't want to criticise the referees because they're all doing a very good job, but....', and then discount everything I'd said until then and blast them in a different way. Then it would be 'Mr Baxter's a marvellous man. He's working very hard to promote football in Japan'. And there's a big difference between the two.

My move to Vissel Kobe in 1994 came about quite surprisingly. Everybody asked me why I wanted to leave when I'd just won the League, and how could the chairman let you go. The chairman apologised to me, and told me that it was his fault. During my second season there, he asked me 'What will you do next year?' And like a typical British coach I said 'Listen Mr chairman, let's be honest with each other. If we lose a few games, you're going to want me out and if we're winning a lot of games and I have to go somewhere else, I'll tell you. Let's just be straight with each other, and if you feel like you want me out, and I feel like I'm going to go then I'll tell you'. He took that to mean 'Oh, he's warning me now that he's going to go'. I then said to him 'Let's be fair, let's be honest with each other. I've been here a year and a half now and we've had a good run, and I'll tell you if someone makes me an offer'. That week I told him I had an offer. He then thought 'Well, I've got to look for a new coach'. So he then started looking at the beginning of the season, when we won the League, at options for new coaches. I believe he then went into a pre-contract agreement with Wim Jansen that they couldn't get out of. So he came to me and apologised. We had won the League and had started the next half of the season when he said 'Look. I will arrange for you to be interviewed for the best jobs in the country. I owe you that because I misinterpreted what you were saying'. I told him there were absolutely no hard feelings on my part. Since I'd done well I could say that there were no hard feelings. So if I'd not done well, it would have looked as if I'd got the sack.

But three big clubs did approach me, one of them being the new club Kobe. It was owned by a very wealthy businessman from Tokyo, who had bought the rights to establish a club in Kobe. So he bought a small team from Kawasaki, an amateur team, and moved it lock, stock and barrel to Kobe. He employed me as the coach, gave me a vast amount of money to spend on the team, and basically he was with me for two and a half minutes where he said 'Mr Baxter, you're the best coach in Japan and please give me a good team'. And then he walked out! That was the last time I saw him, because when the earthquake hit Kobe, he pulled all his money out.

I wasn't actually in Kobe on 17th January 1995, the day of the earthquake. I was supposed to be there, but two days before I flew over with two of the directors to Portugal to sign a player. I was actually with them in Portugal as the earthquake hit. At 6 o'clock in the morning we were supposed to get up very early and meet the agent, the president of the club and the player. The manager of the hotel woke me up and said 'Mr Baxter, have you seen the television?' I turned it on and it was CNN in Portuguese. And I said 'Oh dear me, an earthquake?' And he said 'Yes, in Japan'. I thought that it was the big one in Tokyo, but he said 'No no no, it's in Kobe'.

So I was looking at pictures of people getting pulled out of buildings. I ran next door to the two directors and they were just sitting, open-mouthed, looking at the television in a state of shock. I then had to arrange for them to get back home, and we had to fly virtually all over Europe to fly back into Japan. Fortunately, my family were in Sweden. I got these people back into Japan, but they wouldn't let me go back with them. They told me to go back to my family, and that they would call me. We went there, they called me, I had signed my staff, and we went back to Europe. Then the pre-season training didn't start when it should have done. It was a month late, then it was six weeks late.

Then they called, asking me to go back, and we went back not to Kobe but to a small town just outside it. The big sponsors had pulled out, but the local government were going to give us enough money to keep the team afloat, because they thought that any success that we could get would help the people. So the pressure you had on you then was not football. It was 'We are going to give you enough money for the football team, instead of building houses for these people'.

There were these temporary dwellings all over Kobe, and the city was crumbling. The training field had a split right down the middle, and there were no shower facilities. It was chaos for six months, but right at the end of the summer, things started to get moving football-wise. Up until that time we took three points from ten games. We basically didn't have any players, just this amateur team, but in the last ten games of the season we only lost two games. At the end of the season we played in the Japanese Cup, and we beat Jubilo, Dunga's team, and went to the semi-final of the Cup. This little amateur team basically. It was an incredible achievement.

Our new training ground was strategically built right in the middle of a temporary dwelling block. So we were training every day next to these 'rabbit hutch' type buildings, housing maybe a thousand people. Our training ground was right next to it, and there was a large ravine with a bridge going over it as you go out of the city. One day we saw a family committing communal suicide by throwing themselves off the bridge. Now you've got to put that into perspective and say 'Well look, what am I doing here?' Either you say to yourself 'I shouldn't be doing this' or you say to yourself 'Look, I've got to succeed'. It's not just a case of getting three points because the press will slaughter me. It's not even three points because I'm a professional. It's three points for millions of other reasons much more important than football. I've never had such pressure on myself as a professional, to make sure you do the job properly. It was the most insignificant of all the Championships I've won in terms of the global game, but it was the most pleasing and the most relieving, and probably the most rewarding as well.

The following season they invested a little bit more money and we got a new training ground. We won the Second Division Championship, and with it, won the right to play in the J-League. Four games before the end of the season, we bought Michael Laudrup, which really showed that we went full circle and that the city was back on its feet. It wasn't, but through its football we'd shown that we'd overcome all those difficulties. I stayed one year with the team in the J-League, and that was my five years of residence in Japan. And after five years, you then become taxable for all of your income during that time. I was going to Europe, and I came back with a very nice painting that the City of Kobe gave me, with a huge diploma designed in the Japanese style, thanking me for my services to the city. Again the job at Kobe became something more, and people think I'm being very high and mighty and superficial when I say this, but it was more than just football.

I had to give a speech in the middle of the field after my final game in charge. I spoke in Japanese, and just said that the people had been so kind to me and my family, and that I had seen the Japanese people going through hell with the earthquake. I had seen them show the quality of the Japanese people to bring the city back to life, and the pictures and the feelings that I've had from the people of Kobe are ones I'll never forget. It was very nice, especially as the very last game I coached was against Sanfrecce Hiroshima, my old club! I went into the dressing-room, and the two groups of supporters came in and asked me to come out again. The two sets of supporters had invaded the pitch and I had to go out and have a tossing-up and down in the middle of the pitch from both the Sanfrecce and the Kobe supporters. It was very moving. And then I went to AIK Solna in Sweden.

We won the Swedish Championship in 1998 in my first season back in Sweden, and got to the Cup Final that year as well. The following year we won the Swedish Cup and came second. I think all the experts in Sweden realised in that second season that we had a seven point lead in the League going into the Champions League, but being a small squad and being a normal Swedish team playing in that 'group of death', we just couldn't hack it. The players were on their knees, coming back from Wembley and then going down to Kalmar, and we lost out on goal difference right at the death. But the thing was that being in the Champions League was such a massive event for the club, the supporters and everyone concerned, especially the players, that there was no way you could tell them not to have a go at it. They realised that they were probably or definitely never going to experience anything like it in their careers again.

So the first Champions League game was against Barcelona, with 35,000 at the Rasundastadion. We were leading 1-0 for I think about eighty-eight minutes, and then there was an unbelievable decision by the referee which robbed the players and supporters of a marvellous evening, and robbed the club of an honourable victory, probably the greatest scalp they could have ever taken. Personally it probably robbed me of a chance of working in one of the best Leagues in the world, because you know yourself that a result like that results in the 'phone ringing the whole day after from Serie A, La Liga and the Premier League. So that's the way of the world, but the strongest memory I've got of that match is the mistake by the referee.

We went to Wembley the next game to play Arsenal, and of course with me having been sent off the previous game, I couldn't even sit on the bench. So I sat in the Royal Box instead! And again that was 1-1 after ninety-two minutes. Then Arsenal threw a long ball into our box, and Kanu fell down, and while he was on the ground, he toe-poked the ball to Henry, a typical Kanu sort of situation. So it was 2-1 and we had a corner in the last seconds of the game and we threw everybody forward. The ball was cleared to Henry, who ran the length of the field and scored. And again, a 3-1 result when it had been 1-1 after ninety-two minutes. Then we had a 0-0 draw against Fiorentina at home, which we should have won, and after that we played Fiorentina in Fiorentina. We lost 3-

0 in probably our best game, a match that we dominated more than any other. Their three goals were a free-kick by Batistuta that hit the wall and looped up into the top corner, a thirty-yard strike from Chiesa two minutes later, and then total dominance from our side for about fifty minutes where we missed chances that you couldn't believe. Then in the last minute of the game they broke away and scored a third. It looked like we got trounced but Trappatoni came to me after the game, and was very supportive. He actually said to me 'If you'd scored at 2-0 I don't know how it would have finished'. It was a good game from our side.

The one that we got completely wrong was against Barcelona at the Nou Camp because we knew we couldn't qualify after that. We had the most important game of our season coming up three days later, away at Orebro, where we were virtually playing for the Championship. You go to the Nou Camp knowing that the only chance you've got is to have a great night, play your full team, work yourself to a standstill, and hope that they have a bad night. Well what we did, I went there and we rested three of the players.

We went 2-0 down in ten minutes, so the players know already that the game's lost, they took their foot off the accelerator, and Barcelona played out of their skin. So 5-0 at the end of the night was probably a decent performance for us, because we were 3-0 down at half-time, and knowing that we didn't want to work too hard. That was the only one we got wrong, but it was completely understandable for me.

We took a bit of stick in the press in Sweden from people saying we should have done this or that. I was telling the players, what signals am I giving when I pull the captain off after twenty minutes? You know what I'm saying – this game's lost. I've got to really think now. We've not got it right, so now we're going to go for the one at the weekend. We can't pull half the team off and go at 50% and still think we can go and get a result from the Nou Camp. Leeds went there a year later and got beaten 4-0, and they had a full strength team going full speed. So that was all we got wrong.

But we did go and play a marvellous game out in Orebro, and won the game 2-0. Unfortunately Helsingborg drew 1-1 in

Gothenburg, with an offside goal, and they won the Championship instead of us.

Our last match in the Champions League was at home to Arsenal, which we lost 3-2. A very fine game, where it was cut-and thrust the whole game. Arsene [Wenger] always talks about that game when we meet. It was a very good game of football.

I had some good players at AIK in the beginning. Not Pontus Kamark, because he came after the Champions League games, right at the beginning of the run-in and didn't qualify for the Champions League. Johan Myallby, who's now playing for Celtic, was certainly the mainstay of the side in 1998. Krister Nordin was the captain, and he's at Brondby now, Mattias Asper who's at Real Sociedad, and Tommy Gustavsson who's at Coventry.

But eventually I left the club and people said 'What a good professional he is, and thanks for the three years'. The chairman of AIK Solna said it was the three most successful years in the history of the club, and that was very nice. So I felt like I had left at the right time.

At the moment, I'm managing a side called Lyn Oslo. The owner of the club, Atle Brynestad called me when I left AIK, and asked if I would help him. His ambition was to buy a club in Spain, have a club in Norway and have one other club somewhere in the world. He wanted to make me the general manager of all three clubs, which was fantastically flattering, very impressive, and sounded marvellous. So I then started looking at clubs in England because he was thinking of buying a club there. That went backwards and forwards for a while, we left it at that, and I had this contract with Atle.

Then he called me and his team, Lyn Oslo, were at the bottom of the League. He asked me to take over his team until the end of the year, and I said 'Look Atle, I've not done a pre-season with the players, you're bottom of the League, and really, I'm on a hiding to nothing.' But again, as I usually do, I went in feet first! I said to my wife 'Look, the kids can carry on going to school in Sweden. Atle's got a private jet and he can fly us up and down, so I'm forty-five minutes away, and it'll be like working in Malmo. Let me have a go at it. He's going to pay me very well for these six months [from May to November 2001]'. I've gone up to Norway and scraped them from bottom position up to tenth, despite having some quite hair-raising experiences there! It's been hard, but we're slowly moving forward.

There are lots of things have affected the coaches job over the last twenty years. Simple things like equipment have affected the way we have to coach, and the goalkeeping coach has to work on more things. Number one, the rules of the game have now changed. For example, the offside rule and the positional play for a goalkeeper are now different. Two, the demands on the goalkeeper's footwork are greater. Three, the ball has changed: it flies more quickly through the air and spins more. So the six foot nine goalkeeper that has slow feet and can move and catch balls all over his penalty area doesn't exist any more. David Beckham whips balls in, and it can be dipping down two metres from the goal, so the goalkeeper still can't come and catch the ball. Everything is changing, and if you've got your head stuck in the sand and you don't allow those things to determine the way you're going to coach, then you're going to get it wrong.

So tactically, the game is evolving around the physical, technical and mental capacity of the players. The way you train the players physically is changing, because they're understanding the demands of football more deeply. The psychological approach to the game is changing, as is the social approach to it, and you'll know what I mean by that more in England than in Scandinavia, with the beer-drinking culture that is accepted, as being 'one of the lads'. You're no longer 'one of the lads', you're 'one of the brain-dead morons'. You're becoming an isolated group rather than being a majority. There is now such a large amount of money being invested that people will NOT accept that anymore, and quite rightly too. So now all of those things are making the coach's job different: the rules of the game, the physical and mental capacity of the players and the demands made on the coach.

The last thing that's come out over the last five or six years, which is making the job even more difficult, is the role of the agent. You don't have to be a psychologist, but you have to be someone who can deal with the situation that if you drop a player, his agent calls you the next day threatening that he's going to go to Lazio. So you've got to decide how much you're the slavedriver, how much you're the father figure, how much you're the 'good cop' or 'bad cop', and at the same time they want you to be Attila the Hun at times! They still want you to give the Winston Churchill speeches, and sometimes they'll fall on stony ground because you have to find out what the real motivation of the players is. Are they in this game for the love of football, for the money, for the pride in their performance? Are they in this game because they see that as an immediate way to fame and glory?

You've got to understand that before you start, and Japan helped me enormously in this respect, because people said to me that it would be one-way traffic and I'd just be instructing. It wasn't. It was making me aware of my own ability to unlock boxes, and asking me 'Can you unlock that box? Can you find out what makes him happy?' It was an immense challenge, and it made me assess some of the basic qualities of a coach. I think that Arsene [Wenger] would agree. It wasn't just being an instructor in Japan, it was two-way traffic.

As for further development in football, I think we've scraped the tip of the Iceberg in terms of mental and physical preparation. Tactically I think there are only certain things that you can do on a football field. We talk about width, balance, and penetration. We'll keep moving the numbers and shuffling people around and ending up with variations on the theme, but there are only certain things you can do. And we will go in cycles, and for example play a system that they played ten years ago, but with more pace and efficiency, because we'll break it down into its components and make it better. Having said that, there are only certain things you can do tactically. There are always going to be innovators and copiers, but the greatest gains are going to be physically and mentally over the next five years.

I think at different times different people have influenced me in my football career. Keith Spurgeon was probably the biggest influence on my playing career, because he introduced me to a soft side of the game that I didn't know existed. When I say 'soft side' I mean that Keith allowed me to make a few mistakes, and when he did that I found out that I could play a little bit better than I'd been admitting to myself. I looked at myself as a 'hard man', winning the ball in the air and knocking it off, threatening and intimidating people, and having a whack and being a good professional. Keith allowed me a little bit of space to allow me to find out what else I could do. I realised that that meant so much to me, because I found out that way that there was more than one way to skin a cat. I realised the feelings of anxiety that I felt before certain games, and I could identify them and why I felt that way. So Keith was probably the coach who influenced my playing career, albeit belatedly!

As for my coaching career, Keith was probably the first one to influence that as well. That sort of feel that he had for the game has stayed with me a little bit. In terms of creative coaching, I think that the short spells I spent speaking or working with Malcolm Allison were immensely interesting. And in terms of organisation, I think Roy Hodgson was the greatest influence. I played against [IFK] Gothenburg in the early 1980s when Sven Goran Ericsson was coach. I knew him when Glen Hysen was there, and also when Benfica came over to Sweden and Sven Goran was with them. I did a football camp for a week and he was there too, and because he was Swedish I kept in touch with him. I can't say I was a close friend of his, more a colleague, but I know him well enough to have visited him a couple of times in England since he's been there. I've also been invited to the managers and coaches conference in England, probably because Sven Goran is the national manager.

My advice to British managers with offers to coach abroad is as follows. Evaluate it carefully and with great thought, but don't be too careful or too apprehensive. It can be two-way traffic when you think it's going to be one-way traffic, and learn as much as they can teach you. It may be a springboard to a level where you can be a bit more creative than the environment will allow you to be in England. I think that those would be all the positives I could think of, and it won't be easy".

As already mentioned in this Chapter, Stuart is currently

manager of Lyn Oslo in Norway, the former club of current Premiership stars Ronny Johnsen and Jo Tessem.

Paul Elliott

PLAYER
Pisa, (Italy), June 1987 – June 1989

Paul Elliott's professional football career first began in 1981 when he signed for Charlton Athletic. A move to Luton Town followed in March 1983, as did his first England under-21 appearance. He then signed for Aston Villa in 1985, and we pick up Paul's story in June 1987:

"Well, it was a strange situation because I was at Aston Villa at the time. There was a player at Villa called Mark Walters, a very talented left-winger, and there was a lot of interest from Europe for his services, particularly from Italy. I recall the coach of Bari coming over to various games to look at him. Mark and I were very close friends back from our England youth days in the early 1980s, so he told me about the interest, and I told him to just go out there and do his best. He was quite nervous about the prospect because there were so many agents getting involved and ringing him, and saying that there were clubs interested.

So the bizarre thing at that time was when they came to watch him for Aston Villa, Juventus had just signed Ian Rush. They watched him about four times, and unfortunately in two or three of these games, Mark didn't perform up to expectations and went off with a hamstring injury. In these four games, it so happened that I was playing against Liverpool, was marking Ian Rush, and had done reasonably well. I played against West Ham, and at that moment Tony Cottee and Frank McAvennie were doing very well, and did OK. I also remember playing against Everton marking Graeme Sharp.

So the irony was that in those three games where I performed reasonably well, the Italians had sent a delegation of staff to watch Mark Walters, and he was unfortunate. But it was a fortunate moment for me, particularly with the signing of Ian Rush to go to Juventus. I played against him and did quite well, and I think that was the catalyst – somebody else's misfortune was probably my fortune I suppose. So as a result Pisa pursued their interest in me, and the deal was confirmed in 1987.

I was only twenty-three at the time. I looked at the situation that I was a young man, and it was a wonderful opportunity. Pisa had just got promoted from Serie B to Serie A, and I just said to myself that it would be fantastic to go and play in the best stadiums in the world. Maradona was so significant at that time, and Ruud Gullit, Marco Van Basten, and a lot of great players were also there. So it was just an opportunity that I felt that had I said no to it, I'm sure I would have regretted later on in my career.

What happened was that Aston Villa got relegated that year. So it was a situation where the club had gone down a Division, and like anything else in that situation, they were basically asset-stripping the club, and selling players with significant transfer values. So my move to Pisa was probably best for the club and for me.

Believe it or not, about four months prior to that, we actually played a friendly match against Pisa, and I think that initially opened the door for me. But thereafter it went quiet for a while, obviously until they sent a delegation to watch the game, and I did quite well in the matches they watched.

I hadn't heard of Pisa before I went, but when you go to Italy you hear about your Sampdorias, AC and Inter Milans and Juventus, they were the big significant names. But I looked at going to Pisa as another aspect of my footballing education. It was clearly somewhere where I revelled in the environment, and obviously came back having done a good job there.

I remember when we left from East Midlands airport on the Pisa president's private jet, and we arrived at Pisa. I just remember this mass of people. I probably underestimated the fanatical element and the passion and the love of the game there in Italy. I didn't come to appreciate it until I was in that environment. It was quite spectacular, what with so many people at the airport to welcome me off the plane. I think that it was a big coup for Pisa, because they had got back into the top flight, and had signed me and the Brazilian Carlos Dunga. We were the only two foreign players there, as they only allowed two foreigners to play in each Italian club team at that time, and we arrived more or less at the same time. So there was a big marketing and PR exercise going on, with cameras and everything else doing all and sundry. It was overwhelming.

As regards finding me a house, Pisa were fabulous. The president was a gentleman called Romeo Anconetani, who passed away about six months ago. He was an extremely nice man, and very good to me. He made my family very welcome, looked after them well and paid for all their flight tickets when they came out to see me. He went out of his way to make sure that everything was as comfortable as possible for me. That was on, and more importantly off, the field because he was aware that if things were right off the field then here's a good chance that you're going to progress on the field. He was a super man, and it was a very nice and friendly club with no big pressure, because obviously having just got promoted from the Second Division, it was all about consolidation in our first season as we'd done very well the previous year. The expectation level was obviously greater for the bigger clubs to perform. I must say that it was a wonderful success story there.

I didn't speak any Italian before I went out there, but obviously with the culture and the environment, that was a priority to come to terms with. I was quite lucky that I went there with a very positive attitude and was fluent in Italian within six months.

The club also gave me a private tutor to help me learn the language. I was quite fortunate that two or three of my good friends in Pisa, who I still keep in touch with now, were quite fluent in English anyway. That helped me along when we were out socialising, When we used to go out for meals, we would have a pact that I would speak Italian and they would speak English! So it was a hidden way of trying to educate oneself.

I don't know whether the fans gave me a nickname, but I had

this strange name which the president called me which was 'Biondo'! And I'm still not quite sure what it stands for! I think it was at that time that I was, shall we say, quite 'fashion conscious', and I had a touch of a blond streak in my hair, and 'Blondie' is that strange name that always stuck with me. He also called me 'Jamaicana', which means 'the Jamaican', because he knew of my love for Bob Marley. Probably the latter nickname was more significant, and that followed me up to Celtic and back down to Chelsea. It became like a tradename for me. The biggest thing with Italy is that there was tremendous pressure, because obviously the expectation of the club and the supporters was great, but to have played against some of the players I played against was absolutely phenomenal. I remember on my debut we played against AC Milan, and I was marking Marco Van Basten. Gullit and Rijkaard were also there, and I'd never heard of Baresi, Evani and Maldini. I can tell you something – ninety-odd minutes later I'd heard of them all right! That kind of experience, playing against Maradona and the rest, was quite tough. You can't buy that, and there were so many positive things like that during my time there.

There were a lot of funny media interviews that I did. The initial thing was that when we were all being greeted, some of the players were very cheeky, and I was asking them about certain words. They gave me some inaccurate statements as to how I should greet the president and his wife and other people, and I can assure you that I got stitched up on more than one occasion using certain words which weren't applicable to the situation! That was all part of the banter.

The good thing with the media in Italy is that whilst they are critical, they were constructively critical, and you sense that if they could see you, especially with me as a foreign player, trying to speak the language and adapting to the culture, then they gave you a lot easier time. They knew that you respected the environment you were in. I found that this took a lot of pressure off me in the first seven or eight months, the fact that I went out of my way to mix socially with the locals and speak the language. It was a case of immersing yourself in their culture, because they're such proud people the Italians, and I think without realising that I scored some very good house marks early on. That clearly held me in good stead for my future in Italy.

Our local rivals were Fiorentina, and Roberto Baggio was obviously the main man then. We had some phenomenal games against them. I saw a Celtic/Rangers derby in Scotland during my time there, but the ones in Italy are so passionate, and the difference is there's so much hatred between the two clubs, whereas if you look at all the derbies in England, the players would socialise afterwards and have a drink together. But in Italy that would never have happened. That was so significant to me, the level of competitiveness and of rivalry between not just the clubs but the individual players themselves. We beat them at our place 1-0 and I remember we drew 2-2 away. It was a tremendous game. There were about 50,000 people there, although it seemed like 100,000, because there was so much media frenzy before, during and after the game, and the supporters in Florence, vocally-speaking, made it one of the most intimidating places to play. Their supporters were so wild and passionate about their club that it was frightening. Even now they're known in that kind of way with such a reputation for their vocal passion, which was evident during my term there.

I remember playing against Michael Laudrup when he was on his way up at Juventus. He was a phenomenal player and a wonderful talent. Preban Elkjaer, who was at Verona, had just won the European player of the year award while he was there. He was one of the great players, as was Rudi Voeller at Roma – it just goes on and on, and doesn't stop. Baggio was a top man at Fiorentina, as was Altobelli at Inter Milan. It was during that era when they were at the peak of their career and I was on my way up, as well as the Maradonas, the Carecas and obviously the Dutch contingent over at AC Milan. When we talk about great players in this current generation, I think we use the word 'great' lightly, but they were the true greats in my opinion, and they would certainly be able to play in any era under any set of circumstances.

Carlos Dunga was one of my best mates at Pisa, and we got on very well, probably through our love of red wine! He was a smashing lad, and it was funny that he couldn't speak any English and I couldn't speak Portuguese. But it's funny that when you play football it's a universal language, and that became clear when you've got all these different races, cultures and creeds all in one area and everybody getting on and working for the same objective.

One of the funny things that happened to me was when I first arrived, and I saw all this wine on a table at the training ground. This was at one of my first training sessions, and I thought 'Oh. We're probably not doing anything today. They've called off training'. So me and Carlos Dunga started to drink this white wine, but then we realised a short time later that we were training in about an hours time! None of the other players were having any wine, and they were saying 'Come on, join in!'

So that was the first time that I discovered the benefits of drinking wine, an everyday part of Italian culture. But the players knew that, and it was their way of sending on a message to me to make me realise it was a tongue in cheek situation. That was quite funny, because you never know what to think, and I thought that if this is what's to come, then I'm going to have a very enjoyable time in Italy!

The coach was Guiseppe Materazzi, whose son Marco played centre-back for Everton. A smashing man, and I remember his wife passed away a couple of years ago after having been very ill. His son always wanted to come and train, and I got on really well with him. It's a shame I didn't get to see him when he was at Everton – a very accomplished centre-half. But Materazzi was a good coach, went on to Sporting Lisbon after that and also went on to one or two other big clubs in Italy. He knew I was a good pro and he just let me get on with it. He definitely had a big influence on my career.

Yes, he catered for me tactically, no question about that. But he improved my game, particularly my groundwork, my positional sense, and more importantly in Italy, my concentration. That's so vital when there's a very slow build-up followed by a lot of frenzied movement in the last third of the pitch. But he had a big influence on me, and we had a very good working relationship. When I left, I remember seeing him in England and in Italy when

I was working for Channel Four. We always had a lot of respect for each other.

We worked very hard in training in Italy. The first major difference was the diet. The quality of food was much better, and you ate a lot more. You trained longer hours, and in the evening too. It wasn't so predictable as I found in the UK, and there was a lot more ball work and endurance work, particularly in the early stages of the week. We would always play a practice match against local teams every Thursday prior to a game, and I just found the whole experience so intense. The club paid good money for you, and paid you good money. They had total authority and control, and there was a lot of respect from the Italian players. I also noticed the level of professionalism that there was there: the way they'd look after themselves, how they dressed in all different sorts of climates, and how they would wear the right things. They were so mindful and conscious of always protecting themselves, and I think my single biggest memory of my time in Italy was the high standard of professionalism, and the level of authority and control the club had because you were their product. They wanted to do everything to maximise your level of performance on a Sunday afternoon.

The biggest single areas of improvement for me were my concentration, my groundwork and my technical work, because we would do so much 'keep-ball', possession of the ball, and passing passing passing, because obviously that's 95% of the game. As a defender you're allowed a bit more time on the ball, but then you had to distribute the ball better, and you couldn't afford to concede possession cheaply. I think they were the three significant areas of development in my game.

I wanted to stay because there were one or two other clubs in Italy that were interested in me, but Pisa got relegated that year, which was a similar thing to what happened to Aston Villa just before I left them. They had a few economic problems, and going down a Division meant smaller crowds and a massive wage bill. At that time I knew the manager of Celtic, Billy McNeil, who was the manager at Aston Villa during my time at Pisa. He moved to Celtic and they had just won the Double. Mick McCarthy was a tremendous centre-half at Celtic, but when he moved to Lyon in France, there was a big void to be filled at centre-half. So with him knowing me, he sent a few people out to Italy to watch me and I performed reasonably well. Then it was brought to my attention that there was a possibility of me going to Scotland.

The president of Pisa was a very honest and open man. He always said that if Pisa got relegated and I wanted to go home, he would say that I had done a great job for the club and he wouldn't stand in my way. He said we don't have to accept any offers for you, but we'll keep in touch if any enquiries are made. So it was a situation that was probably beneficial for both parties. Celtic came and agreed terms, and the president had even flown with me to Glasgow and spoke with them. In the end they made a 100% profit on what they paid for me, and it was a good deal for me to get back to Britain with a good club.

The fans were sad and disappointed when they heard I was going but not surprised. But the good thing about Italy is that they appreciate what you do. They knew I had gone there and given everything I'd got. So whilst they were disappointed, they realised that it was in my and their best interests. They're quite sensible in that way are Italian supporters. The funny thing is that even now when I go back to work there with my summarising work with Channel Four, they've got great memories for players, and I always get a very good welcome from people when I go back to Italy.

I got a plaque and a medal from the club thanking me for my services and dedication to the club. It was a sad day, but I think they accept that. You know in the UK when players want to leave clubs, the clubs say that they're not going anywhere, they're under contract. There's always a big drama about all of it, and it's all 'cloak and dagger'. In Italy, the managers always know what they're doing for next season. It's quite acceptable to have a professional way of dealing with it, and there's not a problem knowing in January that come July you're moving on to another club, because they know that within yourself you have high standards of professionalism anyway. That's not going to do your credibility any good if you don't perform, whether you're a player or a coach. Most of the arrangements are pre-contract anyway, subject to a medical, your performance and many other things. They have this very professional way of dealing with things, and that's why I think I admire the Italian culture and outlook so much.

When I boarded the plane to leave, I just thought to myself that I'd had a wonderful journey, and that it had been a wonderful success story so far. I'd enjoyed my time. I had been at Charlton, Luton and Aston Villa before Pisa, went in Italy when I was twenty three, and was thinking at that time that I was on a journey again, I was on the way to Scotland. I thought to myself that I was only twenty five, what a great opportunity I had at Celtic, and to go out and enjoy every moment. I always had a very positive mind, because I thought I was a bit of a journeyman. I had that culture and fire in my belly. What used to make me laugh was that you hear so many players in England saying that if you move up North from the South or vice versa, that 'I can't settle here'. And I thought 'What are you doing that's so different? You're playing football, the game you love and enjoy, you're in a different part of the world. You're still getting well paid for it'. I can never understand that insular mentality from so many people.

One of the highlights of my time at Pisa was when I played against Ruud Gullit. I remember when he scored a goal and I was marking him. He was probably the first player I saw score a header from the edge of the box. I also remember that he had these long dreadlocks. A ball came over from the right, I was competing with him for it, he got in front of me, and his dreadlocks poked me in the eye as he headed the ball! I had a joke with Ruud when he came down to Chelsea, and I said that after that as well as scoring a goal and winning the game 3-1 for them, his dreadlocks poked me in the eye and gave me a bloodshot eye for a fortnight! I think that was probably the high point of the whole thing, playing against a footballer of such great stature, then going on to meet him later, getting to know him as a friend and sharing that kind of joke. That was something I'll always remember.

The best advice I could give for any British player moving to a foreign club is to go there with a positive mind, and recognise that immersing yourself in the culture and the environment is just as important as playing football. It makes life so much easier for you, because you can get so much more respect when you can mix with the locals and speak the language. And you'd be surprised, even in troubled times. If you stick to your task, and go with that kind of open mind and mentality, you'll come through your experience in a big and positive way".

After returning to the UK from Italy, Paul spent two seasons with Glasgow Celtic before signing for Chelsea in 1991, where he remained until injury prematurely ended his career in 1993. He now works as a match summariser for Channel Four's 'Gazzetta Football Italia,' as well as having other media commitments.

John Collins

PLAYER

Monaco, (France), May 1996 – July 1998

John Collins was born in Galashiels, and first played professionally in Scotland for Hibernian. He stayed with Hibs until 1990, when he signed for Celtic, the team he supported as a boy. He spent six seasons with the Bhoys, during which time he won a Scottish Cup winners medal in 1995, and the first of his 58 caps for Scotland, his most memorable international games being his 50th, against Brazil in the opening game of the 1998 World Cup where he equalised from the penalty spot, and his 58th and final cap, against England. We pick up John's story in May 1996:

"I was coming to the end of my contract at Celtic and the Bosman ruling had just come in that November, so I was in a lucky position at the end of that season. I was able to move abroad without a transfer fee being involved, which was unheard of before in football. When I was coming to the end of my contract, my agent Raymond Sparks asked me if I fancied moving abroad, and I said yes most definitely. It would be a great experience for me as a footballer, and for my family, to experience something completely different.

It was strange because one day in January he asked me where I would like to go and play football. I said that well Monaco was quite special and financially it would be nice. Monaco's a beautiful place and it would be a nice experience. And during May 1996, towards the end of the season, I was up North with the Scotland squad, sitting in my room, when all of a sudden I got a phone call from Raymond, my agent. He said 'You're the luckiest guy in the world! Remember what you told me in January about Monaco? Well, they've just contacted me and they want us to come across at the weekend and negotiate terms. I want you to be there and your wife to come across'.

I hung up the phone and was dancing around the room! I couldn't believe my luck. I phoned my wife and she was, shall we say, excited. So we headed across to Monaco for the weekend, with me, my agent Raymond and my lawyer Malcolm McPherson to negotiate the contract. They took my wife around the town to look at apartments, and the contract was pretty much sorted out in that time. We agreed terms and I went to sign a three-year deal, although unfortunately I couldn't sign at that precise time because my contract at Celtic wasn't up for three months. I had to go to Euro 96 first, and after that was finished I went across to Monaco, signed and started playing for them.

So it was quite an amazing weekend. When I came back, I thought to myself what a lovely experience it had been looking at all those beautiful apartments. We eventually got a fabulous apartment overlooking the sea, with balconies all round and plenty of space for visitors, because both my wife and I have big families that we're very close to. So it was important that we had space to welcome them all when they came to visit us. I had two children at the time. One was three years old and just starting school and the other was nine months.

So we moved across and I got stuck into the football, but it's a strange story with my French teacher. It was announced in the Scottish papers that I was signing for Monaco, and the next day, after the news came out, a man named Philippe, a French teacher who'd been living in Glasgow for twenty-three years, approached my agent. He came up to his office and said 'I can teach John Collins French, and he'll be able to get by in fifteen days.' My agent thought that sounded pretty strange. He phoned me right away and I said 'Well I'll arrange a meeting and I'll bring my wife along to meet him'. So we met the next day in my manager's office in Glasgow. My wife and I liked Philippe, liked what he had to say, so we thought 'yes, let's do it'.

So I had it in my contract that the club would take care of any teacher's fees. When I first signed he was there with me fifteen days solid, morning til night. I was there with my family, and then he'd jump in the car with me. I drove him up to the Monaco training ground with him constantly bombarding me with French. He sat by the side of the training pitch and took notes of everything the players either said or shouted, and we jumped back in the car and started on that. He was basically stuck to my side for the fifteen days. Wherever I went, he went, talking French, and I was repeating what he was saying. It was conversational French I learned, stuff that I would need day-to-day, not stuff you would learn at school and never use. So when we were at the post office it would be post office talk, at the beach it would be beach talk, at training, training talk etc.

Philippe spent fifteen days with me and my family. Then he left, and gave me some homework to do. He gave me some great tips, and told me not to listen to CDs or cassettes, but to tune into French radio. Even though you don't understand what's being said, just repeat it as you're driving along to get used to the words and the accents. So I did that, and I read 'L'Equipe', the French sports paper every day, to keep practising reading. I did all these things, and after ten days I did my first basic interview in French with a journalist. It was just a basic one, but I was quite happy with my effort after ten days. Philippe came back in November to stay with me and my family for another six days, and became my friend. It was six days solid work again. Then he left and came back again three months later to stay again for six days. So that was my teaching, and it was pretty intensive, but it worked a treat. I became pretty fluent and my wife was able to communicate better in French as well.

I think that's one of the most important things for any player going abroad: you've got to make an effort to learn the language. If you don't make an effort, you don't get respect from the people in the streets, or the people in your team. Even if you make mistakes when you're first out there, as long as you try means that you've got instant respect. And obviously the first two or three months are difficult. You're in an environment where they're all talking French at the dinner table. You're picking up little bits and pieces and you're not really participating, but as the months go by you get practising and get more confident. We also made a lot of friends, not only on the football side but in the daily life in Monaco. My wife and I had such a great time in fact that our plan is to go back and live in the south of France once my career's finished. That's three years now that we've been away, but the desire's still there for us to go back. We still keep in contact and go back as regularly as we can and stay with friends we've made out there. In fact we've got some Monaco friends staying with us right now.

For me it was a lovely place, and the fact that they had a great football team made it easy for me to join. We went and won the Championship the first year [1996/97], and also got to the UEFA Cup semi-final. The second season, we got to the Champions League semi-final, and beat Manchester United in the quarter-finals. From my point of view it was hard work, because I had to be on my toes and had to play really well to maintain my place on the team, as there were twenty-two players in the squad and they were all internationals. The substitutes bench had five full internationals sitting on it, and others sitting in the stand.

So it kept me on my toes, and took my game up to another level, both tactically and physically. The first training camp I arrived at, we had three training sessions a day. I thought the guys were kidding me on when they said to me 'You'd better get your kit the night before, the bus to training leaves at 7 o'clock in the morning'. This was for a thirty minute jog and stretch in the woods, back in for breakfast, then back out at 10 o'clock, more running more weights, stretching, sleep, back in for lunch, sleep in the afternoon, and then back out at five o'clock for more work. Three sessions a day was hard work, and something I'd never been used to, but it was thoroughly enjoyable.

Obviously my young daughter went to French school. The teacher there said that there was an international school where we could have put her in an English-speaking class, but she said that she's at an age where she'll pick up French very quickly. It'll be difficult for the first month. And it was exactly right. She went and she mastered French within about five months, and she was speaking French like a little French girl, with an accent far superior to mine or my wife's! That again gave me special pleasure, seeing my daughter go off to the French school. She never used to speak French at home with us, but the teacher said that was normal, and he didn't want her to speak French to us in the house. I used to take her up the park every day after training, and hear her playing and talking in French with the other kids. It used to melt my heart, her giving me so much pleasure. But she's back now. She can still understand, but she's lost a bit, but she'll pick it up when we go back to France. So everything went like clockwork really.

I started off and scored in my second game, a friendly, and from then on it just went from strength to strength. Jean Tigana was the manager, and he'd been a great midfield player. I got on very well with him and the coaching staff at Monaco. I think the hardest part is making the effort with the language. It is difficult to start, when you feel isolated with all the changes, and you hear everybody laughing and joking and you're not part of it. But that drove me on even more to make sure that before I leave this place, I'm going to be part of the action, having a laugh and a joke, communicating in their language. And I was joining in, and it was all worthwhile.

And here I am three years later at Fulham and under the same manager. The way it's worked out is pretty amazing. You never know what's ahead in football, and you can never plan ahead, but it was a fabulous lifestyle out there. The training was hard, and a lot of time was spent in hotels before every game which took a lot of getting used to. We played most of our games on a Saturday night, so we'd be in the hotel by 5 o'clock on a Friday night, all day Saturday, play Saturday night and you'd be home on Sunday. Then back again playing on a Wednesday, so back in the hotel again by 5 o'clock on a Tuesday night and all day Wednesday. So there was a lot of time away from the family, which was a little bit hard for my wife to get used to for the first few months. But she adapted and made friends, and we just got on with it.

The diet when we went to the hotel was the same thing every day: plain pasta; rice; mashed potatoes; some chicken; small pieces of meat with some salad and no sauces, and that was hard to get used to. I was always a healthy eater but that took me on another level. No cakes, no ice-cream, no desserts, just plain yoghurts. I think there's no doubt it made a difference. We also had a dietician, a specialist in vitamins and minerals and this doctor would tell us which vitamins and minerals we were all lacking. When I first arrived the tests were pretty amazing. The medical was nothing like anything I'd ever had in my career – it was so strict. They checked every joint and muscle, they stuck me on a treadmill, all wired up and with a heart monitor, and they basically told me to run until I dropped! They then checked my heart and oxygen intake, analysed my blood and my teeth by x-raying my mouth. It was on another level, it was all taken so seriously. But it paid off, because we played beautiful football and won the Championship in my first season. It was fabulous.

When I first arrived, there wasn't a big fanfare at the airport because they didn't know I was coming. At that stage it wasn't definite I was going to sign. It was just the club secretary who met me and the chauffeur-driven car took me to a hotel. It was all pretty hush-hush, because my contract at Celtic wasn't up until the end of the month, and it was only then that I was allowed to talk to them. Obviously Celtic were a bit disappointed because they hoped that I'd go to England and that they'd get a transfer fee for me. They had turned a few bids down just before deadline day, so they actually lost out on some money.

I left Celtic, and had given them six years of my life. They bought me for a million pounds and I had six fantastic years. It was my dream to play for Celtic, and there are pictures of me as a kid from five years old onwards always wearing a Celtic strip. I fulfilled my dream, and it was a special club and special supporters. I honestly don't think there's another club like Celtic. I wouldn't say I left on bad terms, it was just circumstances. I decided I needed a new challenge in my life, and the opportunity came at Monaco. I thought that if I refused it, I might regret it for the rest of my life. It was difficult leaving Celtic, because it was the team of my dreams. But I made the decision and had no regrets, especially after having had six great years at Celtic and two great years at Monaco.

Monaco took care of the accommodation side of things for us, and that was all part of the contract. We got to choose between two apartments, and we were very lucky to find a beautiful big four-bedroom apartment there, with four or five bathrooms and a balcony that looked out onto the sea. Every morning, when I woke up, I had to keep pinching myself to make sure I wasn't dreaming. I was born in Glasgow where the weather's not so great. I'd open up the patio doors, walk out onto the balcony and see the beach, the blue sky and the sea every morning. Well, it was fantastic, and it was based on all the hard work that I'd done throughout my career as a young kid which was paying off.

That inspired me and spurred me on to keep working hard, because I hadn't gone there for a holiday, I'd gone there to play football. I enjoyed the sunshine, but never had time for weekends away or barbecues – we never had a day off. We were training seven days a week, played on the Saturday night, and always had training on the Sunday morning. So from that point of view, there was no spare time to spend with my family enjoying the South of France. That's why I'm looking forward to going back and living there and basically enjoying the whole coastline, because I never had the time to do what the tourists do and see the place. My life was training and eating, even though I did have time with my family, but not at weekends.

L'Equipe was the main sports newspaper over there, and they had a journalist based at our training-camp getting interviews from us every day. There was also Nice Matin, which is the local newspaper. They were the first newspapers I had to deal with. My first major interview was with L'Equipe, and although it was pretty basic stuff, I went through it with my teacher, and had him ask me the questions that we thought the journalists would ask just to practice. And I came across well. But there's always a danger when you're in a foreign country doing interviews if you don't understand the question, you can be misinterpreted. So that's always a danger when you're doing it and you have to make sure exactly what the question is, and that you know exactly what they're asking you. You have to double-check, to make sure they're getting your answer properly and they don't misinterpret it. So you have to be careful, but it went OK.

My first European goal against Borussia Moenchengladbach was especially memorable. It was in an away game in the second round of the UEFA Cup. I managed to smash one into the bottom corner of the net to give us a 1-0 lead. We went on to win the game fairly convincingly, and that was a special goal. I scored a nice volley against Marseille which is always special as they were our big rivals. I scored one from a corner at the edge of the box. I think the game when we won the Championship in my first season was against Nantes, and we needed at least a draw to win the Championship, and they scored in the first half, so we were 1-0 down at half time. But I managed to equalise near the end of the game and I think someone else scored the winner for us right at the end. I think Nantes had to get the three points to get into Europe as well, and I think at the end of the game their goalkeeper and everyone else was up in our box for a corner. We broke away, got the winning goal and clinched the title. But we won it fairly straightforwardly with a few games to spare. We also played Newcastle in the UEFA Cup in my first season there. We won away 1-0 and fairly convincingly at home.

But probably my most memorable and enjoyable game was the one against Manchester United at Old Trafford in the Champions League. We were always confident we could beat them even though they were the big favourites, and we were classed as a small team. We won the Championship the year before but had sold five players which was pretty strange from my point of view. But Monaco's the type of club where if you've got players who want to leave they won't hang onto them, because there's no outside pressure for them to perform. You can walk the streets and there's no pressure. The stadium's never full. It's not like playing for Celtic or Man United where you're under pressure all the time, walking down the streets with fans on your back. In Monaco there's no pressure like that, so you have to be totally committed and motivated within, and psych yourself up because the stadium's never really full. So if players want to leave, more often than not they'll say 'On you go' and they'll bring in some hungrier fresh talent.

So that year Sonny Anderson went to Barcelona for £12 million,

Enzo Schifo went back to Anderlecht, Manu Petit and Gilles Grimandi went to Arsenal, and Patrick Blondeau went to Sheffield Wednesday. So five players of Monaco had gone, but we signed some good players in the summer. That season we finished third in the League, which was disappointing, but we got to the Champions League semi-final. We drew 0-0 at home in the first leg against Man United, but we played well and should have won. After the game, everybody in the English media was saying 'That's the tie over now, and Manchester United should win it at home'. But I think Jean Tigana spoke to the French media after the game, and said that it was fifty-fifty before the game and now I think it's sixty-forty in our favour. And I remember all the media thinking 'What is he saying? We've just drawn 0-0 at home'. But we had so much pace in the team. Thierry Henry just had lightning pace, and whenever we went away from home we knew we were capable of scoring and could get in behind teams that were coming at us. Then we'd hit them on the counter-attack. We were fantastic at that in Europe in both seasons I was there, because we had so much speed up front. David Trezeguet was there, and he'd taken over from Sonny Anderson. He was on form.

So we went to Old Trafford and took the lead after fourteen minutes, with David Trezeguet rifling in a fantastic shot into the top corner. And we started playing some great football. I remember slipping Thierry Henry through half-way through the second half, and he should have put us into a 2-0 lead. But he didn't take it, and during the last ten minutes, Manchester put us under a bit of pressure. They equalised, but we played really well and went through on the away goals rule. So it was a special night for me because the Celtic supporters bought a bus in my home town of Galashiels and the bus was named after me. They had run a bus down from my home town with fifty Celtic supporters, who were with Monaco's fans for the night. They were there, with my father, sisters and brothers. It was a special night, and probably one of my most memorable in football.

There were quite a few famous people living near me in Monaco. Frank Rijkaard lived on the top floor of my apartment building, so we used to see Frank regularly and I'd chat now and again with him. Sergei Bubka, the Russian pole-vaulter, was in the same apartment block as me, and up at the top end of my street there was Boris Becker and Shirley Bassey.

We also used to see the Monaco Royal Family regularly. Prince Albert was in the changing room for most games, wishing us all the best. After the game against Manchester United at Old Trafford, he was in the changing room, slapping us all on the back after a great victory. So Albert is very passionate about the game. His father, Prince Rainier, was always at the big games, but Albert's really keen on football. And yes, I even spoke to him before the 1998 World Cup in my hotel. We had a chat and he wished me all the best for the World Cup.

You'd always see some supermodels walking about the streets, as well as famous actors and actresses. But it wasn't really part of my life – I was there for football. Whenever I had visitors I used to take them up to show them the casinos. Sometimes it was nice to just go and watch, and I used to take my family and friends up to show them. It's a beautiful place, with lots to see and do, so we always had plenty of visitors, let's put it that way! The first six months were tiring for my wife. Obviously I was training so she had the hard job of looking after the guests and showing them the sights. The first couple of months were really tough, because we had a young child and it was very hot at the end of July to August. So it was stifling heat, but my poor wife had to do the tourist bit with all the family and friends around the town.

My team at Monaco was fabulous. Manu Petit was a terrific player, and he played at left-back behind me. Sonny Anderson was a striker who went to Barcelona the first season, a fabulous player. There were two young kids there, and this is a story I often tell, during my last season. The rule at Monaco was that you looked after your own boots and shinpads, not like in Britain where the kids used to clean your boots. You took your own boots in your bag to the games. The kit-man looked after all the strips. He was about seventy-three, and although he packed the hamper he was never allowed to carry it. He was a lovely chap, and one of the nicest people I've ever met in my career, who loved Scotland. He had visited Scotland many times with his wife, and we used to have chats about his trips there.

The rule was, according to Jean Tigana, that the youngest players carried the hamper on all of the buses and planes. So the last season I was there, Thierry Henry and David Trezeguet carried it. They went on at the end of that season to both get World Cup winners medals, but that whole season they carried the hampers. When I tell the younger lads in the team here at Fulham they don't know how spoilt and lucky they are, because we've got kit-men carrying everything on and off the bus. Even though they were both big players who went for huge transfer fees and both got World Cup winners medals, that season their job was to carry the hampers on and off the bus. So it's a great story to tell the young players in this country who sometimes get tired of playing here, where life's so easy.

Thierry Henry was a great player, but when I was there he was in and out of the team, he was just a sub. He's obviously made great progress since then. David Trezeguet went to Juventus, and was another terrific goalscorer. When I first signed for Monaco, we had Enzo Schifo, the Belgian, in the midfield – a terrific player. Ali Bernabia, a French-Algerian guy, was a fantastic little player. The whole team was quality, they were all nice guys and made me feel welcome.

The first game I played in was against Nantes. I was up against this skinny little chap, and thought he was so tricky. And now he's playing for Real Madrid – his name's Claude Makalele. So it was a good first test for me with this little chap jinking about, but there you are, a few years later....I knew he was a good player, but nobody talked about him, and he went on to play for Celta Vigo and Real Madrid. There was a lot of talent in the French League the first season I was there. In Europe I played against Inter Milan and Juventus.

The initial feeling you get when you go there is isolation, and as I said before, it's a strange feeling, when you're used to laughing at a joke and understanding every word. All of a sudden life changes. Everybody's laughing and talking, and you feel completely out of it. In that situation some people go into their shell and it makes them want to come home. It had the opposite effect on me and drove me on because I wanted to be a success there and make my mark, and I like to think that I did. When I go back to Monaco now, I stop every hundred yards to talk to someone in the street. I get well received when I go back and still have lots of friends and contacts over there. And when I go back there it's like going back home. I still know all the guys in the Restaurants, the car parks and the football clubs, and I say hello to them every time I'm there.

I think my game came on, there's no doubt about that. I was always a fit player and a healthy eater but being at Monaco took me onto another level. I think the main thing was that I was playing against better players week in week out, both in the matches and in training. No disrespect to my team in Celtic, but you had to perform every day in training, and every match was a major test, not just to beat the opposition but to maintain your place in the team. And I think that just keeps you on your toes. Some people may say that they get frightened of too much competition for places, but at Monaco it kept everybody on their toes. They had to play to their peak performance every game, or another international would take your place. So you could never ever be complacent, and if you were you were out of the team.

I was coming to the end of my second season at Monaco. The crowds were small, I was thirty years of age, and I did at some point in my career want to play in the Premiership. I went to the World Cup in 1998 and thoroughly enjoyed it. It was a fantastic experience, with large crowds and full stadiums. It made me think that I could have the chance to go and play in England, where every stadium is full. As a thirty year-old I thought that it would probably be my last chance to make another big move back to the UK, and even though my life in Monaco was just idyllic and perfect what with playing in a brilliant team, I decided to move back because I was missing playing in front of full houses with that passion from the terraces driving you on. I also wanted to sample the English game and players, and test myself against them.

I decided after the World Cup that it was time to go back to

England. I spoke to my agent, and during the World Cup several clubs had contacted him to see if I was interested. Walter Smith, who was the 'opposition' manager in Glasgow for six years as the Rangers manager at the time, was manager of Everton, one of the interested clubs. He and Graeme Souness had tried to sign me for Rangers before I signed for Celtic. He came across to France and said that he was desperate for me to sign. He had a lot of money to spend that summer, he'd have more money to spend the following summer, and even more the summer after that. He could then take the club away from the position that it had been in the previous year, away from the relegation zone and build the club up again.

I liked what he said. I spoke to a lot of people and they told me that Everton was a massive club with terrific support. I was thinking long and hard about it, and was in the training camp in Monaco at the time, when I had a phone call from the chairman of Paris Saint-Germain. PSG had also agreed a fee with Monaco, like Everton had. He asked if I wanted to go to Paris. I spoke with my manager and my wife, and she said that she would happily go to Paris, but in an ideal world she would rather stay in Monaco or go back to England. I decided that we'd had such a special time at Monaco, that I didn't want to go to another French team, even though PSG was a massive club. So I decided against Paris and chose to go to Everton.

It was a huge decision and there were a lot of tears shed. The last day that I went to the local park, my head was full of 'Should I or shouldn't I go?' I was never 100% sure, even when I was in the club helicopter that flew me to Nice airport, to the plane that took me to Liverpool. Me and the wife and kids arrived in Liverpool for talks. It was pouring with rain and I thought 'Oh my God! What are we doing here?!' I decided I was there for football, even though my wife and two kids had a fantastic life and great times in Monaco.

The weather was terrible and the football never went according to plan. The chairman there had been telling, shall we say, a few white lies to the manager. He never had the funds that he was told he was going to get, and he ended up having to sell players instead of buying them. Basically I was told a lie. It came from the manager, but the manager had been told a lie by the chairman. So under the circumstances it was disappointing. But my wife and I had two fabulous years there. We bought a beautiful house in the Wirral overlooking North Wales, and there was a big garden for the kids, with stairs from the garden down to the beach. So I loved the house, and we found a lovely school for the kids. They loved it, my wife settled very well and we made some lovely friends in the Wirral. I have to say we've been happy wherever we've been, and I got very attached to that part of the country.

As I said before, the football never went according to plan, and two years later I got a strange phone call from Jean Tigana. He said he was coming to Fulham and I couldn't believe it. I thought that it was a joke, knowing Jean Tigana. He resigned from Monaco eight months after I left there and became a football agent. Then somebody told me he was going to Fulham, and I thought 'no chance' because I knew that big clubs were always wanting him to be their manager in Spain and Italy. He said that he had been approached by the chairman and the board of Fulham, and had got assurances that the club wanted to build a new stadium and training complex and build a big club again.

There was the challenge and excitement at the thought of building a club, not just a football team, and that was a new challenge, as it had been at Monaco with another language and a new culture. So it was a brave decision from him, and he said that I was the first player he wanted to join the club. Once again it was another huge decision, leaving the Premier League to go to the First Division. He assured me that he was going to build a team and get them super-fit, as he was bringing in a fitness coach from France. The whole regime would be a French system integrating all the foreign training methods. So I came down and looked about the place, and my gut feeling said that it was time for me to go and make another move. But again it was a tough decision for my wife and kids, as well as me. They were at school and I had a third child by then, my little boy who was a year old.

My wife really didn't want to come to London to be truthful. She was so settled in the Wirral. But again we came down, and we were lucky enough to find a lovely house. She was again devastated to leave her old house in the Wirral, a special place. It's always been harder for my wife, as she's left with all the work, and whilst I've signed a contract and I've got to be there the next day, she's got to stay there and pack up the house, and the memories. It's an emotional thing, and I'm sure that for anybody who's reading your book and has done it, they will realise what I'm talking about. You're attached to your house, the kids get attached to their school and friends, you get attached to the whole area, and then you're uprooting again.

I'm very lucky to have a fantastic wife, who's intelligent, adaptable, likes a challenge like me and makes friends easily. So she's been working at my side in every single move and without my wife and my family, there's no way that I would have been as successful in any of my moves. She's always been there supporting me. We went down to London, and from day one it's gone like clockwork. The kids are in a beautiful school, which they thoroughly enjoy, and my game and the team just clicked.

We played some great football and broke the club record by winning the first eleven games of the season. we played fabulous football, and people couldn't believe just how well we were playing. Every player was so fit, it was probably the best I'd ever played in my career, and we walked away with the Championship. It was just a memorable season, and here I am. As I told everybody, I was taking one step backwards to go two steps forwards. They all thought I was talking nonsense, and that going down a League could end my career, and I told them to just wait and see. It gave me tremendous satisfaction at the end of the season to have won the League, and win it in style, to take us up to the Premiership in amongst the big boys.

When I left Monaco, they said that whenever I returned I'd always be welcomed back with open arms if I wanted to come back. Before I left, I took all the players out for a lovely meal at the Cafe de Paris in Monaco to have a glass of wine together. I said my farewells, which was very emotional, but it was nice to be able to say goodbye to the lads. What normally happens is that a transfer takes place so quickly in football that you don't get a chance to say farewell to your team-mates. So I made sure that I got everybody there, we had a nice meal together and I got the chance to say farewell. The manager pulled me to one side and wished me all the best, and I left on great terms with everybody. They offered me a new contract and didn't want me to leave. But I thought it was time to try something different. That was probably the hardest decision of my career – to leave Monaco. It was a very emotional move, partly because I'd become so attached to the way of life there. But in life you've got to move on and meet new challenges, and we'll be going back there to life after my playing career is over.

I'll never forget when I told my wife when we went to see the apartment, 'We're negotiating, try to keep a straight face and not look too excited, the deal's not done yet'. And she came back and said 'Well, I've seen two apartments I really like. One's a little bit too small with three bedrooms, but the other one's nice'. And that was the one we had picked. And I'll never forget, the agent took us to the door, opened it up, we went in and saw these huge marble floors. We went out on the balcony. I called my agent Raymond Sparks. It was a beautiful day, about eighty-five degrees, with a huge balcony and I just looked out to the sea and thought 'How lucky am I?!' I looked up to the sky and said 'Thank you God!' I was jumping up and down like a little kid shouting 'You beauty!' And I was thinking that it was going to be special living there after a wet, cold and miserable Glasgow. Scotland's not a miserable place but the weather isn't the best. The people are nice though.

From a footballing point of view, my abiding memory is running round the football stadium in Monaco with the League Championship trophy above our heads, winning the title in my first year, getting presented with my medal from Prince Albert, and lifting up the trophy. That was a special occasion.

Everybody's different, but my advice for any British player that's going and playing abroad is as follows. If you're just going for the money, I don't think you'll ever be successful or happy. I think your attitude's got to be that I'm going to go there and I'm going to learn the language. It's not easy, it can be difficult. There are frustrating moments when you can't get your point across. But if you go there open-minded, and integrate into the way of life and the culture, when you do eventually come back to the UK, you'll find that it's been so fulfilling. You can jump on a plane and travel, communicate in another language, and adapt to a new type of football and training methods. You got to be open-minded. You've got to forget what you've done in the past, and just completely open up your mind, listen, learn, and enjoy it.

You've got to do it with a smile on your face, and realise how lucky you are. Too many football players like to moan and complain. That's just the nature of the way we are. We have got a fantastic life. We train every day, and to go across to a new country, test your skills against foreign players, and learn a new language as well. It's an unbeatable experience, and so fulfilling".

As previously mentioned, John is currently a squad member and first team player at Fulham F.C.

Scott Minto

PLAYER
Benfica, (Portugal), June 1997 – June 1999

Scott Minto was born in Birkenhead in the Wirral. His first professional club was Charlton Athletic, for whom we signed in 1989. He spent five happy seasons with the Addicks, before moving to Chelsea in 1994, winning an FA Cup winners medal in 1997. We pick up Scott's story in May 1997:

"To be honest with you, my agent sorted it out all the contract details. A lot of clubs knew that I was going to be on a free transfer, but at that particular time there were also free transfers abroad. I was having discussions with Chelsea about my contract at the end of the 1996/97 season, whilst we were on our tour of Thailand, Brunei and Hong Kong, straight after the 1997 Cup Final. I then got a phone call from my agent that Benfica had come to watch me, they liked what they saw, were prepared to offer me a three-year contract and would I like to go? I thought about it, it was obviously going to be a big move, and I thought to myself that this was an incredible opportunity. I didn't know much about Portuguese football as such, but everyone's heard about Benfica. So I was playing in the stadium of light, experiencing not just the football side of things but the lifestyle and personal side of it as well. Experiencing a different lifestyle, culture and country really appealed to me, so I didn't think twice about it to be honest, and I just said yes to the move straight away.

Benfica is such a big club and everyone's heard of it, and of Eusebio obviously. They were doing a lot better at that time than before. It was just an opportunity where I thought to myself that these type of things only happen, if you're lucky, once in your career, and that maybe this opportunity wouldn't arise again. I thought to myself that there was a good chance, if it didn't go well, that I could come back to England. I was very fortunate that from the word go everything went really well.

I actually told my family I was going to Portugal when I was away on the tour, so they were probably quite shocked and surprised. They completely understood why I wanted to do it. My Dad and my Brother actually went there to watch me in my first game for Benfica. It was really nice, the whole ambience of the country and the way they played their football. It was just a fantastic experience and one that I really enjoyed. I now go back to Portugal every year.

The first time I went to Portugal was when I played for England in the under-20 World Cup. We were based in Faro in the South. We got knocked out of that competition, but I actually stayed out there for a week after that with my cousin, so that was the only time I'd been in Portugal before that.

Did I speak Portuguese before I went out there? No, none at all. It was quite funny actually because leading up to the 1997 Cup Final I went on the Zig and Zag show on 'the Big Breakfast' on Channel Four with Suggs from Madness, and we had to answer questions about each other. Fortunately we got a bit of information fed to each other beforehand, because he didn't know anything about me and I didn't know much about him either. I had to read a piece in Portuguese, because Juninho was in the Middlesborough side up against us in the Cup Final. So just as a bit of a joke, I had to read this passage in Portuguese with Juninho talking and me saying 'I'm going to kick you!' So that was on Zig and Zag, and it was the only piece of Portuguese that I'd ever read or spoken before going over to Portugal! And less than a month later, I'd signed for Benfica.

There were a few members of the press at the airport when I arrived, which was a bit surprising. I quite enjoyed that, and they were asking me a lot of questions. Luckily I'd been told roughly what the questions were going to be so that went well. Then we went straight to the ground, but before then I had to do a medical and they were quite stringent. I then signed a pre-contract and had to go out and do a two-day medical. Then I came back and signed a proper contract again. It was a new experience, because although Chelsea was obviously a big club, Benfica was the biggest club in Portugal and was known as the club of the people. It was a new experience for me but a very enjoyable one.

The club helped me a lot with setting me up with a house. They didn't actually help me with the Portuguese side of things and learning the language. I looked in a local newspaper, found a teacher and started having lessons quite early. I must admit that I went into the whole experience of it trying to learn the language and find out what Portugal was all about, and that was very important. But I was very surprised at how many people speak English in Portugal. You could easily go there and not try to learn a word and get by without any problems because so many people do speak English. But I wanted to give learning Portuguese a go, and I think I made a good impression by doing that. I was the first Englishman to go over there, and Graeme Souness wasn't yet the manager, so I think it was a novel experience for them and for other people as well, speaking to an English guy, because I think I was probably the first English guy to play in Portugal. I tried to learn the language, but when I couldn't get by, there were a lot of people on hand to give me some advice in English.

There were financial problems at Benfica at the time I was there. It was very rare that we got paid on time, and quite often we got paid a month late. But playing for Benfica was a great experience for me, and I was happy as long as I was getting paid what I was owed, even if it was a little bit late. On the playing side of things, I think they'd finished third the previous season, and had qualified for the UEFA Cup. I was told that it was disgusting for them to finish so low. We played in the UEFA Cup but we got knocked out in an early round. I'm not sure what the situation was football- wise, but financially I knew that they were having a lot of problems at the time. There was also a change of presidency about three months after I arrived.

To be honest with you, I didn't really see or talk to either the first or the second president. The first one didn't speak any English when I started, so we just had translators when I was actually signing. The second one I spoke to now and again, but only very rarely. You're right when you say that the president over there definitely has a bigger profile than they have in England. Going on TV, I was amazed to see football programmes being broadcast almost every single night. It just seemed such a massive thing, and it took me back a bit.

I think nicknames that the fans give players, and being the new great hope, are more for strikers than defenders. Obviously, as a left-back, I'm not going to completely and radically change the team by coming in there, so if the fans did give me a nickname, I didn't know about it because I didn't understand it! I was very fortunate because I probably had the best pre-season of my career when I went to Portugal. I even scored a couple of goals from left-back, and was very happy with how that went.

As for the press, I didn't do any TV stuff when I was over there. After every training session, the press asked for certain players to go and do press conferences, and I did a few of them but again not too many. I think they wanted to talk to the strikers or the attacking midfielders. I did a few other press conferences and interviews that got into newspapers, but as for TV work I tended to stayed away from that.

I'd have to say both the away games against Sporting Lisbon were the most memorable. I was injured for the two games at home over the two seasons, but the two games away we won both times and I set up the opening goal in both of them. As well as this the match at Sporting Lisbon in the second season was my last League game playing for Benfica. We won 2-1, with me setting up the first goal. So probably playing against them, and the atmosphere, were games to remember. Obviously there's such a build-up to the game, and it's like how they treat the FA Cup Final here leading up to the game. It's a must-win game for the fans so it was nice to beat them there. In addition to playing in Portugal, I played in the Champions League in my second season, and I must say that those two games against Sporting and the games in the Champions League were the highlights of my time playing for Benfica.

We had a guy at Benfica called Joao Pinto, who was like the

Cantona of Benfica. But I think they've given him a free transfer now because they couldn't afford his wages. He was an excellent player, and there was a lot of pressure on him as well. I really admired the way he handled it all, because he had a very high profile. A young lad called Nuno Gomes was just coming through as well. I think he'd probably do better in Europe than in England because of the physicality of the English game, but he showed in the last European Championships what a good finisher he is.

There was another guy in the team as well called Colado and during my first season he was without doubt the best player at Benfica. The best player I played against was Sergio Conceicao when he was at Lazio – he's now at Parma. The thing that really surprised me about Portuguese football was that everybody, even the defenders, was very comfortable on the ball and very technically gifted. But the problem with the defenders was that they weren't so good at defending. On the ball they just seemed to have so much time. Their touch was good and their passing was superb, but obviously you do get much more time in Portuguese football than in English football. Having said that, they used that time well.

I did manage to socialise a bit with the players. When I first went out there, there was a guy called Gaston Taumont, a Dutch winger who Benfica had just signed from Feyenoord. I used to socialise with him quite a lot. When Graeme Souness came over he started bringing in some English players. The first one to arrive was Brian Deane and I saw a lot of him, as well as Dean Saunders, Mark Pembridge and Michael Thomas. As for the Portuguese players, I didn't really socialise with them a lot even though in pre-season we got on very well. We went on tour, we were allowed a few nights out and we had a really good time together. But they were quite professional in the way that they didn't really go out that much. It was their culture not to go out and get totally 'off their face' on alcohol, they usually just went out for a couple of glasses of wine. I did that a few times as well. There was also a Belgian guy there called Michel Preud'homme. I think he was voted best goalkeeper in the 1990 World Cup, and I used to go out with him a lot. Also with Martin Pringle, who's now at Charlton and is a Swedish international. I used to socialise with him too. So there were a few guys there, but once there were a lot of English guys over there, we all used to live in the same apartment block, within half a mile of each other, so we socialised quite a lot there.

Graeme Souness was actually the coach from the second half of my first season. The first coach was Portuguese and didn't speak any English. His name was Manuel Jose and he was unlucky. We started off that season with a 4-0 win and everybody thought we were going to go off and win the League. We then got knocked out of the UEFA Cup and perhaps didn't do as well as we could have done in the League. What with the president saying 'I'm going to call a vote, and I'm not going to stand for the next election', and the new president-elect was coming in and saying 'I'm going to bring him in and him in', it was a pretty chaotic situation. He was a bit unfortunate really in that he didn't have that long. He seemed pretty good, and he picked me so he obviously knew what he was doing! Just joking!

Then Graeme Souness came in about November/December time, and I got on very well with him. There was definitely a bond between Souness and the English guys, and I think the fact that he brought quite a few over shows that he had faith in them. But for me I was quite proud of the fact that he didn't actually bring me over, as I was already there. This was because at times some parts of the Portuguese media were trying to create a division between the English and the Portuguese guys, because there were a lot of English guys, about five or six, in the team. As a result there were some Portuguese guys on the bench. We did have a little bit of a 'media blackout', and didn't speak with the Portuguese press for about a month because of this, but I liked the way Souness coped with it all.

The fans were very passionate. I remember my Dad saying to me the other day that there was a time when I was injured, and we sat in the box for the players and their wives. The fans can see you there, and on that particular night we went 1-0 down. There were fans banging on the windows making rude gestures, they were screaming at Graeme Souness, and it was obviously very passionate. Then suddenly we scored two goals in the space of about five minutes, and then everybody was coming up to him, banging on the doors and sticking their thumbs up! So it's very passionate out there, probably to the point of being a little bit crazy. The highs are very high and the lows are very low, but I admired Souness for the way he dealt with everything. We didn't win every game of course, but when that happened he came out of it with a lot of dignity, despite there being a lot of provocation.

As for the tactics and training, it was quite funny because when I was in England I played under Glenn Hoddle. I know he's English, but he probably got a lot of his tactics from Monaco, and then I played under Ruud Gullit, a foreigner. Then I went abroad and a Scottish guy was the coach! So it wasn't really a case of that when I went abroad there was a lot of difference. It was almost the reverse really. Souness was very much into getting the good players together, those who can play and understand the game themselves, with five-a-sides, possession work and set-pieces before the game. Gullit was quite similar like that as well. I think Glenn Hoddle was probably the one who liked to do most on the tactical side. Being an international manager probably suited him a lot, because I think he loved having the cream of the English players and doing something with them. So it wasn't really that much of a difference going abroad, purely because I had a lot of experience of foreign training and coaching methods even before I went to Portugal, when I was at Chelsea, what with Gullit and Hoddle.

My best moment came at the end of my first season there. In Portugal they always have a match at the end of the season between the best-voted Portuguese players, and the best-voted foreign players, and I was actually voted as the best left-back. So that was nice for me, and showed that I'd made a good impression.

I still had a year and a half on my contract when West Ham came in for me. Obviously Julian Dicks being the legend that he was at West Ham, they were thinking about possibly bringing in a left-back, because he had a lot of problems with his knee. Harry Redknapp had known me from my time at Charlton, and they came in for me. And to be honest with you, if it had been a club outside London, I probably wouldn't have gone back to England.

At that time I was on my own, having a great time and enjoying myself, but I was a single guy going in, training, coming home and just being on my own for the rest of the day. A lot of the English guys had their families over there with them. It was often a case of seeing them now and again, but quite often going out on my own for a meal. It was nice to come back to a London club and be near my family where we could be chasing a UEFA Cup slot every year. So West Ham really fitted the bill in every way possible, and they were the club that I needed at the time. I was very happy at Benfica and wasn't looking to move, but when West Ham came in I just thought to myself that this was perfect for me on both a personal and professional level.

Everything happened so quickly that I don't know what the press and supporter reaction was. I went to pick up my boots and the director of football, who was a very famous footballer for both Benfica and Portugal. I'm not exactly sure what his official title was, but he acted as the link between the club officials and the players. He asked me what I was doing, and I told him I was going to West Ham. He didn't even know about it! So it was very hush hush, and kept that way, until I was virtually on the plane home. The nice thing is that whenever I go back there, everyone keeps asking me whether I'm back to sign for them again. When I had my honeymoon in the Seychelles there was a Portuguese family there too, and they asked me whether I would sign again for Benfica, and they'd love to have me back. It was a nice little boost to see that you've left a good impression on a team like that and on a foreign culture and the people there.

The match against Sporting was my last League game, although nobody knew it at the time. We played a Cup game after that the following week. We played on the Sunday, and I got the phone call on the Monday to say that I could possibly be going if I wanted to. Then on the Tuesday I was on the plane back to England! So it really was such a quick twenty-four hours, and twenty-four hours before that I knew nothing about it. We'd played in the Cup and we won 4-1. It was so out of the blue that nobody else knew anything about it.

When I boarded the plane to leave, it was kind of a mixed

emotion. There was definitely a big part of sadness inside me to be leaving Portugal, not just because of the football side of things but the lifestyle as well. It was amazing for someone like me who loves nice weather and living on the coast near to the beaches, because I lived two minutes from the beach. So I was a bit sad for that, but obviously I did have the choice. I wanted to come back to London and be near my family. I also wanted to sign for West Ham and be in the Premier League, where we finished fifth in my first season.

I did score an own goal in the Champions League, which wasn't great. The following day we went in for a warm-down, and for the first training-session of pre-season there were about five thousand people watching, and between two hundred and a thousand watching every day. The day after that own-goal, as we jogged around the pitch, there were people shouting my name and clapping and being really nice, shouting 'Don't worry about it!' in English. The only thing I can say is that after having been there, when I go back, the fact that the people say 'Are you coming back? We want to have you back in the team'. I think that when you've left that kind of impression, it just makes you think that that's really nice that they appreciated you.

If you have offers to play abroad, I would say that you have to be ready to go abroad both professionally and personally, but more personally, because it is a big upheaval moving to another country and being away from your family. I was twenty-five at the time, which was probably the perfect age to go. I would say to anybody up until the age of twenty-three that you're probably better off staying where you are. If there is the possibility that you can go abroad, it may sound fantastic, but it doesn't always work out. You have to be ready for it, and if it doesn't work out it can be a very lonely time. But I think that once you get to that certain age, twenty-three or twenty-four and certainly onwards, I would say go for it, because I'm so happy that I did it. I would look back now if I hadn't done it with complete regret, thinking that I had a fantastic opportunity to experience something different and I passed it up. I would tell anybody who does get the opportunity to be at a good club abroad to go for it."

After moving back to the UK from Portugal, Scott signed for West Ham, the club he is still currently playing for.

Gordon Cowans

PLAYER
Bari, (Italy), May 1985 – May 1988

Gordon Cowans was born in Cornforth, County Durham, and first signed for Aston Villa in 1976. He was to stay for nine hugely successful seasons, winning the League Championship in 1981, the European Champions Cup in 1982, and the first of his 10 England Caps, against Wales, in February 1983. We pick up Gordon's story in May 1985:

"My transfer to Bari was done at that time through an agent who came via contacts in Italy. He just approached me and asked me if I fancied playing in Italy. It was the same agent that two years prior to this had approached me regarding a move to Naples. That ended up falling through because the president of Naples got ousted from the board along with his general manager, who wanted to buy me. It was the same general manager who was then at Bari who wanted me to go there. They came over to watch me play a couple of times. Whilst they were watching me, they also liked the look of Paul Rideout, who was a young lad playing centre-forward, so they ended up taking the pair of us.

I'd always fancied having a go at playing abroad, especially because at the time Italy was probably the best country to go to. To just go and play a different style of football, pit your wits against them, and see how you could cope and get on was appealing to me. My wife was all for it because I wanted to go. It was going to be something totally different for us, and what we hoped was going to be a good experience. The climate was obviously a lot better than over here, so we decided to go for it.

I was getting towards the end of my contract at Aston Villa, and

I made it clear that I wanted to go. I'd come back from a broken leg a year before, had a full season back after breaking my leg, but still wasn't back to what I was before the injury, even though I was getting towards my best form again. They understood my situation and didn't put up too much of a fight. I think Aston Villa got what they wanted financially, and certainly didn't stand in my way.

I'd been to Italy before, on holiday, but not to Bari. I didn't speak any Italian before I went over there. I remember when we went over to sign and to have a look. We arrived at the airport in Bari, Paul Rideout and myself, and the agent, a fellow called Gianni Paladini, who you might have heard of by now because he organised Fabrizio Ravanelli's move to Derby. I think this was probably the first deal he did. So we arrived in Bari and there were around ten thousand supporters at the airport waiting for us! The place was literally jam-packed. When the plane had landed and pulled along the runway, there were just thousands of people everywhere along the perimeter fences of the airport, in red and white. We had to go into the airport and be ushered through the crowd by police: we'd never seen anything like it, the pair of us. It was a very emotional experience, with grown men trying to hug and kiss you. It was certainly a situation I'd never been in before and never likely to be in again.

I did look into the background of the club before I went out to play there. They had been close for a couple of years to getting into Serie A, then finally managed to get into Serie A, and had spent a little bit of money to get new players in. But unfortunately not enough money, because we went over there and found it very tough going. We were playing against very good sides, and Bari was a very average side. They had got promoted and five new players had come in, but they really needed a lot more than that and a lot more quality to really be able to maintain their position in Serie A. They still had the two foreigners per team rule in Italy at that stage.

There was a big press fanfare as well when we first arrived there. We were actually escorted from the airport to a hotel in Bari, and once the signing was completed there was a press conference. It was typically Italian, with lots of photographers and pressmen firing all sorts of questions at us. At that stage we used an interpreter to answer the questions.

We didn't actually go to school to learn Italian, we just picked it up. The agent, Gianni Paladini, was Italian and he stayed with us for long periods, sometimes three or four months at a time, and then came back to England to his family for maybe a couple of weeks. Then he'd come back to see us again, so he really helped us a lot. But neither Paul nor I went for Italian lessons. We picked the language up as we went along, and it came along. There were certain spells when you'd think you were standing still, and then all of a sudden you've have a spurt and then you'd learn a lot more. It kept going on and on like that, until by the time we got to the third year we could understand everything, and make ourselves understood really well.

I spent three weeks at training-camp when we first arrived in Bari, and then we came back down to Bari to our villa, which was about two hundred yards off the seafront on the coast, which was very nice. It was nice too that our neighbours next to us, people we didn't know at all, waved over the fence or the balcony in the morning and shouted good morning to us. They were really lovely people and we're still in touch with them to this day.

We had met the members of the Board when we went over to Italy. The president of Bari at the time was a Signor Matarrese, and his brother was president of the Italian Federation. They were a very powerful family, and we got on well with them. They were very well respected in Italy and in Bari. For instance, they used to take us out for a meal every Tuesday night, and when we went into the restaurant, everybody would stand up and clap him in!

I got injured early on in the Italian Cup, which is played before the season starts. I broke my fibia, which put me out for six weeks. I actually missed the start of the season, which was a massive blow for me. The coach, Bruno Bolchi, worked very hard to get me fit, and spent a lot of time with me after the other lads had finished training doing exercise, and having me run up and down the stands.

We went on local television stations to do interviews, again with interpreters to start with. It was a different situation, because

Bari obviously wasn't a big club like AC Milan where the likes of Joe Jordan, Ray Wilkins and Mark Hateley were playing. It surprised us, the media coverage at everyday training. Every day you went to train, there were six or seven journalists there, and they would just stand around and watch the training, looking for any little story. They actually did stories on how the training sessions went! They'd say something like 'Oh, and Cowans did this in training and Rideout scored a goal'. You would think that it was ridiculous to be writing about things like this. Maybe you'd finish with a five-a-side or some crossing and finishing, but I never understood why they would want to be writing about that sort of thing!

My debut game was against Lecce, our local rivals. I'd been out with a broken leg and came back on the 27th of October, which was my birthday as well. It was quite a big occasion for me, and we won the game. But the hatred between the two clubs and the two sets of supporters was unbelievable. We have derby games here where they dislike each other, but it really was bad over there. Anyway we won that game, and I got lifted off the field by the other players. It was fantastic just to get out there and finally be playing, against a side like that in a local derby, and for us to win was very good. So everybody was made up about it, but for me it was just nice to be back playing again.

I played with, and against, some great players in Italy. For Bari, the lad who is now at Valencia, Amadeo Carboni. He was a youngster they brought in as one of the new players. He was in and out of the side playing at left back, and very quick. It was obvious that he was going to be a big talent. There was also Massimo Carrera, who went on to play for Juventus. He was a youngish lad who was playing centre-half, and was another player who went on to do very well for himself. As talented as anyone there was a lad called Pietro Maiellaro, who I don't know whether people over here would have heard of, but in Serie B over there he was as good a player as was about. But he just couldn't quite come to terms with Serie A. He really should have had a hell of a career for himself, but for whatever reason he didn't quite make it.

We were fortunate enough, and that was the good thing for me, to be going and playing against probably the best players in the world at the time. Unfortunately I was injured when we played Juventus so I missed facing Platini, but I'd played against him prior to that with Villa. Karl-Heinz Rummenigge was out there, and Ray Wilkins and Mark Hateley too. Junior was there too, and I also played against Maradona. When we actually played Napoli. Maradona was injured for the game at Bari, but we went over to Naples, and when we played there our coach put a man-to-man marker on him. But he made this marker look absolutely silly. He tore him apart and totally destroyed him. He was unbelievable on the day, we got beaten, and Maradona ran the show.

I remember that we were under the same stand in the warm-up, in different areas but in the same vicinity, and I was just watching Maradona doing tricks, and all sorts of things, with the ball. I just stood there watching him open-mouthed, because he was just so incredibly talented. To be out there playing against these sort of players is the reason that you go in the first place. You go and play at all the big stadiums against the big names. That was what I wanted to do, go and pit myself against the very best. It was disappointing that the side that I went to was, I wouldn't say inadequate, but there was no way we were going to places and putting on a good show. We were getting narrowly beaten in a lot of games, which always put us under a lot of pressure. There were a lot of 1-0s and 2-1s, but we never really took the game to the opposition, so it was difficult.

We got relegated in my first season at the club, which was a big disappointment for me, and after getting relegated I was totally gutted and disillusioned. At that time Jim Smith, then manager of QPR, came over and tried to buy me. Bari wouldn't have any of it, and they insisted I stayed because they were happy with me. But it worked out well that I stayed, and I had a good experience of playing in the lower League, Serie B, for the following two years.

The president took the team out every Tuesday night, but after games there were a couple of lads and their wives who we socialised with. The goalkeeper, a fellow called Pino, was a similar age to me. We got to know his wife, and he had a couple of kids. We used to go round to their house and they'd come round to ours.

We occasionally went out with Pino, Massimo Carrera and their wives after games, and the lads were really very good to us.

What we used to do for the home games was to stay at a hotel and go in a minibus to the ground. There were times when we were getting stones thrown at us, with people banging on the side of the bus when things weren't going well. It was a very intimidating and dangerous situation. We would pull in and park the bus under the stand, but when you were pulling out after the game, or at times going there when we were struggling, it was very frightening, and a lot of it was down to frustration. They were so pleased to get the chance to play in Serie A, and to be struggling and looking like they were going to be relegated, well, they just couldn't seem to be able to handle that situation. As far as having battered cars, that was true, and a lot of the lads used to have just little run-arounds, because if you've seen the way they drive over there, it's absolutely crazy! They have no respect for anybody giving way or on traffic lights, with everybody sneaking through on red.

The first coach we had at Bari was Bruno Bolchi. He was a fantastic man and I got on very well with him. He had a lot of time for me. He was very patient with me when I broke my leg, which was obviously a blow for him with the two foreigners coming over, and one of them breaking a leg. I was supposed to be the playmaker, so it was obviously a problem, and in the meantime he had to try and put somebody else in there to do that role. He spent a lot of time doing different exercises with me and trying to get me fit as quick as he could. I felt that he had a good knowledge of the game and was a good coach and nice man as well. He lost his job after we got relegated, and a fellow called Enrico Catuzzi came in. He was a different sort of man altogether, with different ideas. He was a much younger fellow, and it was a difficult situation, as he was obviously learning as well. But without being rude to him, he didn't get a great response from the players.

The very first day we went training, we went to a camp right up in the North. They took us to a running-track to do a twelve-minute run round the running track. When we did this sort of twelve-minute training run in England, you went flat out and were trying to get as many laps in as you could. Now we got there, and the doctor was trying to stop me from doing it. I had a temperature the previous day and on the morning before the test, so I felt a little bit feverish and shaky, but I was saying to people that I was fine. We started the run and I went haring off around the track, trying to do as many laps as possible. But the doctor tried to jump out in front of me on the track and block my path! I kept on waving him to one side and kept on going, whilst the other lads were literally just jogging round the track. And Paul Rideout and myself were wondering 'What the hell's going on here?! They're taking the mickey!' It was very much like that, and the build-up was very slow.

So the next day we went training and they took us for a walk and a jog in the woods with these little weight-belts on, weighing only a couple of pounds. They gradually built it up, and the weight-belts got heavier and the running got harder. They really went into it in a very professional way. So what we thought was going to be very easy gradually got harder and harder. I wouldn't say harder than what we'd done previously in England. It was easier, but it was certainly a more scientific way of looking at it over there.

I think playing abroad bettered me as a player. I used to try and play a lot of early balls and put players in early. When I first went over they started getting the ball and I'd try to put a forward in, get a winger in behind a full-back or whatever, and try and play forward early. But everyone kept telling me to just keep the ball until I got into the last third, and then start trying to slip people in from the higher positions up the field. It was a much more patient game. You had to pick your times when you tried to create something, and that was a good learning point for me. Learning to be more patient with the ball, and deciding when the time was right to go for it and when it wasn't, certainly benefited me as a player.

Did Bari want me to leave? That was certainly not the situation, and they wanted me to stay. I came towards the last year of my contract and started to think that I wanted to be back home in the UK, and start playing in English football again. I played for

England prior to going over to Italy, I played a couple of times when I was in Italy in build-ups for the 1986 Mexico World Cup squad, and I played over in Egypt, Russia and got close to getting selected for the Mexico World Cup.

But at the time I was playing in the Second Division in Italy, so it didn't really matter how well I was playing because I was getting no recognition back home, and that was a disappointing thing for me. I wanted to get back, because I'd got myself really fit again, and wanted to get back into the senior international set-up. I played seven consecutive games, broke my leg in England, and was out for a full year, played a full year after that, and went to Italy. So I was missing that side of it, and was probably getting overlooked which was a little bit frustrating for me.

By this time my wife was settled and wanted to stay in Italy. My daughter had been brought up there, what with going over there at fourteen months of age. She spoke fluent Italian, she had all her mates there and really loved it. But as for me, I wanted to get back, and there were a few clubs that came in for me, and fortunately one of those, although very late, was Aston Villa. When John Sillett came over for me, it looked like I might have joined Coventry. Then probably a month before coming back, Graham Taylor came over. He didn't promise anything, but just said he didn't agree with people going back to a club where they had come from a second time. He said that he'd go to watch me play. So anyway, he watched me and said that he wanted to bring me back, but that I needed to be hungry to play for Villa again.

So I ended up coming back to Villa, which couldn't have worked out better for me. I was very fortunate to go back to where I wanted to be anyway. We were back home in Birmingham. I remember coming back, because before I signed he took me straight up to Lilleshall to do fitness tests. After I'd been over there, and after having broken my leg over there and before I went to Italy, he just wanted to check on my fitness, because he was very thorough in everything he did was Graham Taylor. He took me up there, and I ended up on a treadmill with tubes sticking out of my mouth and all sorts, and wires all over my heart. He was delighted with my fitness. They tested the leg that I had broken, and found that it was stronger than my left leg, which I hadn't broken, so he was delighted with my overall fitness.

The Bari fans were very good when I left, and very supportive of me. They were desperate for me to remain at the club, and I had loads of letters and postcards wanting me to stay, and thanking me for my efforts with the club, for what I'd done. The Italian press were good to me as well. I think what they recognised was that I gave my all, and that every time I was out on the field I ran around and did everything I could to get something out of the game, which they appreciated. So I think I had a good relationship with the supporters at Bari. It was nice, but by that time I'd made my mind up, despite the fact that the president wanted to keep me. They had a new coach who was coming in who spoke to me before, and when we left he wanted me to stay. But I had made my mind up, and wanted to get back and try to put myself in the picture to get recognition with the England side.

We didn't get any mementos when I left, but the supporters gave us a great send-off. There were handshakes, hugs and kisses, as the Italians all do, just fond farewells, and they all thanked us. Since then, I've probably seen the president three or four times when he got involved with the David Platt transfer. I came back to Villa, and the president of Bari was ringing me about Platty, three years later. He was desperate to get him over there and was on the phone to me every other day. We actually went over with Bari, with the side and with Platty, and he invited me out for a meal with them up in a restaurant near the city centre.

Last time I was in Bari was three or four months ago. We went over there for a youth tournament that was on. I called in at the club, which is all changed now with the new stadium which they had built for the World Cup, and I saw quite a few old faces there which was nice. Other than that I've been back once, and the wife's been back a couple of times to see the neighbours who are our friends. When I went back three or four months ago, I just popped round unexpectedly and had lunch with them. They were obviously pleased to see me, and we went out that evening with two of their sons as well.

As I boarded the plane to leave Bari, I felt pleased to be going back to England. I did enjoy my time there, although I was disappointed that we spent two years in the Second Division. But overall it was a very good experience, and certainly one that bettered me as a player. The reasons I went there were to play a different style of football, to pit myself against that, to see how I learned, and to play at the big grounds against the very famous world-class players that were over there.

There are a couple of moments I haven't mentioned. The ups and downs of the football, and the high of playing in my first game against Lecce. Then we went up to AC Milan in the Italian Cup when Van Basten, Gullit and Rikjaard were playing, and they tonked us 5-0 – we hardly got a kick. That was a low, coming up against such good sides and really getting the run-around. But overall the memories of just being there were enjoyable. It was what I went for, to try and play against good players. I certainly got that, although I didn't have too much help from our lads and that's with no disrespect to them, because to be honest with you, some of them just weren't up to it. That was a disappointing side to it, but I certainly don't regret it anyway.

If a current player asked me whether he should play abroad, I'd recommend that he go, because it certainly betters you as a player. It gives you a new outlook on life. You see how other people live, and you're only going to benefit from it. But I would go to a good side".

After returning to the UK in May 1988, Gordon had spells with playing with Aston Villa, Blackburn Rovers, Derby County, Wolverhampton Wanderers, Sheffield United, Bradford City, Stockport County and Burnley. He is currently working as the youth team coach at Aston Villa.

Tommy Docherty

MANAGER
FC Porto, (Portugal), February 1970 – June 1971
Sydney Olympic, (Australia), October 1980 – June 1981
South Melbourne Hellas, (Australia), January – June 1982

Tommy Docherty is one of the most colourful and charismatic characters in football. As a player, he launched his career with Glasgow Celtic, and made 324 appearances for Preston North End, winning the Second Division Championship in 1951. He also played for Arsenal and Chelsea, as well as winning 25 caps for Scotland. He began his managerial career with Chelsea in September 1961 and stayed until 1967 when he moved to Rotherham United. Following a brief spell at Queens Park Rangers, he took charge of Aston Villa in 1968, and we pick up Tommy's story in February 1970:

"To be quite honest with you when I was at Aston Villa, and got the sack there, I was on my way to Athletic Bilbao. We'd agreed terms with the president, and on my way over there the president was unfortunately and rather sadly killed in a car crash. So the new people who took over the club obviously wanted to appoint their own coach, which was fair enough, so that plan went out of the window. Then FC Porto came in for me. I went over to Portugal for the interview, got the job, and had two lovely years over there.

Well it was one of those things, and decision-time, and I decided that this would be good for me, going abroad to a new environment, a new culture, and new players, and learning about a different type of mentality. I thought that it wouldn't do me any harm, because

I've always been a person that when I'd lost a job, I always wanted to find another one and get back into work as quickly as I possibly could. Not always necessarily the right job mind you! Maybe I was too impetuous at times and should have waited for a bigger and better club, but then how long do you wait?

I'd been over to Portugal on holiday beforehand. I went to Cascais when I was manager of Chelsea and had a lovely time. Portugal is one of my favourite countries and the people are so nice there. But no, I didn't speak any Portuguese, not when I went, although by the time my two-year contract was up I was managing quite nicely.

Well of course I had heard of Oporto before I went there, and at the time the Portuguese national side consisted of players from Benfica, Sporting Lisbon and Oporto. The whole squad of twenty-two was more or less from these three clubs. And Eusebio, Simoes, Graca and Mario Coluna, they were the top Portuguese players in the 1966 World Cup.

I didn't really deal with the Portuguese media as such. It was a strange time because they had a PR man there and you dealt through him. So I didn't really speak to the press, hardly at all in fact. When you spoke to the press attaché that belonged to the club, you told him your ideas and he related them to the local press. The interviews out there were mostly done through the club, because they felt that it took a lot of responsibility off your shoulders, through good and bad results.

The club were excellent with finding me accommodation and helping with language lessons. They put me in a nice hotel until such time as I got my own house, which didn't take us long. They also signed me up to go into school for Portuguese lessons twice a week, so they were very helpful.

Oporto were about fourth or fifth in the League when I arrived there. They were a bit like, how can I liken it at the moment, you could say they were like Chelsea are now. But Benfica and Sporting Lisbon dominated the scene at that particular time. They were the big rich clubs, with Eusebio, Simoes, Coluna, and all the top stars.

I met the president, Joao Eduardo Pinto Matos Dias for the first time in Oporto when I arrived at the hotel. We discussed terms and the deal was done. I was always called 'Mister' by the fans. Bobby Robson and John Toshack would probably say the same thing. They call the coach out there 'Mister', especially if you're English. And of course, you're just the coach there, and not the manager.

Well of course being out there for the first time, they were all big games for me. Benfica, Sporting, Belenenses, Braga, and Boavista, which is the local derby, were the major ones. But Porto were always a UEFA Cup team, but not quite getting into the European Cup as it was at that time, or the Cup Winners Cup.

I had a player at Oporto who was the captain of the first team – he's dead now unfortunately. He died quite young after taking some pills prior to a match about four years after I was there, and unfortunately the lad died during the course of the game. His name was Pavon. A Portuguese international, a great player and normally an outside-left who played for Oporto as well. We had a good hard-working well-organised side, with a couple of Brazilian lads in the team as well. But as I said before the big scalp at the time was Benfica.

I used to go out quite a bit over in Portugal. Well actually what I used to do was to go into the restaurants or I would have a meal at home at night, and I would switch down the sound on the television, because it was all subtitled. So say if an American film came on, or a British one, there were Portuguese subtitles, and it was tremendous help for me to pick up little bits and pieces of the language. And yet if you went out for dinner to a little restaurant or whatever, you picked up all sorts of bits and pieces of the language by listening to the Portuguese people chattering away to themselves. It was very interesting actually. Everybody, and even the supporters, was very helpful and very loyal. They were always there – nothing like you get today.

I'll tell you a strange thing that happened to me. Going out there at the beginning as a football coach, they called them a trainer as well, you had to learn the football terminology first. So you were learning the language upside-down if you like, and learning words like corner-kicks, penalty-kicks, goal-kicks, and offside. Sometimes of course you would get things wrong grammatically, and the players would turn round and burst out laughing because you'd said something! You would maybe inadvertently put in a swear-word and they're all turning round laughing like anything, and I was saying 'Well, what have I done wrong?!' They were terrific, but of course there was a tiny snag as well. A lot of the Portuguese players, in fact most of them, wanted to learn English. So they didn't want me to speak Portuguese, because they wanted to learn English! And I wanted to learn as much Portuguese as I could. They were asking me about the football over here and the players over here, and I said 'Nao intereso. Parlo Portugues!' So I only spoke in Portuguese to them.

The mistake I made to begin with was that I thought I'd get them fit, and train them very hard with a lot of physical work. But they weren't used to that, and didn't take too kindly to it. So I had to readjust my ideas and methods, because in the morning they did what they called physical work, but it wasn't in the same class or as hard as the British player's training. In the afternoon it was technical work, whereas in England there was no technical work in the afternoons. They just did a bit of physical and technical work in the morning, and have the afternoon off. But over there you worked in the afternoon as well, after a light lunch and three hours rest, and then you were out again working on the technical side of the game.

When I took over at Oporto, we were fifth from the top and just missed a European place. I went there in the February before taking over in the June. So when I came back after the 1970 World Cup in Mexico I took over at Oporto. I had an interpreter for about three months, and I don't know whether that can be a good thing or not because sometimes you tell the interpreter in an aggressive manner what you want to tell the player, and he might be a nice placid type of gentleman. So the player gets the same instructions, but in a different way, in a much nicer way than the way you want to tell them. Whereas you maybe want to be telling someone off, and he puts it in such a nice way that the fella thinks you're paying him a compliment! That can be a difficulty with an interpreter.

But gradually there were one or two of the players who spoke a fair bit of English as well and that was a tremendous help to me concerning the tactics and the playing side of things. I also picked up things at school, little sentences and the time of the kick-off and stuff like that. As for the players, they all have about five names, but you only address them as one name. I found it, I must say, in later years when I come back, I found it very interesting, and I was delighted that I went.

Of course having been on holiday, you're there for two weeks and you think 'Oh, I'd love to live there, you know'. But when it gets a bit longer, you obviously think 'Well, maybe I would like to live here'. Portugal is a lovely country, and of course after the first six weeks there, you get into a way of life because all you are over there is the trainer. You go in for training in the morning about half past nine or 10 o'clock. You've got the doctor there weighing them, taking their weights, and the players sign in at a specific time to make sure they're not late for training. Their kit is put out for them. They go out themselves and warm up and do a few stretches. They're very organised, and then you come out and explain to them want you want, and they would go about it. Sometimes they came up to me and say 'Mister, too hard! Too much running without the ball!', because they loved to play with the ball. It was quite true when they said that 'Mister, the ball is for playing with, and when we've got no ball we cannot play and win matches!'

It was then that you realised that you had to get the training right and get them fit first of all. They always admired the physical attributes of the British player. The Portuguese would say that technically the British are not as good as them but they're physically stronger, and of course their eating habits were right even then. They had a dietician there with the club as well, who would let the players know what they could and couldn't eat. He did the menu for the players, and the surprising thing before the match was that at about 12 o'clock when the players were having Lunch, the game was usually at 4 o'clock, they could have a glass of red wine!

The club were very good to me when I left Porto, and they could learn a lot from it here, the way things were handled. There is no hassle. For example, when my contract was finishing in May, they brought in a new coach to work with me in about March, to give him some idea as to what had been going on. They were great believers in that it was easier to change a coach than to change the team. Maybe a coach comes in and he doesn't fancy the players that he's got, but it's easier to change just one man than it is to change eleven or twelve. So they got the new coach to come in and work with the outgoing coach, as they did with me, with an eight-week run with the current coach, successful or not successful. They copy him, they make notes and they see what you're doing right, and doing wrong, in their opinion. So in that way, he gets an insight into everything before he actually takes over. I think it's a great idea.

I went home first before going to Hull City, but I'll tell you the good thing about over there in Portugal. If they sack you, maybe say six months before your contract finishes, i.e. for bad results, they pay you your full salary and there's no haggling. So if you were a failure, they felt that it was their fault and not the coach's. They picked the wrong coach, and they paid you your full salary. There's no hassle, aggravation and no fighting like they have over here right now. When I came home, I must have been back for about a month, and Terry Neill who is a friend of mine, was the player/manager at Hull City. He wanted me as a sort of consultant/assistant, he asked me if I would go with him and I said yes. But I said that if there was another job that came up as a number one, and I had never been an assistant before, would it be alright to pursue it? And he said yes, no problem, so I went to Hull City and they were a lovely club.

In Portugal, they were brought up to expect coaches to come and go, so it was no big disappointment to them when I left. It's a case of 'The king is dead, long live the king'. So they accepted the new coach coming in, and that's the way Portuguese football works. It's exceptional to get a coach in Portugal to stay four or five years with the one club – most unusual.

My last match in charge of Porto just went off as another game. We went out with the team and got a terrific reception. Well it wasn't just for me, the team did as well. But I got an exceptional send-off, and after the game as well. The following Wednesday, the club held a big function at a large hotel for me. All the players were there, and they made a presentation to us. I must admit they did it wonderfully well. They thanked me for my services, and wished me bon voyage and good luck for the future.

Well I didn't fly home to the UK – I drove home. I had so many presents and bottles of wine and port wine from well-wishers, that my car was absolutely loaded to the brim! I drove home through Portugal and Spain.

I would have to say that initially I was a bit apprehensive when I signed the contract, and wondering whether I would ever return to English football again. And I wondered whether I would I learn the language, because my English wasn't all that good at the time! So what chance would I have of learning Portuguese?! But gradually I could see things improving and getting better. But I missed the banter at home, the aggravation if you like, at home. I guess I missed the whole scene at home, and although I enjoyed my stay in Portugal – I wouldn't have missed it for the world – when I switched the car engine on to drive back to the UK, I was looking forward to coming home."

Following his spell at Hull City, Tommy was the Scottish national manager until December 1972, when he became manager of Manchester United. He was in charge at Old Trafford until July 1977, during which time he won the Second Division Championship in 1975 and the FA Cup in 1977. After leaving Manchester United, he managed at Derby County and again at Queens Park Rangers. We pick up Tommy's story in October 1980:

"Before going to Sydney Olympic in October 1980, I'd actually been out there twice before. I went with Chelsea in 1965, and we went there for about nine weeks. We played about eleven matches all over the place, which was fantastic, and then we went with Man United in 1975, and played about four or five games there, mostly against select elevens and national teams, because the club football wasn't strong enough. Whilst I was out there, I met a little fella who'd been a friend for life called Johnny, a little Scots fella who many years ago was demobbed from the Army, and on his way home he'd jumped off the ship at Sydney and never went back to Scotland because he liked it so much. He got into business there and did well.

So when I finished at Derby in May 1979 he rang me up and asked me whether I had ever thought of working in Australia. I said that quite honestly I hadn't actually, because the football set-up out there wasn't big enough, and he said 'Well, it's improving all the time, and if you fancy coming out for a job and a bit of a holiday, see how it goes and I can fix you up with a lovely little club called Sydney Olympic'. Which was Johnny's local club.

So my wife and I flew out there, and we met up with little John and the president of Sydney Olympic, John Constantine. We talked things over and I said I'd give it a go for a bit. I got to like it, but for me it was part-holiday part-football. It was like the Vauxhall Conference here, in terms of the level of football, and we trained on Tuesday, Thursday and Friday and played on the Sunday. The best way I could describe it was that there was a lot of excellent talent out there, but it was like the Vauxhall Conference, and you had to sort of, well, some games, you had to remove the cattle from the field before you started! It was strange actually, but the Greek people out there were fanatical. They're brilliant winners but not good losers and they're not good for drawing either. But winning – there's nobody better when they win. We were getting gates of about twelve to fourteen thousand at Sydney Olympic, because the Greeks are football mad, and this for a part-time football team.

When I arrived I asked them 'When do I meet the players?', and they said 'We've only got one!' He was a lad called Graham Jenkins, and I remember him vividly, because he was an outside-left. I turned him into a left-back, and later on he went on to play forty-nine times for Australia. He was a great player. Anyway, my friend John, the little Scottish gentleman who I met, said he had some great contacts, and after one thing and another, we got going and I signed some great players.

We had a great first season and finished runners-up in the

Championship to Sydney City, who used to be called Hakla. They had a lot of good players as well. It was during that time they changed all the names of the clubs, because there were so many ethnic clubs out there. I had a great spell out in Australia, and I had it in my contract that if anyone ever came in for me, I would be at liberty to return to the UK I had a great time and it was a great holiday. I recharged my batteries, we did ever so well, produced a lot of good players for the national team, and then Preston North End came in for me.

I went back to Preston and it didn't work out. Then I went back to Sydney, to South Melbourne Hellas, the same team that Man United played in the World Club Championship in Brazil last year. I think it's going to take a long while for the game to go anywhere in Australia at club level, but they've got marvellous talent. If I was the manager of Man United, I'd have a full-time coach in Australia, because the talent out there was unbelievable.

Australia only just missed out on the World Cup Finals in France, but they might have a great chance of going in this time because they are producing so much talent. Most of their players are playing in Europe now, particularly with English clubs. Take Harry Kewell at Leeds – he's world-class.

I took a couple of Man United players over there as well. One of them was Stevie Patterson. He did very well out there, went on to play in Tokyo and is now the manager of Inverness Caledonian Thistle.

The attitude of the players in Portugal was fantastic. They were absolutely brilliant and true professionals. In Australia, they were semi-professional and all had decent jobs. They didn't get any money for playing except a bonus as a premium for winning. So if they won a match they got some money, and if they didn't win they got nothing. The attitude out there was semi-professional, because we had a few British players who were brought out as well. They had jobs and were playing part-time or non- League in England, or were failed professionals for want of a better word. They were coming out there, so you were dealing with a different type of animal altogether. Some wanted to do really well, and for others it was just a game of football.

With the situation in Melbourne and the Aussie players, it was like a pub team. But they were smashing lads – they weren't 'bad lads' at all – and when you went to play a game, it would be like a social weekend. If you won great, and if you didn't 'so what'. They had a few jars afterwards, go back to the ground and pick up their car and go away, and apart from match days on Sunday, you only saw them for training on the Wednesday because they all worked.

This was on a rented ground. So after being at Man United especially, and coming out to Sydney Olympic, I found it a bit different. The English media made a big thing of me going out there, because I'd gone out to Sydney, and they took a film of me coaching and working. For me personally, it was a big long holiday to recharge my batteries after all the turmoil I'd had in England.

I would say to any young manager who gets the opportunity to go abroad and work and coach abroad to snap it up with both hands, because it's a fantastic experience, which will surely stand him in good stead in years to come in the future. You'll learn about how to work with directors of a club, how to work without the press, but through a media advisor in your own club. You don't have the chairman telling you who to buy and sell, in terms of players. They buy the players, and you coach them. You are a coach and nothing else. You don't have any press conferences before, during or after a game, and as I said that's done by your attaché. For example, you spoke to the attaché and he gave the news to the press. It was like a sporting club in Oporto rather than just a football club, with the football, the hockey, skating and basketball. So you had great coverage of all sports, even cycling, every sport that you can think of – except synchronised swimming! In the Portuguese paper 'A Bola' they had coverage on every conceivable sport. And so you're there as a bona fide coach, and if you do that to the best of your ability and you're successful, you're a hero".

After returning to the UK from Australia, Tommy managed Wolverhampton Wanderers from 1984 to 1985 and Altrincham from October 1987 to February 1988.

He now lives in the North of England, and divides his time between numerous media commitments and maintaining his position as the much sought after doyen of the after-dinner speaking circuit.

Kelly Smith

PLAYER
Philadelphia Charge, (USA), July 1999 – Present

Kelly Smith has been called the 'Michael Owen' of British women's football, and at the age of 22 has so far accomplished more than most players have in an entire career. She began her playing career in the UK with Arsenal ladies, most notably scoring two goals in the 3-0 win over Liverpool to clinch the 1995-96 women's Premier League Title. By that time she had won the first of 26 England Caps (correct at time of publication). Kelly then went to the USA to study, and played for Seton Hall University, where she performed so well, scoring 76 goals in just 51 games, that the University retired her Number 6 shirt! She also played for two summers for the New Jersey Lady Stallions of the W-1 League. We pick up Kelly's story in 1999:

"I first heard that I had a professional contract when my agent told me that I had been picked to play for the Philadelphia Charge. I either wanted to play for New York or Philly because I wanted to stay near to my friends from Seton Hall. I had always wanted to play professionally so I wasn't going to turn this opportunity down. My family were happy for me to play for Philadelphia, just as they were while I was playing in college over there. At that time I had just finished college, and was working for Seton Hall as the assistant women's coach. I worked there for a year. When I signed for Philadelphia, we knew about the formation of the women's League, and Seton Hall were very happy for me to go, and were good in not standing in my way.

It wasn't the first time I'd been to Philadelphia, because I have some friends from Seton Hall who come from there, and I'd been to visit them. I didn't know anything about the Philadelphia Charge side because it was a brand new team. Everything and everybody was new. All the members of the team met in California for pre-season training. Flights were scheduled for us, we all met in the airport and then drove to the hotel. This was the first time the team had met, and we spent a month training and preparing for the season at the San Juan Capistrano training camp. Our coach is Mark Krikorian and we play at the 11,800 capacity Villanova stadium

The new women's League, the WUSA (Women's United Soccer Association), was made up of eight teams based in Atlanta, New York, Philadelphia, Boston, San Diego, San Francisco Bay Area, Washington DC and Carolina. Almost all of the US national team members play in the League, and each team has had at least one squad member allocated from the US side. For example, Brandi Chastain plays for the Bay Area CyberRays, and Mia Hamm and the Brazilian Pretinha for the Washington Freedom. The League allowed for sixteen non-US players to be drafted, making two per team. I was picked with the German player Doris Fitchen and we were second in the draft.

I think it surprised a lot of people that Philadelphia picked Doris and me instead of some of the household names of women's football such as the quartet of Brazilians, Sissi, Pretinha, Roseli and Katia, or Charmaine Hooper from Canada. Unlike the others, including Doris, I didn't have the global TV exposure the others had during the 200 Olympics in Sydney because I didn't play there.

The club didn't find me any accommodation for me because I wanted to do it by myself. I lived in New Jersey, so each weekend I would take the two-hour drive to Philadelphia to hunt for an apartment. So it was easy for me to find somewhere to live, but for the girls who came a long way the club made sure that accommodation was found for them.

My most memorable game has to be my first ever professional game out in San Diego. Nobody expected us to beat them, but we won 2-0. I was brought down in the box for a penalty, which we scored, and I scored the second goal. So things were going very well for me, but a very sad moment was hearing that my manager Norman Burns had had a heart attack and died while I was in college, so I immediately flew back for the funeral. I played all my youth football for this man. He was a great guy who I loved and had so much respect for.

My best ever goal was the one I scored for England in the European Championship play-off against the Ukraine. It was during the first leg, which was held in the Ukraine on the day of my twenty-second birthday. Since I hadn't played in the previous qualifying games, coach Hope Powell wanted to use the same eleven players for continuity and I wasn't one of the starters. I came on in the second-half as a forward. In the 58th minute I took a cross from the right, and I hit a left-foot volley from just inside the top of the box. Even though it was the first international goal I had scored in a while, I didn't think of it that way. It was just such an important goal, because we didn't play well in the first half and then I came on and felt like I made a difference. I was just happy that we'd scored, rather than thinking about my own statistics. Later in the second half, I took the ball from the right, cut in and fed it to Karen Walker. She had a shot from outside the box, and the Ukrainian keeper fumbled it and it went through her legs. We felt pretty pleased at that point, but the Ukrainians scored in the last ten seconds, which was disappointing because we felt we'd blown it a bit, and given them a chance of getting through in the second leg in England.

The anticipation for the second playoff match back in England was tremendous. It had been five years since England had qualified for a major Championships, so there was a huge amount of pressure on us the whole week, and even though we had a 2-1 lead from the first leg, everyone was nervous. The media coverage was much more intense than usual, there were photographers and journalists at every training session, and there was an expectation for us to win.

We heard that there would be a 9,000 crowd at Leyton Orient's Brisbane Road ground, so the excitement was definitely building by the time we played. I started the match on the right side of midfield, a position I had never played before because I am left-footed, but I was in the side replacing the injured Karen Burke. Despite that, I felt that I played well, created a lot of chances had a few good shots, and just ran at them with the ball. I ran them ragged.

We eventually won the match 2-0, and the tie 4-1 on aggregate, to qualify for the 2001 European Championships. It was a fantastic moment, and I'd never seen everyone come together so much as a team and celebrate so much. We did a lap of honour around the pitch and I threw my shirt into the crowd – although I was wearing a T-shirt on underneath! Then we had some champagne in the dressing-room afterwards, and it felt great because we'd actually qualified for a major tournament after so many near misses, and only playing in qualifying games.

When we heard the draw for the European Championships, we knew it was going to be tough. We were drawn with Germany, the defending champions, Sweden, and Russia, but we were determined to show people that we weren't just going to make up the numbers, and I think we had a point to prove. The England squad met up at the Burnham Beeches hotel, not far from where my parents live in Watford. After dinner we tried on our England suits, and all looked very sharp in our black trouser suits with a purple shirt – we looked the business!

We went to Germany on June 18th, and some of the girls decided to wear purple nail varnish to match their purple shirts. The England goalkeeper Pauline Copes' excuse for not wearing the varnish was that she felt it made her hands too heavy! The whole table fell about with laughter, but she was dead serious and insisted that her hands did feel really heavy! I thought it was hilarious.

The whole squad went to the first game of the tournament, between Germany and Sweden, two of the teams in our group. On the bus to the game, all the England players and myself had small bets amongst ourselves as to which minute the first goal would be scored. I put down the 14th minute, as I had a good feeling about that number. And lo and behold the first goal was scored....in the 14th minute, so I won! That was a good start to the tournament for me!

We trained after that game in the Jena stadium, and unfortunately I hurt my ankle during the session. Nobody was around me and I just rolled it while I was tracking back. That was a very frustrating moment because it meant that I would miss the opening game of the tournament.

Our first game was against Russia on June 24th. Angie Banks opened the scoring for us with a very well worked goal, but I felt that we took our foot off the pedal and allowed the Russians to come back into the game, which you can't do in international football. I came on as a sub for the last twenty minutes and didn't play particularly well. We came away disappointed with a draw because it was a game that we knew we could have won, but at least we came away with a point.

Our second game was against Sweden on June 27th, and they were by far the better team on the day. They were a quality side, we struggled to match their intensity, and even though we were 2-0 down at half-time, we were still in the game. I came on five minutes into the second half, but they scored soon afterwards and that was the killer blow. I played much better than the previous game and was more relaxed, but the Swedes won 4-0.

Everybody was really up for the game against Germany on June 30th as we felt we had nothing to lose, and this was reflected in our performance, which was probably the best I have been involved with in an England side. Although we lost 3-0 the scoreline didn't tell the whole story about the game. The Germans panicked when our forwards, including myself, ran at them, we hit the post twice, and I had a penalty saved. Germany qualified for the semi-finals, and eventually beat Sweden 1-0 in the Final to regain their title. So I was pleased for Doris Fitchen and her team.

Overall I think it was a great experience for me, and I can only grow as a player given the experiences I had. Our only major fault as a team during the tournament was that at times we had periods where we lacked concentration, for example during the ten-minute period against Germany. I hope that we learned as a team during the tournament, because football is a ninety-minute game, and you cannot afford to switch off or you will get punished. I'd been itching to play on the big stage, and since having that chance I am hungry for more! Our next aim is to qualify for the women's World Cup in China in 2003.

Who are my favourite players? When I was growing up, my favourite player was Ian Wright for his determination, goal scoring ability and his energy for the game. My current favourite player is Zinedine Zidane because he is so skilful with the ball, and has amazing awareness of where his team-mates are. The best player I had ever played with has to be Doris Fitchen, who has over 100 caps for Germany as a centre-back, and also plays for the Philadelphia Charge. She is a great defender who reads the game so well, and is a leader by her actions. The main difference I have found between college and professional football is that everybody is so much quicker, stronger and smarter in professional football, so that has been a learning curve for me.

As for media appearances, I recently did a commercial for the Wendys food chain last May along with fellow Philadelphia Charge players Lorrie Fair, Heather Mitts, and Jen Tietjen. We did a promotion for Wendys which gave the fans a chance to win tickets for Charge games and be honorary captain for a game.

Even though things have been going really well for me in Philadelphia, my major lows this season have been my injuries. I was diagnosed with a stress fracture of the right ankle after only the second game of the season, and had to sit out six weeks of the season. Then I sprained my left ankle very badly during my first game back after injury. After that, I then missed two weeks of the WUSA (the US Women's League) through international duty with England at the 2001 European Championships in Germany, even though I was still struggling with my sprained ankle.

At the moment (August 2001), it's the WUSA playoffs and me and my team-mates can hardly wait. It is such a nice position to be in, considering all the pre-season polls ranked us eighth out of eight, the worst team in the League, and gave us no hope of reaching the play-offs. Our team is so proud to be here because we have all worked tremendously hard both on and off the field, and proved everybody wrong. We feel confident that we can beat Atlanta and go all the way to the Finals in Foxboro. It will be a special game for me, because with my ankle injury I've only played once against them. It should be a great game on the 18th August.

My career targets are to win the WUSA League with the Philadelphia Charge, to finish top scorer, and to qualify this year for the women's World Cup with England. As for the women's game in general, I think it has developed a lot within the last four years, and has a great future.

If any young English girl asked me for advice on whether to play abroad, I would say you have to do it, as it is a once in a lifetime opportunity. The WUSA is without doubt the best League for women to play in, because all the best international players are here."

Kelly Smith, as previously mentioned, is still playing for the Philadelphia Charge in the WUSA. For more information about Kelly, readers are free to visit her website, ***KellySmithSoccer.com***

Allan Harris

MANAGER
FC Barcelona, (Spain), 1984 – 1987 (coach)
Sporting Club, (Kuwait), 1992 – 1993
El Aly, (Egypt), 1993 – 1996
Izmir, (Turkey), 1997 – 1998
Malaysian national team, 1999 – Present

As can be seen above, Allan Harris has an impressive managerial CV, but before moving into the coaching side of football, he also enjoyed a distinguished playing career, starting off with England schoolboys.

He began his professional playing career with a six-year spell at Chelsea in 1958, as one of 'Drake's Ducklings'. A move to Coventry City, at the time managed by Jimmy Hill, followed before he went back to Chelsea for a season in 1966. He then went on to play at QPR for four happy seasons, and Finally Plymouth, where he ended his playing career.

Allan's first coaching job was at Crystal Palace where he teamed up with fellow coaching newcomer and former Chelsea and QPR team-mate Terry Venables, a partnership that was to enjoy much success both then and in later years. Promotions from the old Third and Second Divisions followed in the late 1970s, before Allan (and Terry) moved to QPR in 1980. He spent four years at Loftus Road, during which time the team was promoted to the old First Division and were FA Cup Finalists in 1982. We pick up Allan's story in May 1984:

"It was towards the end of the 1983-84 season that Terry had the offer to go to Barcelona. He then asked whether I would like to go there with him or stay and take over at Queens Park Rangers. I had already played at Barcelona with Chelsea in the Inter Cities Fairs Cup. We got to the semi-final one year and we played Barcelona. I saw the stadium and the wonderful facilities they had over there, so when Terry asked me whether he would like to come with me, I had no hesitation in saying yes. This was because I feel that there are a lot of players and coaches in this country who bury their head in the sand somewhat, whereas I wanted to open my mind to the different experience of continental football. So when you get an offer like that from Barcelona, it was a case of there being no turning back or second thoughts. If I can describe it, looking back, it was a bit like having a small part in Eastenders and then getting a part in a film in Hollywood! It was that big a jump, and that's no discredit to Queens Park Rangers because I had four very happy years as a player and four more as a coach there. So Terry had decided what he was going to do, and I went to see Jim Gregory, the chairman of Queens Park Rangers, who I got on very well with. He was OK about me going, because he knew that I was ambitious, and he gave me his blessing. It was a very amicable departure from the club.

My family were very supportive when I told them that I was going there. They knew what a big club Barcelona was, and I don't think people realise how big a club it is until they either work or live in this beautiful city. But what I liked most about Barcelona is that they kind of 'brainwash' you in some way, and I don't mean that in a bad way at all. I mean that in as much as they treat you so well, that their idea is that when you go away from the club and out into the world, you only speak well of Barcelona with everybody you meet. I've found that ever since I left the club in 1987, everyone always says to me that I'm always going on about Barcelona! But they do treat you so well. Two years ago, we had a Centenary Dinner, and they flew all the ex-players and ex-coaches over to Barcelona for a three-day gala event, so that's the sort of club they are. Our average attendance for League games in the year we won the League title (in 1985) was 99,000, and for the big games it was 120,000.

It was a great experience, and looking back now I just wish I could have gone there as a player. Their motto is 'more than a club' [AUTHOR'S NOTE: 'mes que un club' in Catalan], and you realise this when you look at things like them not having a sponsor's logo on their shirts. I mentioned this one day to Nunez, the president, and he just said 'We don't need the money'. I've coached clubs that have played in the San Siro, and you can talk about the top Brazilian, Italian and Spanish teams, but I still say that in my opinion, Barcelona is definitely one of the biggest clubs in the world.

As for the language, I didn't speak any Spanish before I went out there but Terry spoke a little bit. I don't know whether he had got wind that Barcelona might have been after him! But we had lessons out there, although I didn't find it a problem working with the footballers because they knew what you meant straight away, and little by little you pick up words. The only problem I did have at the beginning was that I had to use an interpreter, and sometimes you do get a bit misquoted, even though he was very good. A lot of the people in the city spoke English anyway, so I never had any problems on that score.

When we arrived at the airport, there was a big reception for us. They're very much into the media side of things over there, and that's the first lesson you learn. When I went to Malaysia two years ago, the locals told me that I'd have a lot of pressure from the media, so then I explained to them that I'd been at Barcelona, and no-one had more pressure on them than there. Until you go there, you don't realise how intense it is.

The first thing we had to do after our appointment was to be introduced to the crowd. We had a training session and nearly 70,000 people turned up, just to see us, greet us and watch the training session. That was an ordeal in itself. But 'Barca' is not like any other club where I've coached or played, with regard to their fans. They're not vibrant, or like some fans in Turkey where there is a lunatic element, but in Barcelona it's very much like going to the Theatre or the Ballet. My wife used to come to the games with her nicest coat on, and she said it was very much like going to the Opera. In a way it was sedate, in spite of the massive crowd. I found that the people there were lovely, and the club officials were tremendous.

The domestic side of things was handled very well for us by the then vice-president, now president, Joan Gaspart, a wonderful man who I got on with very well. He also struck up a good friendship with Steve Archibald. I actually lived in one of his hotels, and had two suites there, so he certainly made sure that everything was OK for me. It's nice to know that he's now been made president of Barcelona, and he's deserved that success because he's a nice man, very honest with a lovely family, and has worked very hard. I also found him a great guy to get on with, so if I had any problems I would go to Joan Gaspart. He helped deal with any problems the 'Brits' had.

When we first arrived at Barcelona, there was an interesting story concerning Diego Maradona. During one of our first meetings after we signed, the directors asked us 'What do you want to do with Maradona?' Now the true story, and I always went to all the meetings with Terry, was that Maradona had been 'tacked', so to speak, by Napoli, so I was under the impression that he wanted to go. I think he'd deliberately upset a few of the directors, as well as a section of the crowd, because he wanted to get away from Barcelona. The directors then asked us what our decision was concerning Maradona, and that they would support us whatever we chose to do. So Terry and me had a chat, and we thought that if he was unhappy, and we forced him to stay at Barcelona and play against his will, he wasn't going to be the same effective player that he had been at Boca Juniors.

We then went back to the board of directors and put forward the name of the player to replace Maradona – it was Steve Archibald. I'll never forget their response – 'Who?!' They were very keen for us to sign the Mexican international striker Hugo Sanchez, a very good player, but me and Terry knew all about Archibald, what a good player he was, and how he would have a positive impact on the team, which he did. I remember us leaving that meeting, and the board saying to Terry that if we let Maradona go and we brought in Archibald, that he would have to sign a legal disclaimer saying that it was his responsibility and decision, and not theirs!

That was to make sure they didn't take any stick if it went wrong.

After we'd finished our pre-season training in Andorra, our first away game was at Real Madrid. Talk about a baptism of fire! You can't get any tougher than that. So we went there, to a packed house of 90,000 fanatical fans, and Terry and me realised it was no time to be messing about! But we won 3-0, and that was another occasion when you saw people's reactions to you change from being a little bit hesitant, wondering what these two new English guys were going to do, to being ecstatic after we'd won 3-0, and deserved to win 3-0. I think that set the standard for the rest of the season, and was a big reason as to why we won the League in our first year. That first victory, where we absolutely slaughtered Madrid, got everyone excited. The directors and the supporters were right behind us from that moment, and I remember Brian Clough telling us that we could walk on water from then on. So we won the League the first year we were there, with Archibald and without Maradona, and after that we knew that we could walk on water for two or three years.

With regard to the media, both out in Spain and in general, I've always made a point of saying that I think everybody has a job to do, and they've got a particularly difficult one. The only thing I did find after leaving Britain was that the Spanish press never printed 'muck-raking' stories, or stories about your private life. They just dealt with football, and your involvement with that side of things. So you knew where you stood: you were joining a big club, a great club, and you were defined on results. If the results were bad, you knew you would get the sack.

I remember a story the English press printed that bears all this out. A lot of the English press had gone out with Menotti, we then went out with Menotti and he had said to us 'You two won't last a year. You won't be able to handle the pressure, the press and people stabbing you in the back'. But to be fair he was a very nice guy and he wished us well. I also remember Maradona coming over to our table and wishing us well for the future, and he too seemed a very nice guy. So we started everything off on the right foot, but we knew that we were going to be judged on results. If you were doing well the press were OK, but I find in England that the press do delve into the 'muck and bullets' side of things, and not just on the results.

So it was a welcome change, not least because of the era we were going through in England which made me say yes to the Barcelona job, because I was sick and tired of the hooliganism at football matches. There were a lot of problems at that time, at Heysel and other places, and there was always an undercurrent of violence. In my opinion, the people in charge weren't dealing with the problem, and it was just nice to go to Spanish games, particularly their away games, where you had no riots or crowd trouble and women brought their kids to the game – it was a family affair. When you were in your seat during the game, you could order a Havana cigar or a brandy, and they'd bring it to you. The waiter service, and all their other facilities, was ten years ahead of anything we had over in England at the time. I spent three and a half years over in Spain and I never saw any crowd trouble whatsoever at the games.

As for the needle games, our matches against city rivals Espanol were probably the equivalent of Arsenal versus Millwall today, with Barcelona being at the Arsenal level. They were only a small club, but as it was a local derby they were always difficult games. But the two games that stick in my mind and stand out were firstly our European Cup semi-final second leg game against IFK Gothenburg. We'd already lost 3-0 in the away leg, and then we won 3-0 in the Nou Camp, Finally beating them in extra time to get into the final of the European Cup. The other game, which was interesting even though we lost it, was the one against Steaua Bucharest in the European Cup Final in 1986. We didn't play well, but that was the first time I'd ever been involved in a game where the opposition seemingly wanted to play for a 0-0 draw right from the first whistle to the last, and take their chances after extra-time in the penalty shootout. I'd loved to have known whether their coach told them to play for penalties right from the start! We lost the penalty shootout, and that was the biggest disappointment.

One of the greatest memories for me was after winning the League title in 1985, with about four or five games to go, Terry and me came back to Barcelona not knowing what sort of celebration they had planned. The trip from the airport to the stadium usually took about twenty minutes, but that night it took us about seven hours! There must have been about five million people there to greet us. When we eventually arrived at the stadium, at about midnight, we found that it was full of fans who had literally waited all day, just so they could greet us. It was mind-boggling, and just brought home to me that it was a big club in every sense.

Winning the League was a great fillip for us, and gave us time to bring in new players like Lineker and Hughes, but we were always under immense pressure at Barcelona. After we won the League title in 1985, and Barcelona hadn't won it for eleven years before that, we had what we thought was a good set of results the following season. But even though we won the League Cup and finished runners-up in the European Cup, the Spanish FA Cup and in the League, behind Real Madrid, I remember that the directors said to us in a meeting that we'd had a poor season! So that gives you a good idea of the pressure we were under.

Another memory I have of my time there dates back to the last season that me and Terry were there. We'd played about six games in the League and had just lost our second home game. Now what the fans do in Spain, if they want you out, is to wave their handkerchiefs in the stands. So when they do this it's a case of them 'having a go' at the president, but of course the president never leaves! We were losing this particular game 2-0, the away side had just scored, the handkerchiefs were swirling all around the ground, and I turned round to Terry and we both laughed and said 'We'd better start packing our bags – I don't think we've got much time left!' And within a week we had gone. Looking back now, we survived a lot longer than we thought we would. I don't know what Terry would say, but football-wise they were three and a half wonderful years for me. It was also a wonderful city, and a pleasure to have worked for FC Barcelona.

Of all the funny things that happened during my time with 'Barca', there is one that stands out. We were sitting on the bench during a game in Santander which we were winning. It was one of those benches where you weren't undercover, as it was only a small ground. Terry was sitting next to me, and all of a sudden an old woman of about 80 started hitting him over the head with a handbag!!

Another funny thing took place at our first training session. We were introduced to the players, we shook hands with them, and then we asked them to go the training pitch to do all our talking there. We went out there, and with us being English and not used to the sun out there, and saw all the players standing underneath a tree which was near the training ground. I remember saying to Terry that this looked like our first 'revolt', and that they already didn't like us! But when we got to know them, it was simply a case of them not wanting to stand in the very hot sun.

One of the things I noticed back then was that the players were very professional in every way. They'd just have their one glass of wine and celebrate with their wives in a cafe or a restaurant. Schuster was the player of the year when we won the League title – he also spoke about seven languages. But I was amazed, after having just left the English League, to see how dedicated they were and how they wanted to train and learn. I think that it wasn't the case in the UK because at that time there weren't a lot of foreign coaches in the English game. I think it has changed somewhat now, but in those days I found it a joy to take the Barcelona training sessions. You organised a certain aspect of the training, you wanted it done, and they would do it.

Barcelona also had their own private clinic in the stadium, and if you were a season ticket holder, or 'soci' as they're known in Catalan, and you fell ill, you could go to the clinic in the stadium as well. Everything at the club was 'double' there, and by that I mean that there were two physios, two doctors, two trainers and two kit guys. I think their attitude was 'We'll give you everything. All we want you to do is perform'. The whole set-up was all so meticulously planned and run.

I've been at many clubs where you're eventually sacked or you leave, something which every manager goes through, but I particularly remember the day we left Barcelona. All the players were made to line up in a big banqueting room, and all the directors and very important club officials came in. They shook our hands, everything was settled, and they wanted you to go away with no bad feelings or grudges about the club. That's what I meant about the 'brainwashing' thing I was talking to you about earlier. They didn't'brainwash' you deliberately, but you can see how enthusiastic I still am about FC Barcelona.

My links with the club certainly didn't end there. I'd been back a few times to see some games and a few friends. I then got an invitation to the European Cup Final at Wembley stadium in 1992 to see Barcelona take on Sampdoria. I didn't ask for these tickets – they just sent me two tickets for me and my wife to go. We also had dinner afterwards at the Hilton, again provided for by the club. They are so meticulous with the small things, and if you ever play for Barcelona they will never forget you. None of the people I've come across who in some way have been involved with FC Barcelona, whether they were a player or a coach, have ever held a grudge against them or moaned about them – it's uncanny. I wrote to Bobby Robson when he went to coach Barcelona. I told him that he would enjoy it there, and I also asked him to tell me what he thought of it after he left. He's always said to me that I was right and that it was fantastic.

After the European Cup Final in 1992, I went down to the dressing room to see the then vice-president Joan Gaspart just to say hello, and he and Johan Cruyff invited me into the dressing-room because, as he said, 'You have coached some of these boys'. I went into the dressing-room, and in one corner the players were celebrating. But in the other corner there was Jose Carreras and Seve Ballesteros! They were such nice guys and they told me how they remembered me and Terry when we were coaching there, just small talk really but still fantastic.

The best player I coached in my entire career was Bernd Schuster, because I felt he had everything needed to make a world-class footballer. People said he was moody and was a bad influence, but I never had a problem with him at all, either on or off the pitch. I don't know whether that was down to my man-management or motivational style, but we used to have long talks about lots of things. He was a very clever boy and the best striker of a ball I've ever seen. The pitch always seemed to be very big at the Nou Camp, but he could hit balls across it that were like Scud missiles!

There were a lot of other great players there as well, but unfortunately since I've been in Malaysia, I've heard about the death of the goalkeeper who played during our time at the club, a guy called Urruti. Now he was a real character. I think all 'keepers have got a screw loose, but he was such a lovely guy and so friendly. He would take you back to meet his family and would make you welcome. Urruti was also a big friend of Steve Archibald's, and helped him a lot when he first arrived at the club. He was a good goalkeeper, and I was very sad to hear of his sudden death. Everyone would say, regardless of whether he was a good player or not, and he was, that he was such a lovely person and very well liked at Barcelona, so it was particularly sad for me when I sent my condolences to his family.

As for our coaching style, we basically kept the same tactics and way of playing that we'd used in England. Funnily enough, because I was quite fit and I used to play in the training games with the players, I found that my first touch improved! We didn't change a lot of things, and like I said before they always did what we asked them to. We made them more disciplined, and infused them with a bit more fighting spirit, which was something you didn't always find with Spanish and Italian sides at that time because they would let their heads drop if things were going against them. We had a good bunch of lads, with a similar team spirit to what Manchester United have now, and I had a fantastic time.

Just before we left the club, I remember Terry had gone back to England for a couple of days and there were lots of different rumours. I thought to myself that we'd better be prepared for the sack. It wasn't a situation like it is nowadays where if the manager leaves a club, the assistant takes over. I was prepared to go straight away and there was no hesitation on my part, because I believe that if you are an assistant to the manager, you are just as responsible for the success or failure of the team as the manager. I'd had three and a half very happy years, the directors called us in and said the results hadn't gone well, and the crowd wanted a change. But we couldn't moan about anything because the club treated us very well. We'd had success but couldn't keep going forever, and the club was very honest with us. It certainly wasn't a case of us reading things in the newspapers first and then being told about them later: it wasn't like that at all. The club always met things head on, and we took the parting of the ways with good grace, which I think went down well with them. Whenever I go back they make me feel welcome.

I remember one day when Terry rang me and said that we'd both been invited to Rome to meet the Pope! The story was that ten years before the Pope had said Mass at the Nou Camp, and even though it was pouring with rain there were 120,000 people in the stadium and another 100,000 outside. And the story was that he had told the directors that if the team ever wanted to go to Rome to meet him, then he would arrange it! As Barcelona also had a basketball and an athletics team, there was a group of about fifty of us who eventually met him. Terry couldn't make the trip because he was commentating on a game for the BBC, so I took the team. To meet the Pope was the most fantastic thing, because he had such an aura around him. There was also a massive crowd out in Saint Peter's Square, the Vatican officials instructed us as to what to say, and he is such a knowledgeable guy. He spoke in Spanish to the players, and then suddenly switched to English to speak to me and said 'You're the English guy'. His assistant told me that the Pope is a mad-keen football fan. The photograph of us together and the rosary that he gave me are things that football gave me, even though they aren't necessarily 'football' moments if you know what I mean. The fact is that Barcelona were so big that the Pope gave them a private audience, and there aren't many, if any, other clubs who can say that.

I also noticed that the Catalans are a very proud people with strong traditions. This came across forcefully when we played Real Madrid, because of all the politics connected to the Spanish Civil War. There's a little bit of hatred there, but although it's the big event in Spanish football there's no violence. There would be firecrackers, cheering and dancing in the streets, but you wouldn't have people getting drunk or stoned out of their mind. Their pride showed itself after we lost games, and we'd get seventy or eighty year old women coming up to us in the street asking 'Alan. Why did you lose yesterday?' The two things they're fanatical about are religion and football, and not necessarily in that order! I've got so many happy memories that it's always a pleasure to go back.

After leaving Barcelona, I went back to England to work with Terry at Tottenham. By the early 1990s I had worked with Terry for thirteen years, and I felt that it was time for me to branch out on my own, having done all my homework so to speak and learned a lot from Terry. I then had a job offer from Espanol, the Tottenham chairman said I should take the chance, I was ambitious and I went there.

I then came back to the UK again, never thinking that I'd end up visiting and working in so many countries. Now there's two ways of looking at it. What I find in England, and I'm not being detrimental, is that when you start coaching people tell you to get as much experience as you can, and that if you then go to work abroad you get forgotten. So in a way I was 'pushed' abroad, in spite of all my achievements at Barcelona.

I went to Kuwait and won the League Cup with a side out there, but it wasn't on a par with coaching in Egypt. I went to Egypt after Kuwait, and didn't realise how fanatical they were about their football. I managed a top club called El Aly, the translation of which is 'The national club'. It's the biggest club in Africa and the 'mother club' of football there – everyone supports them! We regularly got crowds of 90-100,000 at home games. I did the Double two years in a row with that club and also won the African Cup Winners Cup, so we enjoyed a lot of success. That was a wonderful experience and I had three great years there. Then I had a spell in Turkey with Izmir. I also had a couple of spells away from football during this time, because I think that when you come away from football you see it in a different light. I took a job as a consultant/agent for a year, but I never really enjoyed that as much as being with the players and training, and I kept myself fit. I was yearning to get back into football, but I'm glad I had those two year-long spells out of the game because it recharged my batteries. This was good for me because what happens is that you're under a lot of pressure, especially at the big clubs, and this can damage your health as unfortunately has been demonstrated in the past. I took a year out, and saw so many things differently away from the game, even though I was still involved as a sports consultant organising tours and dealing with players.

After my second one-year spell as a consultant, I went out to Malaysia to mark the papers of the coaches there, for their UEFA licence equivalent exams, and on my day off they asked me whether I would like to come back. I fell in love with the country, and nine months later they contacted me and asked whether I would like to coach the under nineteens and the under twenty-three national sides, and I said yes. I eventually became national manager in December 2000. I've had two great years out there, they haven't interfered, and I've got some good youngsters coming up. Football in Malaysia is not on a par with Europe, so it can be a bit frustrating at times, but it's a lovely place to live and the people are wonderful.

Thailand, who beat Malaysia recently in the final of the South East Asia games, are a rung above us on the football ladder. They're also managed by a Brit, Peter Withe, a lovely guy. In Asia, you've got the top teams who are Japan, South Korea and China, then you've got teams in the middle band such as Thailand, and we in Malaysia are in the third group on the bottom rung of the ladder. But we're working our way up, and in a lot of the tournaments I've coached in I've put a entire team of under twenty-three players out on the pitch, with a view to the long-term development of the Malaysian game. So I think that in the next two years, and I'm there for another year, we'll have a good team, one that will certainly be much better than the ones they've had previously.

As for the world game, when I was coaching in Egypt we toured Africa a lot and I saw so many good players there. I remember saying ten years ago that I saw African countries becoming a major force in world football. I think Asian countries are a little bit behind them at the moment, but they will catch up and will get a kick-start with the World Cup being held in Japan and South Korea. There are already quite a few Chinese and

Japanese players over here in Europe, and I think Asia will one day be like what I said Africa would be ten years ago. It's definitely moving in the right direction.

How do I see football developing in the future? When you go back to how football was in my day, the game has changed completely, and changed for the better. I think that what has been created, is that when you get fitness coaches, dieticians and psychologists there are more people involved with the game. Fitness wise, I don't see how the players can get any fitter, because it's obvious now that if you play football and you aren't fit, you won't make the grade – it's as simple as that. Years ago, if you were skilful you could get by and that was it, but now the fitness is essential. From my point of view my wife is a hypnotherapist, and I think that were will be a lot more of that side of the game coming into the equation. There is a place for sports psychology and that sort of thing now, because now it's so intense and the players are under more pressure, although the players earn fantastic money now – and good luck to them! I certainly don't begrudge them that. Particularly with the television cameras, you can't get away with doing certain things on the pitch like you could in years gone by, and I say that thinking of my brother Ron. If he was playing now, he'd be caught on video and suspended for six months!! So bodychecks and dirty tackles have gone out of the game now, because you'll get fined heavily and suspended if you're seen doing it.

I must say that I've got a soft spot for Chelsea, Tottenham and QPR, but the team that I do like watching is Manchester United. They toured Malaysia in July and August and to a man they conducted themselves extremely well. I also spent two long sessions talking with Sir Alex Ferguson, who I played against as a player. I knew him just to say hello, but I didn't really know him until I got to Malaysia. I like meeting people who aren't on an ego trip, and if ever a guy should be on an ego trip it's him, especially with what he has won in the game. And he is one of the nicest guys I've met in football. We had a two-hour discussion one night, and the next evening he invited me to have dinner with the team. He was absolutely brilliant and I can't speak highly enough of him. Forget those who say he's ruthless and rules with an iron fist, I just found him to be such a nice guy. There are a lot of people in football who are on ego trips and on a different planet, and he definitely isn't one of them. The Manchester United boys conducted themselves well, they hammered our team 6-0, but I had a lot of young boys in the side. Then they went to Singapore and won 8-1. I do like watching his teams play. On a more general level, I go to games now, I look at the football, and I think that it has improved out of all recognition. They are very good professionals, and I don't come away from many games now thinking 'This was boring'.

The greatest influence on my coaching career was Dave Sexton. He was such a nice guy, his footballing knowledge was exceptional, and he was a good coach. What I've learned from my time on the coaching side is that coaching is just one facet of the game. You've got to be good with the press, you've got be a good man-manager with the players, you've got to start off with being a bit hard with the players at first, because if you start off too lightly with them they'll trample all over you! You've also got to have a good knowledge of the game and be a good coach. So it's not just about good coaching, because I've seen good coaches who've been dismissed from football clubs and never got back into football. It's a mixture of being confident, of how you handle players one on one, and how you get your points over. So much of the job is psychological. Dave Sexton would be the one who first 'sparked' me into thinking about coaching. We used to coach together at Spencer Park school in Wandsworth.

My second big influence in coaching was of course Terry Venables – a great coach. I spent thirteen years with him, but it was definitely a two-way street – he helped me with some ideas and I helped him back. So it was a good relationship and partnership.

I've enjoyed coaching on my own as well, working in some lovely countries, but I just feel now sometimes, in spite of all the money in the English game nowadays, that for the good players in England, it would not be a bad thing to go and play abroad. I'll tell you who springs to mind, as an English guy who some people may have thought was a bit childish at times – Steve McManaman. He went to Real Madrid, and he's come back and really grown up. He's learned a language and a different way of life and that shows in his character. He can still go back to clubs in Liverpool and earn a lot of money, but he's earning, and learning, a lot in Madrid anyway.

If I was a player, I would advise anyone now to go and live and play abroad for five or six years – you can always come back. I've spoken to people who have been players, people like Graeme Souness, who said to me that he wished he'd left and gone to play abroad five or six years before he did, and I'm sure that 'Butch' Wilkins, Mark Hateley, and the majority of the people you've interviewed for your book have said the same thing. The thing is, it opens up your mind. It's about learning things and I think that you get a bit closeted in the UK – you put your head in the sand when you're here. That's my advice, and even if players in the Premiership are earning the same amount of money as those at, say, Real Madrid, the actual experience of learning a new language and culture is an incredible one. I look back on where I've been as a coach, and I've still got friends in these places who I talk to and can go out and stay with. I've learned how to deal with different peoples after playing and coaching in all five continents, and it's given me an education in every sense".

As previously mentioned, Allan is still working as Malaysia's national team manager, after recently receiving a one-year extension to his contract.

Final Score

And so we come to the end of this wonderful journey. Nineteen countries, twenty- three players and managers, and a million memories later. And for me, a journey of twenty years has come to a temporary end. Twenty years in which the world, football and I have become less innocent places, but twenty years which have transformed my views and understanding of life and its strange rules.

I cannot but help a wry smile thinking back to my early exposure to football. It was during break-times at Primary school, when we would race to the assembly hall to see the playground rota for who could play in the front and back playgrounds. No ball games were allowed in the front playground, but they were in the back one. The rota was split along gender lines, alternating between Boys and Girls, and was marked 'B' and 'G' (can you imagine the backlash in our PC-obsessed times if that were to happen today?!) But remember, these were more innocent times. The back playground became the boys 'Wembley', and the rota was changed on more than one occasion by delicately crayoning in a few extra lines on the 'G'! This was arguably my first exposure to squad rotation! The rules were also strict in the back playground: no high balls, for fear of knocking the ball into the adjoining road or breaking a window. So good habits were established early – no long balls and no balls above shoulder-height, or an automatic free-kick. Only balls along the ground and to feet. Brian Clough would have approved – but not Charles Hughes!

It was there, in the melee of fifteen v fifteen, that I felt the exhilaration of dribbling, close control and passing, and out of all the great players on display throughout the footballing world at the time, there was one above all others to whom I aspired – Glenn. Forget 'Diamond Lights' and his contributions on Chas and Dave Cup Final records, he was the player I idolised. He was tall like me, he had blondish hair like me, he had a bit of a lolloping gait like me, he had modelled his game on the Brazilian World Cup squad of his childhood like me (him in 1970, me in 1982), but above all he had the defining mark of genius – making the impossible look incredibly easy – that mesmerised and tantalised all those entranced by the way football should and must be played. People of any generation under twenty-five must tire of their elders blathering on about the heroes of their day, but for those youngsters who only know Glenn Hoddle as England manager and much more besides, they missed out on witnessing the elegance, grace and beauty of a thoroughbred, chastised by the British press for lacking 'work rate' and 'commitment'. Yet again, the triumph of the artisan over the artist. It was the ultimate treachery at the time, hoping that Glenn would do well against Saints, but that's how I felt.

Fast forward nineteen years. Nineteen years and a lot of growing up later in my life. The time, July 2001. The place, London Arena. The event, Masters football. A great Sunday evening's entertainment lay in store as I took my seat waiting for events to unfold. But in spite of all the other former football legends on show, there was only one player there. Yes, HE was playing.

After a few goodish games between other teams, he came onto the pitch, playing against Arsenal. The roar of the crowd spoke more eloquently than a thousand lines of poetry. Even the Gooners, in spite of booing him, had respect for the greatest, most mistreated and most outrageously talented English player of his generation.

And then they happened. Two magic moments of Glenn perfection, each of them worth the admission fee alone. A cheeky yet sublime back heel to a colleague brought everyone, and I mean EVERYONE, to their feet. And then, when pinned against the wall by two Arsenal players, a slight of foot, a shimmy and a dummy later, and the Gunners duo were grasping at air, watching him disappear over the horizon towards the Arsenal goal. By squinting slightly, I was taken back in time to the television in my living room twenty years before, watching him weave another spell on the pitch, and in spite of outward maturity I was again jumping up and down with child-like appreciation of exquisite beauty.

And that, dear reader, is the essence not just of football but of life. Many moments of hard work building for the future, with little immediate reward and often no recognition, interspersed with incredible moments of exhilaration, energy and success. In a world ever more isolated, suspicious of fellow human beings and downright lonely, we desperately need some sort of connection, not just to ourselves but to others. Every day in Paris and London, I look into the eyes of those sleepwalking to the station to catch the train to their job, shuffling towards another day of stress and pain. Their eyes are without exception either dead or afraid – afraid of what? Living? Just remember this folks – a rut is a grave with the ends taken out.

I'm no rah-rah-happy-clappy merchant (as hopefully you've realised by now!), but if you take anything from this book, take the message of hope, dreams and being all you want to be in life. It isn't a dress rehearsal, it's here and now, and the stories of all the contributors demonstrate this wonderfully well. Above all be passionate and enthusiastic, each to their own, whatever turns you on. Whatever you do, don't be boring, don't just exist, don't let the joy of life pass you by, don't die regretting what might have been but for a smidgen of guts and a small risk or two taken in the pursuit of happiness and fulfilment. It's life – be in it.

As we get older, the years and the months seemingly pass ever more quickly (we all seem to forget the quarters and halves in our ages once we hit thirty!) and it's hard to believe that next summer will be my sixth World Cup. As already said, much has changed in my life, but no doubt I will be shouting, screaming, shrieking, laughing and crying whilst watching two teams of eleven chase after a pig's bladder in a far flung corner of the globe, just as I have done during a multitude of matches played in and watched throughout the course of my passionate life.

No doubt you will be doing the same too.

With best wishes for your future success.

Nick White

PS – I was back where I grew up a few weekends ago. I switched on the radio, tuned in to Radio Solent, and heard the melodic Hampshire burr of Norman Murphy reporting on a game at Bashley. Some things never change.